TABLE OF CONTENTS

Editor's Note

This year the St. Louis Cardinals and Boston Red Sox met each other in the World Series for the fourth time since 1946, and after falling behind, two games to one, the Red Sox stormed back to take the Series in six games. It was an exciting, if at times sloppy, showdown between two storied franchises. But it was that first meeting 67 years ago that I kept coming back to. The Cardinals had won 98 games, propelled by the likes of Stan Musial, Whitey Kurowski, and Enos Slaughter. The Red Sox, who had won 104 games, countered with Ted Williams, Dom DiMaggio, and Johnny Pesky. The Series went the distance, with Game 7 ending in a 4–3 Cardinals victory a half-inning after Slaughter's "Mad Dash."

But as the readers of this journal know, there were two other league champions that met that year. Their rosters, too, were filled with greats. The Negro National League's pennant-winning Newark Eagles, for instance, had Leon Day, Monte Irvin, Larry Doby, and Max Manning, along with an aging Biz Mackey. Their counterparts in the Negro American League, the Kansas City Monarchs, had Hilton Smith, Willard Brown, Hank Thompson, and Satchel Paige. Their matchup, like the one between the Cardinals and Red Sox, went seven games, and the Eagles emerged victorious.

There was, of course, never any chance that these great teams from white baseball and black baseball would square off. However close they might have been to seeing Robinson break the color barrier, they still inhabited different, and determinedly separate, worlds.

Yet I can't help wondering what would have happened had the champion Cardinals played the champion Eagles. Or imagining a St. Louis–Kansas City matchup nearly 40 years before the Cards lost to the Royals in the I-70 Series. How, for that matter, would a Boston-Newark showdown have turned out?

A bigger question might be this one: Who else, in looking back to 1946, even thinks of the Eagles or Monarchs? How many among today's baseball fans know what these teams accomplished that year? The likely answer is a big part of what motivates me as a Negro Leagues historian.

If you're holding a copy of Black Ball as you read this, maybe it motivates you, too. So dig deep. With each new issue of Black Ball, it's a little easier to construct our own, imagined highlight reel.

In this issue—our first as an annual—Chris Lamb gauges the influence of the much-discussed Charlie Thomas incident on Branch Rickey, and in particular his decision to sign Jackie Robinson. Chris Baas and Geri Strecker share their experiences working with a group of Ball State Students to document ball parks where black baseball was played in Indianapolis, Indiana. Working through the Historic American Landscape

Survey, the group rescued these parks from obscurity. Courtney Smith examines the relationship between Ed Bolden of the Philadelphia Stars and the newspaper that covered his team, the *Philadelphia Tribune.* Newcomer Shawn Morris provides an in-depth look at the Cleveland Tate Stars, their fortunes, and the off-field struggles of their owner, George Tate. In his article, David Krell considers the intersection of events in 1945 that saw the Cleveland Buckeyes' finest moment overshadowed by baseball's great experiment. Neither the Buckeyes nor baseball was ever the same. Joe Dorinson writes about Paul Robeson, Larry Doby and Monte Irvin—three men from New Jersey (site of this year's Jerry Malloy Negro League Conference, where this piece was presented) who fought for social justice and fair play. James Brunson provides another excellent set of primary materials from the 19th century, this time focusing on Chester, Pennsylvania. Finally, Robert Cvornyek gives us a glimpse into the black baseball world in Boston from the 1870s through the 1940s.

Readers can marvel at some of the excellent artwork submitted for this year's Jerry Malloy Negro League Art Competition. In addition to the winners and runners-up in the professional, amateur and youth categories, we present recipients of the People's Choice Award, which debuted in 2012. In keeping with past issues, we have included an idea for further research, focusing this time on the West Coast Negro Baseball Association and one of its entrants, the Seattle Steelheads. As always, a selected bibliography is included for those who might like to do further research into any of the topics highlighted in the journal. There are also author and subject indexes for the first five volumes of *Black Ball.*

Enjoy this plump new issue, and let it whet your appetite for the sort of historical research and writing that this (now annual) journal and the Jerry Malloy Negro League Conference have long supported.

Leslie Heaphy

Did Branch Rickey Sign Jackie Robinson to Right a 40-Year Wrong?

CHRIS LAMB

Abstract

Branch Rickey's signing of Jackie Robinson has generated a great deal of interest in and historical literature exploring the events and people involved. One area of continued controversy has to do with the motivations of Mr. Rickey. Did he sign Robinson simply to help his Brooklyn Dodgers win? Did he first consider the possibility of integration only a few years before the signing, or was this event the culmination of a much longer process? Did Rickey's concerns date all the way back to his days at Oberlin, as he often claimed?

ON OCTOBER 23, 1945, THE MONTREAL ROYALS, the Brooklyn Dodgers' AAA team, announced the signing of Jackie Robinson, bringing down professional baseball's color barrier, which had barred blacks from the national pastime for six decades. In his story, Associated Press reporter Gayle Talbot said that the signing of Robinson was the culmination of a three-year search by Branch Rickey, the Brooklyn Dodgers president, who had sent scouts through the United States, Mexico, and Latin America searching for blacks with big-league potential. Rickey explained his motivation in signing Robinson as follows: "I have never meant to be a crusader, and I hope I won't be regarded as one. My purpose is to be fair to all people, and my selfish objective is to win baseball games."[1]

Rickey, however, also said that he had given a lot of thought to racial discrimination since his days coaching baseball at Ohio Wesleyan University in 1903. Rickey recalled that during one road trip to South Bend, Indiana, to play the University of Notre Dame, a hotel clerk denied the team's black ballplayer, Charles "Tommie" Thomas, a room. Rickey asked if the ballplayer would be allowed to sleep on a cot in his room. The hotel obliged. Later that evening, Rickey saw Thomas rubbing his skin, tearfully saying, "Black skin. Black skin. If only I could make them white." Rickey said the scene haunted him. "I vowed that I would always do whatever I could to see that other Americans did not have to face the bitter humiliation that was heaped upon Charles Thomas," Rickey said.[2]

Black Ball / DOI: 10.3172/BLB.6.5 / Volume 6 / 2013 / pp. 5–18 /
ISSN 1939-8484 (Print) / ISSN 1939-8379 (Online) /

Talbot reported that Rickey had foreshadowed the Robinson announcement in a speech to a Brooklyn Rotary club in April six months earlier, where he raised the issue of racial equality in baseball. It was inevitable that blacks would play in the major leagues, Rickey said.[3] A month earlier, Rickey confided in Brooklyn broadcaster Red Barber, telling the Southern-born Barber that he planned to sign at least one black player. During the conversation, Rickey shared the Thomas story. When Barber remembered the anecdote in his 1984 memoir *1947: When All Hell Broke Loose in Baseball*, he said that all the players took turns registering with the hotel. When it was Thomas's turn, the clerk pulled the registration book away. "We do not register Negroes here," he said. Rickey told the clerk that the Ohio Wesleyan team was the guest of Notre Dame and that Thomas was the best player on the Ohio Wesleyan team. The clerk did not budge. Rickey asked if Thomas could sleep on a cot in his room. The clerk agreed. Rickey handed Thomas the key. When Rickey came up to the room, he found Thomas pulling at his skin and crying: "It's my skin, Mr. Rickey ... it's my skin! If I could just pull it off, I'd be like everyone else... It's my skin, Mr. Rickey!" Rickey then told Barber, who had grown up in rural Florida, "That was forty-one years ago. And for these forty-one years, I have heard that fine young man crying, 'It's my skin... If I could just pull it off... It's my skin.'"[4]

Branch Rickey signing Jackie Robinson to a contract with the Brooklyn Dodgers (Negro Leagues Baseball Museum).

Rickey recounted the Thomas story often in the days, months, and years after he signed Robinson. Gayle Talbot's Associated Press account was, in all likelihood, widely circulated. Writer Mark Harris included the Thomas anecdote in a story he wrote for *Negro Digest* in September 1947.[5] In 1957, Arthur Mann, in a profile in *Look* magazine, quoted Rickey recalling the 1903 incident and saying, "I never felt so helpless in my life."[6] In his 1966 biography of Rickey, David Lipman added the following detail after Rickey saw Thomas crying. "What if they won't let me play," a tearful Thomas said. "They'll either let you play or we all go home," Rickey replied.[7] A.S. "Doc" Young wrote in a November 1968 *Ebony* magazine profile of Rickey that Rickey was moved by the racism he saw directed against Thomas. "From Charlie Thomas," Young said, "Rickey learned about the terrible degradation of racial prejudice, and that one's race, or color of skin, had nothing whatsoever to do with one's ability."[8]

In his 2007 biography of Rickey, Lee Lowenfish wrote that while Rickey knew little of racial discrimination himself, he "instinctively empathized with Thomas's pain of rejection." Rickey tried to console Thomas by telling him that there would be a time when there would be racial equality. He gave Thomas a pep talk. "Come on, Tommy, snap out of it! We'll lick this one day," Rickey said. "But we can't if you feel sorry for yourself."[9] Arnold Rampersad's biography of Robinson referred to the quotes in the Talbot account and to the inferred historical reference. "The story begged comparison to another, lodged in American lore," Rampersad said, "about Abraham Lincoln going down the Mississippi and seeing slavery, and vowing to see it end one day. Indeed, a portrait of Lincoln hung in Rickey's office."[10]

The Thomas anecdote has become an obligatory piece of the Rickey-Robinson narrative, appearing in newspaper articles, magazines articles, and books. But it deserves a closer look. Did the incident really have the profound impact on Rickey's decision to sign Robinson that so many writers have claimed? Was it, as some said, the inspiration for Rickey signing Robinson? If witnessing Thomas trying to rub the blackness from his skin had such an impact on Rickey, why did he wait so long to sign a black player? Rickey, in fact, showed little interest—at least publically—in the color line during his long tenure as a baseball executive, rarely, if ever, talking about the heartbreaking scene in the South Bend hotel in the decades before the spring of 1945.

Jules Tygiel, author of *Baseball's Great Experiment*, which examined the integration of baseball, expressed doubt over the role the Thomas incident had on Rickey's decision to sign Robinson. "The Charlie Thomas story, though based in fact, is vintage Rickey," Tygiel wrote. "The allegory is almost biblical and the sermonlike quality of the tale invites skepticism. Many people place little stock in the episode as the primary rationale for his actions. Even if one accepts the Charlie Thomas story at face value, it does not fully explain why the Dodger president chose to challenge the color barrier four decades later."[11]

This raises the question of whether Rickey created the story, embellished it, or at least exaggerated its significance. Did Rickey use the Thomas story to insert himself into the campaign to desegregate baseball so he could take full credit for breaking baseball's color barrier? When Rickey signed Robinson, he ignored those activists—including blacks and communists—who had long worked to pressure the baseball establishment to allow blacks. To Bill Mardo, sports editor of the Communist newspaper the *Daily Worker*, which campaigned for the integration of baseball in the decade before the signing of Robinson, Rickey was an opportunist who sat on the sidelines while others fought the good fight, then desegregated baseball when he saw that it was inevitable. "There was the pre–Robinson Rickey who stayed shamefully silent for much of his baseball life," Mardo wrote. And there was the other Rickey, he added, "whose extraordinary business and baseball sense helped him seize the moment, jump aboard the Freedom Train as it was getting ready to pull out of Times Square, catch social protest at its apex, and then do just about everything right once he signed Robinson."[12]

Beginning in the 1930s, black sportswriters, black activists, and white social progressives confronted the baseball establishment with newspaper columns and petition drives, taking their campaign directly to the offices of commissioner Kenesaw Mountain Landis, league executives, team owners, and spring training camps. The campaign to desegregate baseball was most active in New York City, which had a strong progressive political presence that included mayor Fiorello La Guardia and city councilmen. In addition, in early 1945, the New York State Legislature addressed the issue of racism by passing the Ives-Quinn Act, which banned discrimination and in hiring and created a commission to investigate complaints. The law went into effect in July 1945. When Rickey signed Robinson, one sportswriter, Dan Daniel, said that it was "unquestionably" an effort by Rickey to comply with Ives-Quinn.[13]

Lowenfish argued that Rickey's interest in integrating the national pastime was sincere. While Rickey may have exaggerated the South Bend details for dramatic effect, "there is no doubt that the incident occurred," according to Lowenfish.[14] Thomas confirmed that it happened.[15] Furthermore, Rickey and Thomas, who met on a football field at Ohio Wesleyan, remained close to each other and close to the college that had deeply impacted them. The friendship between a prominent white man who spent much of his adult life in St. Louis and Brooklyn, and a black man, who spent much of his adult life working as a dentist in Albuquerque, New Mexico, was, of course, rare, if not remarkable, given the racial climate of the first half of the century. Neither the incident itself nor the friendship between Thomas and Rickey confirms Rickey's claim that he signed Robinson to right a 40-year wrong. But perhaps the Thomas incident and his long friendship with Thomas reveal something about Rickey's genuine interest in racial equality—something that inspired him to end the color line in baseball.

Before being hired as president of the Brooklyn Dodgers, Rickey had served for nearly a quarter-century as president of the St. Louis Cardinals, where he apparently had the freedom to sign whomever he wanted and promote them to the big leagues. But that freedom stopped short of signing a black player for a team that played their games in a former slave state in a segregated stadium, Sportsman Park, owned by a man, Sam Breadon, whose attitudes on race represented that of most of the players on his payroll, the sportswriters who covered the team, the spectators who attended the games, and organized baseball itself. When Rickey signed Robinson, Breadon called Rickey and complained.[16] Breadon later served on a committee of baseball executives who issued a report condemning the integration of baseball.[17]

Even if Rickey wanted to break baseball's color line while working for the Cardinals, he knew his limitations. In his 1950 biography of Robinson, New York sportswriter Bill Roeder supported Rickey's version of events. Roeder observed that Rickey appealed to Breadon to drop the restrictions against blacks at Sportsman Park. But Breadon would not budge. Rickey did not have a reputation for racial sensitivity. "He would make his casual inquiries about Negro athletes, it's true," Roeder wrote, "and friends would hear the Charley Thomas story. But this was a side of Rickey that did not exist in the public mind."[18]

Therefore, simply because Rickey did not publically talk about Thomas or integration before he joined the Brooklyn Dodgers should not suggest that he was not interested in racial equality until he joined the Dodgers. In addition, Thomas may not have directly influenced Rickey's decision to sign Robinson, but knowing Thomas may have shaped the baseball executive's racial attitudes. Rickey was a profoundly complicated man, and anyone searching for simple explanations to describe why he did what he did when he did it will find himself on a fool's errand. "A moralist some people found insufferable, Rickey was a dedicated, Bible-loving Christian who refused to attend games on Sundays," Rampersad wrote. "He was also a master of rhetoric, a grandiloquent speaker whose high-flown locutions overwhelmed most opposition and often obscured or embroidered key facts; reporters called his office the Cave of Winds."[19]

While it is probably impossible to ascertain whether or not the Thomas incident inspired the signing of Robinson, one can examine the friendship between Rickey and Thomas to find that Rickey's interest in confronting racism did not begin with Jackie Robinson; racial equality was a long-standing interest. Secondly, while Rickey may have rarely, if ever, mentioned Thomas to reporters in the decades preceding the signing of Robinson, Thomas was more than a passing acquaintance in Rickey's long and significant life. Rickey was more than a baseball coach to Thomas; he was also a friend, who shared his belief that blacks and whites should not be kept separate on baseball fields or anywhere else.

Moreover, to understand the Thomas story requires not just looking at the relationship between the two men, but also at Thomas specifically. Thomas was not merely one of relatively few black players in college baseball; he was a talented ballplayer who could have perhaps played in the big leagues, if his skin had not been so black. Thomas played for a number of black teams, including briefly in 1904 for the Philadelphia Giants, considered one of the greatest black teams in history, whose manager was Sol White and whose lineup included such stars as Rube Foster, Charlie Grant, George "Chappie" Johnson, Pete Hill, and Bill Monroe. According to one account, Thomas batted .619 during his short time with the Giants. On September 1, 1904, Thomas played first, batted last, and went 0-for-4 in a game where Foster pitched a no-hitter and struck out 18.[20]

If Thomas was playing for the Giants during the summer of 1904, this meant he was playing professional baseball while playing baseball and football at Ohio Wesleyan. This adds irony to the Rickey-Thomas story. Rickey became coach of the Ohio Wesleyan team after being declared ineligible for playing professionally. It is quite possible that Thomas went undetected because he was playing in the obscurity of black baseball or that black baseball was not considered professional. Thomas later played for the Columbus Black Tourist. Thomas was never given the opportunity to play in organized professional baseball. Unlike so many other blacks, who were forced to work in marginal jobs, Thomas became a successful dentist.

Both men maintained ties to Ohio Wesleyan, which possesses a significant amount of material on Rickey, one of the college's more famous alums. This file includes a number of articles that refer to Rickey's years at Ohio Wesleyan, including how his experience as the college's baseball coach foreshadowed his long and successful career in big-league baseball. The articles refer, of course, to the Thomas incident. The college's file on Thomas includes, among other things, 1903, 1904, and 1905 photos of the Ohio Wesleyan baseball team, scorecards of the school's 1904 baseball season, and Thomas's student identification card. It also includes articles from the *Delaware (Ohio) Gazette*, the Delaware *Daily Journal Herald*, and the *Times Recorder* of Zanesville, Ohio, where Thomas grew up. It also includes Ohio Wesleyan's yearbook, *Le Bijou*, the college's alumni magazine, *OWU Magazine*, and other campus publications, including, notably, the *Ohio Wesleyan Transcript* on microfilm. This latter resource made it possible to examine newspaper coverage of Thomas during his three years at the college to see what, if any, attention was paid to his race.

Charles Thomas was born in Weston, West Virginia, in 1881, the same year that Rickey was born in the southern Ohio town of Lucasville and three years before Moses Fleetwood Walker of Steubenville, Ohio, became the first black to play in the major leagues. Walker's brother Welday played a few games with his brother in 1884. No other blacks would play in the major leagues until 1947. Fleet Walker was one of five blacks playing in the International League, a top minor league, in 1887, when the league's executives agreed to allow no more contracts for black players. This "gentlemen's agreement" held firm until Rickey signed Robinson.

When Thomas was three, his family moved across the Ohio River to Zanesville, Ohio. In high school, Thomas, or "Cha," as he was known, excelled in both athletics and academics.[21] Thomas then attended Ohio Wesleyan in Delaware, Ohio, 20 miles north of Columbus. Rickey began attending Ohio Wesleyan, a Methodist college in Delaware, Ohio, in 1901. Rickey had a strong Methodist upbringing, which had a lifelong influence on him. His mother also had a strong influence on him. To address his mother's fears about the secular nature of baseball, Rickey resolved to stay away from the ballpark on Sundays. Rickey's decision to sign Robinson was consistent with his Christian beliefs.

Thomas and Rickey met as teammates on the college's football team. Rickey, who played fullback on the football team and catcher on the baseball team, was declared ineligible from participating in collegiate athletics after it was revealed he had played for a semiprofessional baseball team during the summer of 1902. Rickey admitted to school officials that he had compromised his amateur standing. The Ohio Wesleyan president then hired Rickey to be the school's baseball coach. Rickey asked Thomas, who also played fullback, to join the baseball team, where he played catcher, first base, and outfield.[22]

Thomas was the only black player on the team (the team's mascot also was black). Thomas reportedly was one of the few blacks attending Ohio Wesleyan,[23] and he was one of relatively few blacks playing college baseball. William Clarence Matthews was a star second baseman for Harvard who also faced bigotry during his playing days. The University of Virginia refused to play Harvard if Matthews was in the lineup. The game was canceled.[24] After leaving Harvard in 1905, Matthews played for Burlington, Vermont, in an independent league, where he was reportedly the only black in professional baseball. There is some evidence that a major league manager was interested in signing Matthews but did not pursue the matter because of opposition from the league executives and other teams.[25]

Thomas said he faced little outward prejudice from classmates and teammates—in part, he added, because of Rickey. "From the first day I entered Ohio Wesleyan, Branch Rickey took special interest in my welfare," Thomas said.[26] The Ohio Wesleyan student newspaper, the *Transcript*, in a preview of the season, mentioned Thomas but did not mention his race.[27]

In an April 11 article, the *Transcript* criticized the "sluggishness" of the infielders and outfielders but said that Thomas, as catcher, had "acquitted" himself well.[28] On April 22, the newspaper praised Thomas for the three runs he scored in a win against Western Reserve.[29] On May 6, the newspaper reported that Thomas "played his usual good game."[30]

While Thomas was apparently treated well by his coaches, teammates, fans, and the college newspaper, he regularly faced hostility from opposing teams and fans. When Ohio Wesleyan played the University of Kentucky in Lexington, during the spring of 1903, some of the Kentucky players and fans began chanting, "Get that nigger off the field!" Rickey, who was then 21, reportedly ran across the field to the Kentucky dugout and shouted at the opposing coach, "We won't play without him!" When it appeared that there might not be a game, some of the spectators began cheering, "We want Thomas! We want Thomas!" The game was then played without incident.[31]

Two years later, the University of Kentucky forfeited a game against Ohio Wesleyan rather than take the field with a black player. The Kentucky team "was left to pay their bills and get home at their own expense."[32] Rickey later referred to the bigotry that Thomas faced during a game against West Virginia in his interview with Gayle Talbot.[33] Thomas also remembered the constant onslaught of racist epithets he heard during the game. "I tried not to notice," Thomas said. "Rick said to forget it, ignore it. But it was hard to forget, ignore."[34]

There is some question about whether the incident at the South Bend hotel happened in 1903 or 1904. A number of sources mention the game as happening in 1904. The 1903 Ohio Wesleyan baseball schedule, however, says that Ohio Wesleyan played a game at South Bend on May 12, 1903.[35] Newspaper accounts also refer to the game. According to Ohio Wesleyan's 1904 schedule, the team did not play Notre Dame. There is also some question over the name of the South Bend hotel that refused to admit him. According to a number of sources, the incident happened at the Oliver Hotel, which was called "the most magnificent hotel in Indiana, one of the finest in the United States."[36]

Newspaper accounts at the time do not mention the incident. Even if a reporter had been aware of what happened, it is unlikely he would have reported it; such incidents were commonplace and, as such, not considered news. The racial climate would worsen over the next two decades, as the Ku Klux Klan's influenced spread from the South to the lower Midwest and beyond — as the organization expanded its bigotry from blacks to Jews, Catholics, and immigrants. Leonard J. Moore called Indiana "the epicenter of the national Klan movement." Moore estimated that between a quarter and a third of all native-born men in Indiana belonged to the Klan.[37] In 1924 a riot ensued when Notre Dame students confronted Klan members who were in South Bend for a rally.[38]

After the hotel clerk told Rickey that Thomas would not be allowed, Rickey asked to see the hotel manager. While he waited, he sent his equipment manager to find other housing options for Thomas. Rickey once told black journalist Carl Rowan that it was common for a black servant to stay in the same room as his master. "I later realized that in many cases a Negro could stay in a white hotel if he were a servant traveling with a white man," Rickey said, "and that so long as this relationship of master and servant was obvious, then it was perfectly all right with whites who otherwise would object to a Negro's staying in the hotel."[39] Thomas later said that the incident repeated itself again during other road trips, and when it did, Rickey responded as he did in South Bend. "When we went on trips, Rickey was the first one to see if I was welcome to the hotel where we went to stop," Thomas later said. "On several occasions, he talked the management into allowing me to occupy a double room with his roommate."[40]

Ohio Wesleyan lost the game against Notre Dame, 11–0. The Delaware *Daily Journal Herald* reported that Thomas went hitless in four plate appearances.[41] On June 10, three weeks later, OWU defeated Notre Dame, 5–2, in a game in Delaware. The *Daily Journal Herald* praised Thomas in its story: "The feature of the game was witnessed in the first inning when Thomas stepped up to the slap and slammed the spheroid against the back-yard fence for a home run."[42] The *Ohio Wesleyan Transcript* reported that Thomas had hit a first-inning home run and had gone 3-for-5 in the game, scoring three runs. The newspaper also reported that Thomas had been involved in a trick play. When Notre Dame had runners on first and third at one point, the man on first stole second. Instead of throwing the ball to second, Thomas threw the ball back to the pitcher, who threw the ball back to Thomas in time to get the runner out at home.[43]

During Rickey's first year as a coach in 1903, Ohio Wesleyan went 8–9–1. A year later, the team's record was 14–5.[44] Rickey graduated in June 1904 and then left the college for a teaching and coaching job at Alleghany College in Allegheny, Pennsylvania. Upon his resignation, the *Ohio Wesleyan Transcript* praised him as "one of the most capable athletes that ever wore the Ohio Wesleyan uniform."[45] Rickey's successor as coach was Ben Davis. Thomas, who reportedly became the first black to receive a varsity letter at Ohio Wesleyan, excelled offensively and defensively.[46] According to one account, he hit .300 or better in each of his three years.[47] Score sheets show him batting fourth in the batting order.[48] In a review of the 1905 season, *Le* Bijou called the pitcher-catcher battery of Cleon Webb and Thomas one that "was known and feared all over the state." The article mentioned that "Tommie" Thomas was one of the team's best catchers in years, going on to say that "He knew the game thoroughly and was of great assistance to Webb because of his judgment of opponents' hitting."[49]

Thomas was praised for both his skill as a ballplayer and for his grace under pressure. A letter to the *Transcript* referred to the difficulties Thomas faced because of his race. In a letter to the *Transcript* on May 27, 1905, an Ohio Wesleyan alumnus wrote the following after watching a game the school played against Ohio University in Athens, Ohio: "The only unpleasant feature of the game was the course slurs cast at Mr. Thomas, the catcher. But through it all he showed himself far more the gentleman

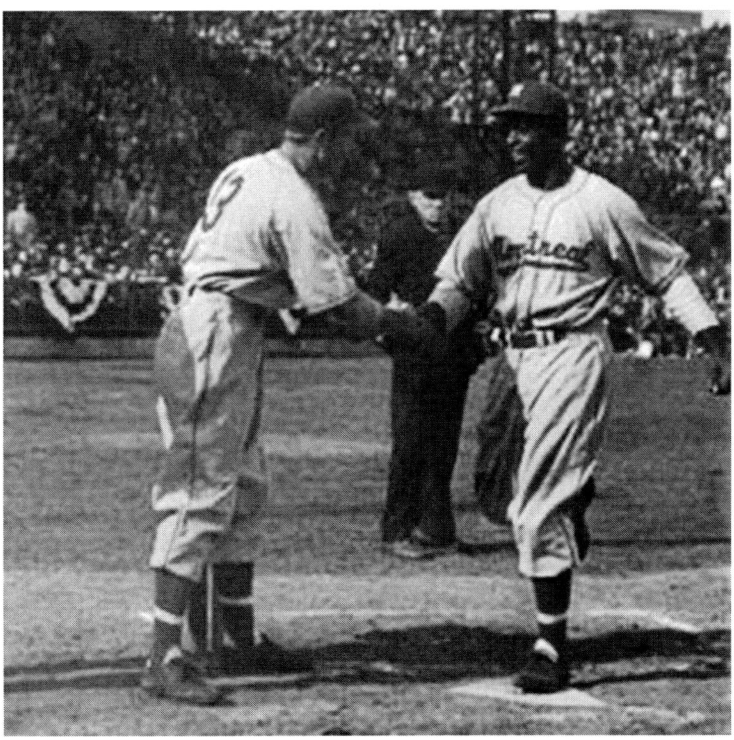

Jackie Robinson shakes hands with George Shuba after homering in his Montreal Royals debut, April 18, 1946 (Leslie Heaphy Collection).

than his insolent tormentors though their skin is white."[50] When Thomas finished his last season at Ohio Wesleyan, a writer for the Wesleyan *Transcript* said, "we can hardly hope to find a man who is as strong an all around player as Tommy. Success to him in whatever he may do."[51]

Thomas's student ID mentioned that he was initially listed as a "special student."[52] During the 1905-1906 academic year, Thomas was enrolled in the business school. It is not known whether he graduated. He withdrew from the school in 1906, presumably without graduating.[53] Thomas left Ohio Wesleyan and moved to Columbus, where he attended dental school at Starling Ohio Medical College, which later became known as the Ohio State University Medical School. Thomas played for the Columbus Black Tourist and then again briefly with the Philadelphia Giants in 1910.[54] Thomas told Mark Harris he thought he had the ability to play in the major leagues. He said that Hank Gowdy, who grew up in Columbus up and played catcher in the majors for 17 years, once told him so.[55]

Thomas graduated from dental school in 1908. He began practicing dentistry in St. Louis, Missouri, in 1912. Nine years later, he moved to Albuquerque, New Mexico, where, according to one account, "he was one of the first black dentists in the state."[56] In 1939, Thomas returned to Zanesville for a visit, which was covered by the city's newspaper, the *Recorder.* The article described Thomas as a "leading colored dentist." The article also mentioned that Thomas excelled as both an athlete and a student while attending high school in Zanesville. It mentioned that Thomas attended Ohio Wesleyan where he played for Rickey.[57] While Thomas lived in New Mexico, he returned to St. Louis to see Rickey. Thomas remembered visiting Rickey but the two were unable to sit together in the segregated stadium. "I called Rickey and he invited me down to his office at Sportsman's Park. We talked about old times, but we didn't go to the ball game together that afternoon. You see, Negroes weren't permitted in the lower grandstand at the time. Rick said, "Tommy, some day, we'll have that changed."[58]

Young blacks had little reason to think social conditions would be any different for them than they had been for their parents. Art Rust, Jr., who grew up near the Polo Grounds in New York City, remembered in his book, *Get That Nigger off the Field*, that a police officer told his father that New York Giants manager Bill Terry did not want any "nigger cops" working at the stadium. When Rust asked Washington Senators outfielder Taft Wright of North Carolina for an autograph outside Yankee Stadium, Wright called him a "black son of a bitch." Rust found St. Louis Cardinals players particularly bigoted. Pitcher Clyde Shoun of Tennessee rubbed Rust's hair for good luck as he left the team's dressing room. Rust had a collection of photographs and asked players to sign their names to their respective photos. After Enos "Country" Slaughter signed Rust's autograph, the outfielder said, "How did that little nigger get all those photographs?" Rust remembered thinking, "With all those crackers, ain't no way a black guy's gonna play in the majors." Branch Rickey once put his arm around Rust, however, and told him that blacks would one day play in the big leagues.[59]

The Cardinals decided not to renew Rickey's contract and its high salary in 1942.

He was subsequently hired by the Brooklyn Dodgers. Shortly after arriving in Brooklyn, Rickey began talking about integrating baseball. He raised the issue of signing black players during a meeting with the Dodgers' board of directors in early 1943. "You might turn up something, so go ahead," he was famously told. This began Rickey's secret plan to scout black players with the objective of finding the right one — or ones— to sign for the Dodgers.[60] More than two years later, Rickey invited Robinson to his office and signed him to a contract. The Dodgers announced the signing of Robinson on October 23, 1945. Rickey recalled the Thomas incident in interviews with journalists, including Gayle Talbot. By the time Robinson played his first game in the major leagues on April 14, 1947, Thomas had become a part of the story of why Rickey had signed Robinson. In the September 1947 issue of *Negro Digest*, Thomas told Mark Harris: "Please don't give people the idea I'm claiming credit for the signing of Jackie Robinson. That's Rick's doing."[61]

Thomas and Rickey remained friends until Rickey's death in 1965. After retiring from dentistry, Thomas moved to Los Angeles. He died in April 1970 at age 91. He was born in 1881, three years before Moses Fleetwood Walker became the first black to play in the major leagues, and died in 1971, a year before the death of Jackie Robinson, who broke major league baseball's color line in 1947.

Thomas's brief obituary in the Albuquerque *Journal*, which appeared on April 6, mentioned that his college baseball coach was Branch Rickey. The article, however, said that he played at The Ohio State University instead of Ohio Wesleyan.[62] A day earlier, the Albuquerque *Tribune* published a lengthier obituary of Thomas, which mentioned his friendship with Rickey. "He and Rickey were such close friends," Herman Schulman, one of Thomas's friends said. "Every time that Rickey would come to Albuquerque he would always get hold of Dr. Thomas and they would have dinner." The article reported that Thomas "was instrumental in the movement to get Negroes accepted into the Major Leagues."[63]

Nearly three decades after Thomas's death, the city of Delaware, Ohio, honored him with Charles Thomas Day on June 29, 2008. The proclamation by the city's mayor, Windell Wheeler, stated: "Whereas, during an OWU baseball trip, Thomas was denied lodging at a South Bend, Indiana, hotel but Rickey was able to convince the hotel manager to allow Thomas to stay in his room as an unregistered guest; and whereas, the event was burned into Rickey's memory and more than 40 years later, proved to be his inspiration in signing Jackie Robinson with the Brooklyn Dodgers."[64]

It is an exaggeration to state that Thomas "was instrumental in the movement to get Negroes accepted into the Major Leagues." It also is an exaggeration to state that Thomas and Rickey were "close friends." Lee Lowenfish said that the two men were "certainly good acquaintances and shared believers in the belief in equality of opportunity for all."[65] Finally, it is an exaggeration to say that the Thomas incident in 1903 was the catalyst for Rickey signing Robinson in 1945. Rickey, in fact, may have broken baseball's color line without ever witnessing the Thomas incident or knowing Thomas, for that matter.

This should not, however, erase the significance—and particularly the symbolism—of Rickey seeing Thomas trying to rub off his skin in that South Bend hotel. For Rickey, the scene came to represent the unfairness and even cruelty of segregation, whether in baseball or in society. Rickey understood this more than his fellow baseball executives—and this understanding played a big part in why he confronted baseball's color line by signing Robinson. The sight of a sobbing Charlie Thomas became both a reminder and a metaphor for the cruelty of segregation. But more than this, Rickey's friendship with Thomas gave the baseball executive a perspective of racism that no other baseball executive had. Indeed, perhaps relatively few white Americans had had it. Yes, Rickey realized the economic opportunity that came with desegregating baseball. But it's important to acknowledge that for Rickey, the breaking of baseball's color barrier was less a business decision than a personal one, based on a friendship with Charlie Thomas that helped shape his belief that blacks should have the same opportunities as whites.

**Chris Lamb would like to thank Lee Lowenfish for his suggestions for improving this article.*

Notes

1. *Miami Herald*, 24 October 1945.
2. *Miami Herald*, 24 October 1945.
3. *Miami Herald*, 24 October 1945.
4. Red Barber, *1947: When All Hell Broke Loose in Baseball* (New York: De Capo Press, 1984), 49–50.
5. Mark Harris, "Branch Rickey Keeps His 40-Year Promise to a Negro Dentist," *Negro Digest*, September 1947, 4–7.
6. Arthur Mann, "The Life of Branch Rickey, Part I," *Look*, 20 August 1957, 79. Quoted in Lowenfish, *Branch Rickey*, 23.
7. David Lipman, *Mr. Baseball: The Story of Branch Rickey* (New York: G.P. Putnam and Sons, 1966), 10.
8. A.S. "Doc" Young, "The Black Athlete in the Golden Age of Sports: Branch Rickey Launched Negroes to Stardom With a Signing of Jackie Robinson," Ebony, November 1968, 154.
9. Lee Lowenfish, *Branch Rickey: Baseball's Ferocious Gentleman* (Lincoln, NE: University of Nebraska Press, 2007), 24.
10. Arnold Rampersad, *Jackie Robinson* (New York: Alfred A, Knopf, 1997), 121–122.
11. Jules Tygiel, *Baseball's Great Experiment: Jackie Robinson and His Legacy* (New York: Oxford University Press, 197), 52.
12. Bill Mardo, "Robeson-Robinson," in *Jackie Robinson: Race, Sports, and the American Dream*, eds. Dorinson and Warmund (Amonk, NY: M.E. Sharpe, 1998), 102–103.
13. *Sporting News*, 1 November 1945.
14. Lowenfish, *Branch Rickey*, 24.
15. Rampersad, *Jackie Robinson*, 24.
16. Harvey Frommer, *Rickey and Robinson: The Men Who Broke Baseball's Color Barrier* (New York: MacMillan, 1982), 112.
17. Maury Brown, "MLB Committee Fought to Keep Blacks Out Even after Robinson Signing," Biz of Baseball.com, http://bizofbaseball.com/index.php?option=com_content&view=article&id=4372:mlb-committee-fought-to-keep-blacks-out-even-after-robinson-signing&catid=26:editorials&Itemid=39.

18. Bill Roeder, *Jackie Robinson* (New York: A.S. Barnes and Co., 1950), 22.

19. Rampersad, *Jackie Robinson*, 121.

20. Sol White, *Sol White's History of Colored Baseball: With Other Documents on the Early Black Games, 1886–1932*, ed. Jerry Malloy (Lincoln: University of Nebraska Press), 58.

21. "Former Star Athlete Visits in City," Zanesville (Ohio) *Recorder*, 12 September 1939. Charles Thomas Archives, Ohio Wesleyan University, Delaware, Ohio.

22. Lowenfish, *Branch Rickey*, 123.

23. Ibid., 22.

24. Atlanta *Constitution*, 31 December 1902.

25. Karl Lindholm, "William Clarence Matthews," *National Pastime: A Review of Baseball History* 17 (1997): 67–72.

26. Young. "The Black Athlete in the Golden Age of Sports: Branch Rickey Launched Negroes to Stardom With a Signing of Jackie Robinson," 156.

27. *Ohio Wesleyan Transcript*, 18 March 1903, 368.

28. Ibid., 11 April 1903, no page number.

29. Ibid., 22 April 1903, 419.

30. Ibid., 6 May 1903, 453.

31. Murray Polner, *Branch Rickey: A Biography* (New York: Atheneum, 1982), 7.

32. *Ohio Wesleyan Transcript*, 21 June 1905, 25.

33. *Miami Herald*, 24 October 1945.

34. Harris, "Branch Rickey Keeps His 40-Year Promise to a Negro Dentist," 4–5.

35. *Ohio Wesleyan Transcript*, 12 May 1903.

36. "Oliver History," Northern Indiana Center for History, http://centerforhistory.org/learn-history/oliver-history.

37. Leonard J. Moore, *Citizen Klansmen: The Ku Klux Klan in Indiana, 1921–1928* (Chapel Hill: University of North Carolina Press, 1991), 1–3, 7.

38. "Fighting for Inclusion," *Indianapolis Star*, 6 January 2013, B1.

39. Quoted in Lowenfish, *Branch Rickey*, 29.

40. A.S. "Doc" Young, "The Black Athlete in the Golden Age of Sports: Branch Rickey Launched Negroes to Stardom With a Signing of Jackie Robinson," *Ebony*, November 1968, 156.

41. *Delaware (Ohio) Daily Journal Herald*, 13 May 1903. Charles Thomas Archives, Ohio Wesleyan University, Delaware, Ohio.

42. Ibid.

43. *Ohio Wesleyan Transcript*, 10 June 1903, 548.

44. Lowenfish, *Branch Rickey*, 22.

45. *Ohio Wesleyan Transcript*, 13 April 1904, 408.

46. *Columbus (OH) Call and Post*, 18 December 1971, 10a.

47. "Charles Thomas Day," *Delaware (Ohio) Gazette*, June 28, 2008. Charles Thomas Archives, Ohio Wesleyan University, Delaware, Ohio.

48. "Spalding's Official Baseball Scorebook," Ohio Wesleyan 1904. Charles Thomas Archives, Ohio Wesleyan University, Delaware, Ohio.

49. 1907 *Le Bijou*, annual yearbook, Ohio Wesleyan University, 251.

50. "Charles Thomas Day," *Delaware (Ohio) Gazette*, June 28, 2008. Charles Thomas Archives, Ohio Wesleyan University, Delaware, Ohio.

51. Ibid.

52. Ibid.

53. 1939 Identification card, Charles Thomas. Charles Thomas Archives, Ohio Wesleyan University, Delaware, Ohio. The card mentions that Thomas attended Ohio Wesleyan from 1902–1906. It says he withdrew in 1906. No graduation year is indicated.

54. James A. Riley, *The Biographical History of Negro League Baseball* (New York: Carroll and Graf, 1994).

55. Harris, "Branch Rickey Keeps a 40-Year Promise," 7.

56. "Former Local Star Athlete Visits in City," *Zanesville (Ohio) Recorder*, 12 September 1939. Charles Thomas Archives, Ohio Wesleyan University, Delaware, Ohio.

57. Ibid.

58. Harris, "Branch Rickey Keeps a 40-Year Promise," 4.

59. Art Rust, Jr., *Get That Nigger Off the Field* (New York: Delacorte, 1976), 6.

60. Lowenfish, *Branch Rickey*, 326.
61. Harris, "Branch Rickey Keeps a 40-Year Promise," 6.
62. "Retired Dentist Dies at 91," *Albuquerque Journal*, 6 April 1971, B16.
63. "Dr. Thomas Was an Avid Sportsmen," *Albuquerque Tribune*, 5 April 1971, A2.
64. "Charles Thomas Day," *Delaware (Ohio) Gazette*, June 28, 2008. Charles Thomas Archives, Ohio Wesleyan University, Delaware, Ohio.
65. Email correspondence with Lee Lowenfish, 18 February 2013.

Discovering Forgotten Ballparks

Documenting Black Baseball Landscapes through the Historic American Landscape Survey

CHRIS BAAS, GERI STRECKER, *and* BALL STATE STUDENTS*

Abstract

Black baseball in Indianapolis has a long and storied history. In 2011 a group of Ball State students set out to discover where those games took place. Using Historic American Landscape Survey (HALS) documentation, the students wanted to look at these stadiums as unique cultural landscapes. The focus was on parks that had historic events happen, represented a unique architectural style or became the common everyday place for teams to play. Documenting their place in the urban landscape allows a deeper understanding of segregation, migration patterns and other aspects of socioeconomic change. Students documented the current conditions of the ballparks that are still in existence and noted others no longer extant. All this provided the framework for the narrative required for HALS documentation. This story explains the evolution and role of these ball parks in the African American community.

Introduction

WITH BASEBALL COMMISSIONER KENESAW MOUNTAIN LANDIS, American Association President Thomas Hickey, four former pennant-winning skippers, and 7,500 fans in attendance, Indianapolis Indians starting pitcher Bill Burwell fired the first pitch in the team's new Perry Stadium. Through the ensuing 65 years, 1931–1996, the stadium was home to the minor league Indians as well as the city's ABC's, Crawfords, and Clowns black baseball teams. During the summer of 2011, a team of Ball State University undergraduate and master's degree students produced Historic American Landscape Survey (HALS) documentation for ballparks where black baseball was played in Indianapolis, Indiana. The students represented the university's Landscape Architecture, Architecture,

**The Ball State University College of Architecture and Planning students that made up the HALS documentation team are Kyle Boot, Brian Grover, Austin Blomeke, Ashley Williams, Ethan Coverstone, Eric James, and Benjamin Doane.*

Black Ball / DOI: 10.3172/BLB.6.19 / Volume 6 / 2013 / pp. 19–36 /
ISSN 1939-8484 (Print) / ISSN 1939-8379 (Online) /

and Historic Preservation programs, and the multidisciplinary course incorporated an immersive pedagogy where students participated in a real-world, experiential project.

The National Park Service created HALS in 2000 to identify and document historic cultural landscapes. The program uses writing, photographs, and measured drawings to document significant landscapes, and the Library of Congress archives these records for the benefit of future generations. The program offers researchers of black baseball a unique and mostly untapped means of documenting ballparks.

Ballparks as Cultural Landscapes

Cultural landscapes are geographic areas associated with historic events, activities, or people. The National Park Service divides these into four types: historic sites, historic designed landscapes, historic vernacular landscapes, and ethnographic landscapes.[1] Historic baseball parks and stadiums are unique cultural landscapes, and their ever-moving geographic locations within our cities illustrate the progression of the game's stature through time. As historic sites, stadiums are considered significant when they, (1) are associated with noteworthy historical events such as the inaugural game of the Negro Leagues at Indianapolis's Washington Park on May 2, 1920; (2) represent a distinct design style like the Art Deco detailing of Perry Stadium; or (3) characterize vernacular (common or everyday) landscapes like Northwestern Park, a sandlot that evolved into an early home for organized black baseball.

The Landscape of Black Baseball[2]

The landscape of American cities is constantly in flux. This was especially true through the first half of the 20th century. Since much of this change was responding to socioeconomic and cultural issues following the Great Migration, documenting locations where black baseball was played also helps track and understand the geography of urban segregation. More important, it illustrates how black business owners and local communities moved beyond color barriers to create and support their own institutions.

Previous documentation of black ballparks has been accomplished at a variety of scales and with an assortment of research methods. Phillip Lowry's *Green Cathedrals* (Walker & Company, 2006) relies on the accuracy of local historians to document major league and Negro League parks. In "The Rise and Fall of Greenlee Field" (*Black Ball*, Fall 2009), Geri Strecker documented the Pittsburgh Crawfords' ballpark, demolished in 1938, by using aerial photographs, maps, newspaper accounts, and construction reports. In a fall 2011 *Journal of Sport History* article, Christopher Baas and Angie Gibson used Geographic Information Systems (GIS) to locate and document Washington Park in Indianapolis.[3] The HALS documentation process engages all these methods, and learning to use these tools provided a valuable experience for students participating in the black ballparks project.

HALS Documentation

HALS originated from the Historic American Building Survey (HABS) program formed during the 1930s to document the nation's architectural resources. As the HABS program evolved, historians struggled to document and describe the significance of buildings without including the context of surrounding landscapes. As a result, HABS documentation began including detailed drawings of gardens, farmsteads, and agricultural fields. Today, the HALS program provides an opportunity to recognize and document landscapes for their own merits, whether they contain buildings or not.

The mission of the Historic American Landscape Survey is to document historic landscapes in the United States and its territories through measured and interpretive drawings, written histories, and photographs. These must be accurate, verifiable, and capture the essence of the historical landscape. The HALS motto of "preservation through documentation" affirms the most basic level of preservation, ideally followed by restoration or rehabilitation.

The National Park Service oversees the daily operation of HALS and formulates policies, sets standards, and drafts procedural guidelines in consultation with the American Society of Landscape Architects (ASLA). The user-friendly National Park Service website explains HALS documentation in detail (http://www.nps.gov/history/hdp/standards/halsguidelines.htm). At a minimum, HALS short-form submissions require documentary photography and written histories.[4] As an added level of documentation, measured and interpretive drawings illustrate and interpret landscapes in even greater detail.

Researchers report a site's history in a short-format template, which includes the site's location, significance, physical description, and history. Since HALS documentation must be verifiable, applicants must list their sources, including all books, articles, surveys, brochures, government documents, websites, and other materials. HALS-documented ballparks must still be standing, and the physical description should include any major changes to the site, such as the addition or removal of stadium parts, plus the site's current physical condition. The short-form template also provides space for current photographs and historic images. Since this documentation is made available to the public, copyrighted images belonging to others require permission, and applicants grant the HALS program permission to use their personal images and images of privately owned documents.

In addition to the short form, HALS drawings record sites so future researchers can understand their appearance, materials, and construction methods, should part or all later be altered or demolished. These drawings can be completed in a variety of sheet formats depending on the character of the landscape being documented. Researchers may hand-draw plans and details, but most use CAD programs. Drawings display a title block and border template provided by the HALS program.

A set of HALS drawings starts with a cover sheet displaying the project title, the park's location, and a brief history and description. To establish the theme of the drawings, cover sheets often include embellishments like Perry Stadium's limestone Deco reliefs of Native Americans and athletic baseball players. Subsequent pages illustrate significant park details, usually communicated in plans, sections, and elevations. While the park's current layout and details are required, additional sheets can illustrate any significant changes over time. For Indianapolis, students included locations and layouts of ballparks predating Perry Stadium.

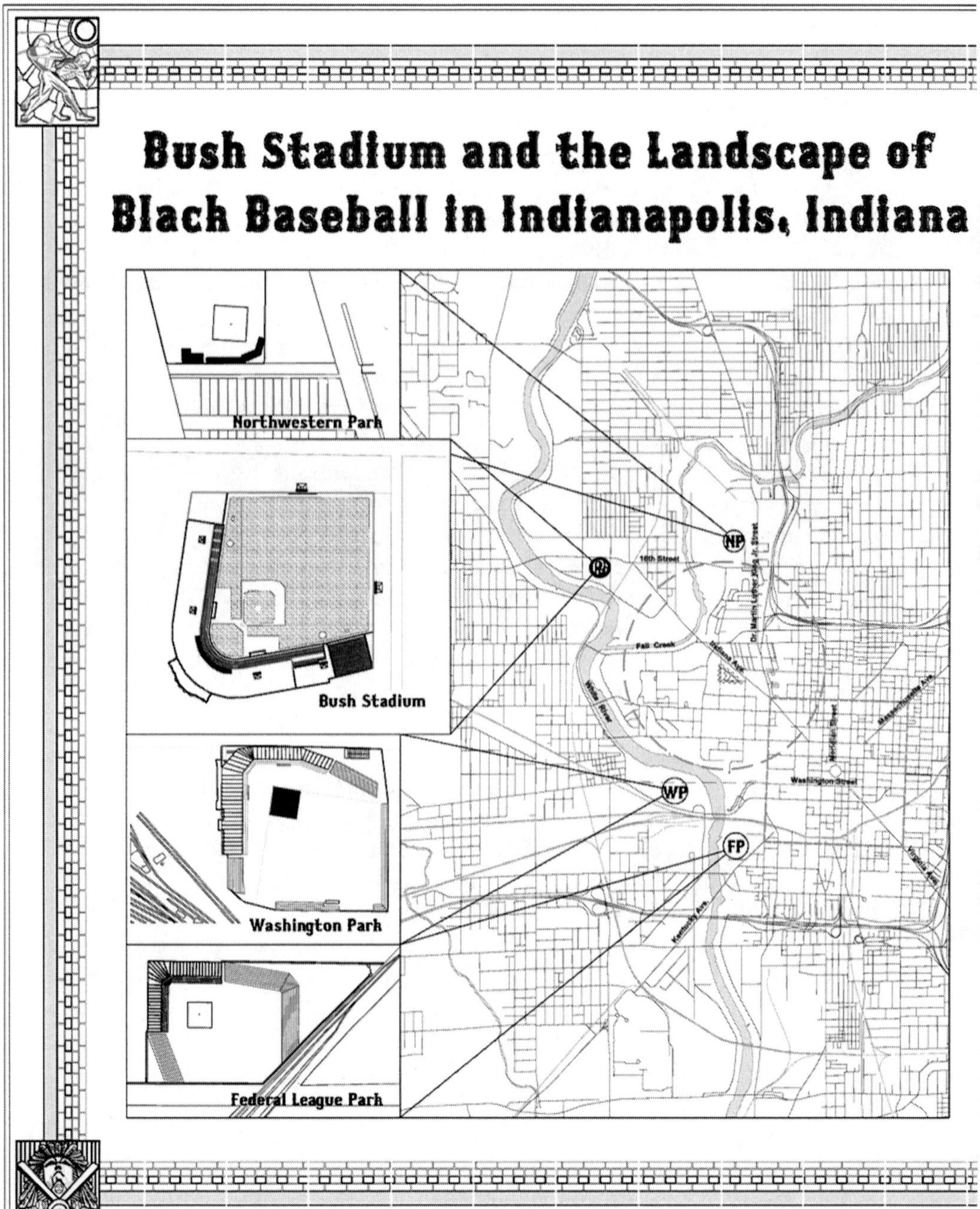

Above and facing: An example of a HALS cover sheet, as prepared by Ball State students.

Project Statement

Bust Stadium is the last remaining landscape where African Americans played Negro League Baseball in Indianapolis, Indiana. At different times, four teams represented the city in the Negro Leagues: the ABCs, Athletics, Crawfords and Clowns. This survey documents the ballpark and its landscape through text, maps, drawings and phtogoraphs. Bush Stadium is being rehabilitated for a new apartment complex that would attempt to maintain some of the structure's original styling along with most of its façade. The act of archiving this national treasure has become a necessity, especially considering this drastic change of uses. Three other ballparks associated with black baseball that existed before Bust Stadium have been researched and documented to better share the story of the landscape of professional black baseball in Indianapolis. These parks are Northwestern Park, Washington Park and Federal League Park.

Bush Stadium

Bush Stadium is located approximately 2.2 miles northwest of Indianapolis's city center and is bound on the north by West 16th Street, on the west by factories along Riverside Drive, on the south by Waterway Boulevard and on the east by Harding Street. Home plate is located at 39° 47'16.38"N, 86° 11'19.70"W.

Bush Stadium, which still stands today, was constructed in 1931 and opened on September 5, 1931. Pierre and White of Indianapolis, Indian, served as the architects, and the major construction materials included reinforced concrete, steel, brick masonry, and Indiana limestone. The park is enclosed by twelve-foot-high brick walls adorned with ivy and capped with limestone. The main entrance is located at the southwest corner, where fans entered through a grand Art Deco gate pabilion of Indiana limestone with bas-relief carvings of Perry Stadium (the original name of Bush Stadium) and Indianapolis Indians motifs. Steel posts hold the steel frame roof over the grandstands and support the box seats above. The original scoreboard was located along the left field wall, but was later replaced by an electronic board on the right field wall. Currently, the structure suffers from a lack of maintenanace, but the city is committed to adaptive reuse on the site to create an apartment complex. After decaying for more than a decade, the stadium may see permanent residents some time in the future. The six steel light towers surrounding the park were moved from Washington Park in 1932, and drainage tile was installed under the playing field to keep the surface dry. Several teams played at Bush Stadium, including the American Association, Indianapolis Indians and the Negro League Indianapolis ABCs, American Giants, Athletics, Crawfords, and Indianapolis Clowns.

Northwestern Park

Northwestern Park was named for its proximity to Northwestern Avenue, A major road that led northwest out of downtown along the Indianapolis Water Company Canal. The ballpark's construction date is unknown, but it was fully functional by at least 1908. Wooden grandstands were located along the third base line, but the fan base soon outgrew the field's seating capacity. In 1914, about 3,000 fans attended an ABCs' game, and 500 more seats were added soon after. The entrance to the park was located at the southeast corner of the park behind home plate and facing toward downtown. The Indianapolis Water Company canal plu housing for its workers were both located nearby. The Indianapolis ABCs were the most influential team to play at Northwestern Park.

Legend

African American Neighborhood
Downtown (Square Mile)
Railroad
River

N

Scale: 1" = 2,000'

2,000 0 2,000 4,000

Washington Park

Washington Park was located approximately 1.3 miles directly west of the center of Indianapolis. The site is now home to the Indianapolis Zoo. The park was bound on the north by old Washington Street, on the west by the Indianapolis Power and Light Company, on the south by railroad tracks and east by a vacant field. Home plate was located at 39° 46'01.40"N, 86° 10' 53.95"W.

Washington Park was built in 1905 and opened on April 3 of that year, but by 1932 the Indianapolis Indians had moved to Perry Stadium (later named Bush Stadium). The park was constructed of wood. Wood columns supported a wooden roof and box seats above the grandstands. Originally the park seated 11,000 fans, with an additional 4,000 seats added in 1909 when the grandstand roof was raised; fifteen feet and 1,000 skybox seats were added. The main park entrance was located at the northwest corner and faced old Washington Street. Inside, a single level of grandstands wrapped around home plate and lined the first (west) and third (north) baselines with dugouts below grade. High uncovered wood bleachers ran along the left field foul line and wrapped around the entire outfield wall with the scoreboard located on the corner of right field. Six large steel light towers were added to the park for the city's first night game in 1930, but were moved to Perry Stadium in 1932. The park was immersed in the city's industrial center, and it was common for railroad switchmen to park a line of freight cars adjacent to the right field fence which allowed youngsters to watch the games from atop the parked rail cars. The Indianapolis Indians played more than 2,300 games at Washington Park between 1905 and 1931, and the Indianapolis ABCs played frequent games at the ballpark between 1917 and 1926. The inaugural game of the Negro National League was played here on May 2, 1920.

Federal League Park

Federal League Park was located approximately 0.8 miles southwest of the city center and was bound on the north by Greenlawn Cemetery, on the west by a slaughterhouse, on the south by Henry Street and on the east by Kentucky Avenue. Home plate was located at 39° 45' 39.56"N, 86° 10'15.87"W.

Federal League Park was also called Greenlawn Park for the cemetery that previously occupied the site and remained to the north. The park opened on April 23, 1914, but it only lasted three years. A modern terminal freight station replaced it.

The grandstands around the park were 252 feet long on the first base line and 268 feet long on the third base line. The were 60 feet wide by 70 feet high and covered by a green metal roof to provide shade for the entire grandstands. The stands were constructed of steel, concrete and heavy timber to it would be fire resistant. The dugouts were made of concrete and sunk four feet below the grade of the playing field. The field itself was constructed on a bed of cinders to help shed water. Many amenities were included for the comfort and pleasure of the fans, including nice men's and ladies' lounges equipped with telephones for long distance calls, rooms with gas heaters, and refreshment stands with refrigerator rooms. The Federal League Indianapolis Hoosiers and the Indianapolis ABCs both played baseball at Federal League Park.

Prepared by: Ball State University College of Architecture and Planning
Professors: R. Christopher Baas and Geralyn Strecker
With contributions from: Austin Blomeke, Kyle Boot, Ethan Coverstone, Benjamin Doane, Anthony Gary, Brian Grover, Eric James, and Ashley Williams

<u>Drawing Set Index</u>

Sheet 1. Project Overview
Sheet 2. Associated Baseball Parks
Sheet 3. Bush Stadium Plan and Details
Sheet 4. Bush Stadium Section, Elevation and Details

HISTORIC AMERICAN LANDSCAPES SURVEY IN-6
SHEET 1 OF 4
BUSH STADIUM AND THE LANDSCAPE OF BLACK BASEBALL IN INDIANAPOLIS, INDIANA
INDIANAPOLIS MARION COUNTY INDIANA
LANDSCAPE OF BLACK BASEBALL IN INDIANAPOLIS
BALL STATE UNIVERSITY
NATIONAL PARK SERVICE
UNITED STATES DEPARTMENT OF THE INTERIOR

The Prints & Photographs Division of the Library of Congress preserves HALS documentation for posterity and makes it available to the general public through its digital collections website (http://www.loc.gov/index.html).

Because of its disciplined research, writing, and drawing components, HALS documentation is a wonderful project for university students or other groups of baseball researchers, encouraging them to invest in preserving local history. Learning more about their community also helps individuals understand changes in the landscape over time.

Black Ballparks of Indianapolis

One set of HALS documentation addressed four Indianapolis ballparks. Information about these sites came from primary and secondary sources. The most influential primary sources were historic maps and construction drawings. Early Sanborn Fire Insurance Maps provided park locations and the layout of ticket offices, entry gates, locker rooms, grandstands, and bleachers. Most of these maps also identify predominant construction materials, so researchers can discover whether ballparks were primarily wood or concrete and steel. For Northwestern Park, the Sanborn map offers the only detailed location for the field. None of the maps included home plate and foul line locations, but aerial photographs provided this information for Washington Park and Bush Stadium. The Ball State University College of Architecture and Planning Archives contain blueprints from when the city considered converting Perry/Bush Stadium into a dual baseball/football facility in the 1970s (the project was never completed). These measured drawings of the existing structure provided a template for plan and section drawings. Additionally, local newspapers provided firsthand accounts as new ballparks were constructed. Most secondary sources came in the form of team histories. Paul Debono's *The Indianapolis ABCs* (McFarland, 1997) laid the framework for understanding the historical context of black baseball in the city plus the team's use of ballparks through the mid–1920s.

To document the current condition of the ballpark sites, the students visited and photographed the exterior of Perry Stadium (deteriorating structures made the interior of the park unsafe to enter), plus former locations of the three parks that are no longer extant. The Northwestern and Federal League Park sites are now part of industrial and warehousing complexes; the Indianapolis Zoo's administrative offices and staff parking now cover Washington Park.

The narrative history of the HALS documentation includes all four sites. However, since sites must still exist to qualify for the Historic American Landscape Survey, the submission focuses on Bush Stadium (still mostly intact during summer 2011) but includes general information for Northwestern, Washington, and Federal League parks (all demolished long ago) as part of the larger context of black baseball in Indianapolis.

African American baseball teams have been recorded playing in Indianapolis as early as 1867. In the decades after the Civil War, the city's black population grew quickly. The 1890 census reported 11,000 African Americans living in Indianapolis, and by 1910 that number had more than doubled to 23,000. This sizable community

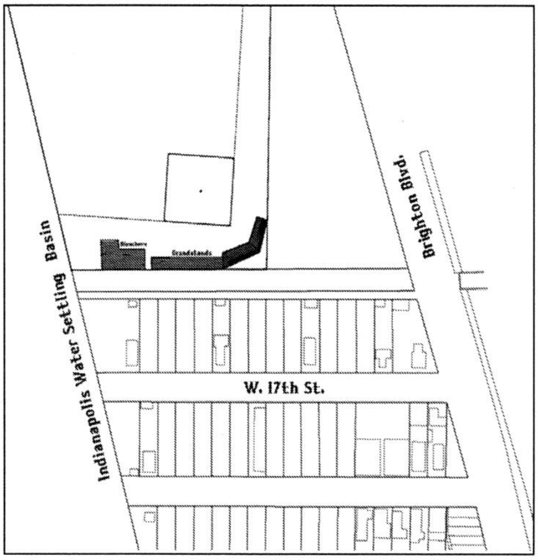

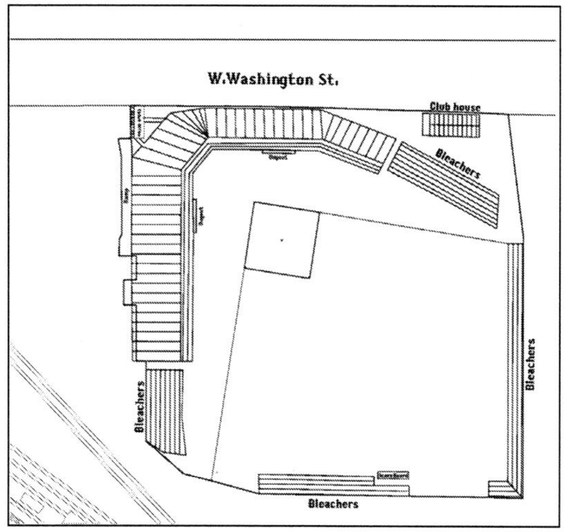

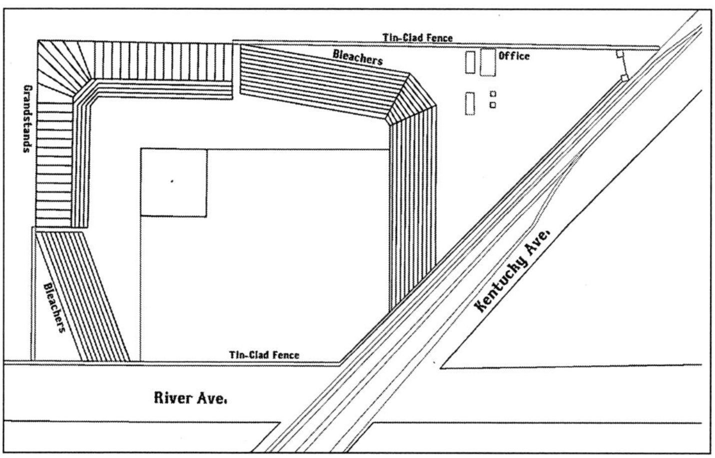

Clockwise from upper left: Plan views of Northwestern, Washington, and Federal parks reconstructed by Ball State students from Sanborn insurance maps.

has remained at about 10 percent of the city's total population since the late 1800s, making Indianapolis unique among Midwestern cities, most of which did not gain substantial black populations until the Great Migration after World War I.

This stable population also allowed the black community to develop its own economic and social systems, and Indiana Avenue on the northwest side of downtown became the middle-class African American section of the city. Among other businesses, Indiana Avenue once held the offices of Madam C. J. Walker, the nation's first African American millionaire, who made her fortune in the cosmetics and hair care industry. In the late 1910s, Indianapolis ABCs owner C.I. Taylor had a pool hall just down the street.

Near the confluence of the White River and Fall Creek, the area around Indiana Avenue was also industrial. The Indianapolis Water Company had an extensive canal and water works system throughout the northern section of the region, and the Indianapolis Power and Light and railroad companies worked out of the southern section. Also worth noting, this area is located between downtown and the Indianapolis

Motor Speedway, which boosted the city to a major automobile metropolis in the early 1900s.[5]

Baseball provided a wholesome form of entertainment during the late 1800s and early 1900s, but in Indianapolis, like many U.S. cities, African Americans were not permitted to play ball with whites on organized teams. Segregated black teams formed at every level, and as social and economic situations improved, local semiprofessional teams developed, often sponsored by local businesses.[6] In 1902, the Indianapolis ABCs (named for the American Brewing Company) emerged out of this African American community and began playing at Northwestern Park.

Northwestern Park

Northwestern Park was named for its location near Northwestern Avenue (now Dr. Martin Luther King Jr. Street), a major road leading northwest out of downtown along the Indianapolis Water Company Canal. This was and still is a predominantly African American working-class community.

The ballpark evolved from a former sandlot. Exactly when the wooden grandstand was built is unknown; however, early newspaper accounts and later aerial photographs indicate the park was fully operational prior to 1905 and was demolished prior to 1937. The park's exact dimensions and seating configurations are also unknown because the site was on the northernmost edge of the neighborhood, and the Sanborn map only shows the southern portion of the park.[7] The entrance was located behind home plate at the southeast corner of the park, closest to downtown. Grandstands were located along the third base line (south), and it is unknown if permanent seating was available along the first base line or the outfield.

Northwestern Park was fine for ABCs' games until 1914, when C.I. Taylor arrived from West Baden, Indiana, to transform the team into a premier professional organization. To facilitate this shift, Taylor brought with him several of the West Baden Sprudels, widely acclaimed as one of the strongest professional black teams in the Midwest. With high-quality players, the ABCs were able to schedule games against other strong black teams from around the Midwest, including Rube Foster's Chicago American Giants. For Sunday doubleheaders against top competitors, the ABCs drew far more fans than the small park could hold. Many had to sit along the outfield fence, sometimes getting in the way of play. After 3,000 fans attended a game in 1914, Taylor quickly invested his own money to add over 500 more seats, including box seats to comfortably accommodate well-to-do female spectators. From this section, Olivia Taylor and Madam C.J. Walker could cheer on the home team in relative comfort. Even with the additional seating, Northwestern Park was not large enough for major games, so Taylor started leasing ballparks from other teams.

In 1914, Indianapolis boasted two professional white baseball teams. Founded in 1902, the Indianapolis Indians were in the minor league American Association, playing their home games at Washington Park on the west side of downtown. Just a few blocks south, a new major league team — the Indianapolis Hoosiers—claimed the 1914 Federal League championship.

Federal League Park

The Hoosiers played at Federal League Park, a new concrete-and-steel ballpark a few blocks southwest of downtown, just west of where Lucas Oil Stadium stands today. Also called Greenlawn Park for the cemetery that previously occupied the site, the stadium was constructed during the winter of 1913-1914 to be the gem of the new Federal League. It was designed by Indianapolis Architect Victor H. Winterrowd and built by contractor Lynn B. Millikan, one of the Hoosiers' club directors.[8]

The park entrance was located at the northeast corner, closest to downtown, and a covered macadam passageway led fans to the northwest corner of the stadium, where they entered the stadium up an incline that opened to a dramatic view of the field. The park could accommodate a total of 23,000 fans in grandstand, box, and bleacher seats. Constructed of steel, concrete, and heavy timber to resist fire, the single-tier L-shaped grandstands were 252 feet long on the first base line and 268 feet on the third base line. The tiers were 60 feet deep by 70 feet high and shaded by a green metal roof. Ensuring unobstructed views, each row was 16 inches higher than the one in front of it. The 6,800 wooden grandstand seats were treated with paraffin so spectators would not have to risk splinters. To accommodate wealthier fans, a band of 62 field-level boxes with concrete floors offered more private seating. To keep out people who only held bleacher tickets, access to grandstand and box seats was through a single grandstand entrance behind home plate. To prevent "knot-hole" spectators and offer plenty of low-price seating, a 12-foot steel fence lined with bleacher seats surrounded the outfield. These bleachers extended out from the grandstand 227 feet along the third base side, 280 feet across the outfield, and 182 feet along the first base side.[9]

Underneath the grandstand, many other amenities ensured fans' comfort, including nice men's and ladies' lounges equipped with telephones for long-distance calls, rooms with gas heaters, and refreshment stands with refrigerator rooms. Since cars were already becoming popular in Indianapolis, land for parking was reserved behind the east bleachers.[10]

The park also offered state-of-the-art locker rooms for players. The dugouts were lined with concrete and sunken four feet below grade. Left field was 280 feet, center field 400, and right field 310. The playing surface was constructed on a bed of cinders to shed water. The press and club officials were accommodated in five boxes perched above the grandstand directly behind home plate. On opening day — April 23, 1914 — a sold-out crowd watched St. Louis defeat the Hoosiers, 3–0. The *Indianapolis Star* compared the day's festivities to Barnum's circus.[11]

While the Indians' Washington Park (described below) had segregated bleacher-only seating for African Americans and prevented them from using restrooms and other facilities, Federal League Park allowed everyone access to all areas, as long as they held the appropriate ticket. Park directors used this information in marketing Hoosiers games to attract the black community.[12] This open policy also made the park ideal for the ABCs.

Federal League Park cost more than $100,000 to build, and Hoosiers games alone were not sufficient to satisfy investors. To generate revenue when the team was out of town, they leased the ballpark to C.I. Taylor for the ABCs. Even after the Hoosiers left Indianapolis in 1915, the ABCs continued playing major home games at Federal League Park for two seasons. But then Federal League Park was demolished in 1917, less than three years after its construction, to make room for a modern freight station to relieve downtown congestion.[13] The fact that the ABCs were playing in a nicer facility than the Indians might have also influenced the decision to demolish the stadium.

One last bit of architectural information is relevant to the history of black baseball. Federal League Park had six exits: four along Kentucky Avenue (left and center field) and two along Oliver Avenue (right field). Knowing this helps us picture an October 24, 1915, incident when Oscar Charleston punched a white umpire during an exhibition game against Donie Bush's All Stars, a team of white major and minor leaguers. To flee a charging crowd of white players and spectators, Charleston and Bingo DeMoss escaped through a center-field gate along Kentucky Avenue.

Washington Park

After the demise of Federal League Park, Washington Park—home field of the American Association Indianapolis Indians—continued as the city's premier ballpark. The Indians had played their first three seasons (1902–1904) at a 1,200-seat wooden ballpark on East Washington Street. In 1905, team owners sought a larger venue and leased a site on West Washington Street, just across the White River from downtown. The new location was readily accessible by streetcar and a short walk from businesses, hotels, and residential neighborhoods. Its proximity to Union Station (1.3 miles) was convenient for visiting teams and out-of-town spectators. Plus, proximity to the Indiana Avenue African American neighborhood also made the facility a convenient site for professional black baseball games when the Indians were out of town.

Constructed in 1905, Washington Park was the city's first large-scale wooden ballpark. It originally seated approximately 11,000 fans, but the Indians' early successes caused the team to add an additional 4,000 seats for the 1909 season. They accomplished this by raising the grandstand roof 15 feet, nearly doubling the seats beneath. The expansion also added 1,000 box seats above the grandstand roof, much like today's skyboxes.[14]

The park's formal dedication was an April 3, 1905, exhibition game between the Indians and John McGraw's New York Giants, the defending National League champions, who were barnstorming their way home from spring training. Giants pitching great Christy Mathewson pitched six innings, and the visitors won, 7–3. The Indians' first official league game at the park was the April 19 American Association season opener against the Milwaukee Brewers. On a blustery spring day, a crowd of 4,500 suffered through a 5–4 loss.[15]

In late March 1913, a catastrophic flood sent the White River over its banks and poured 10 feet of water on the Washington Park playing field. At first, people feared the ballpark might be a total loss. The flood completely wrecked the right field bleachers, pushing the structure back and out of the park. Damage was so severe that the American Association had to rearrange its schedule so the Indians could play all of their games out of town until April 24, when sufficient repairs had been completed to make the park safe. In addition to replacing the bleachers, crews had to replace wooden grandstand seats ruined by the water. The flood had also ruined the dugouts and stripped the turf from the field. Repair crews built new dugouts, but the Indians played without grass until it could grow back. Everything stored under the grandstand was a total loss, including the team uniforms.[16]

Beginning in 1917, the ABCs leased Washington Park from the Indians for occasional games up through the early 1920s. The most notable of these events was the inaugural game of the Negro National League on May 2, 1920. The ABCs defeated Joe Green's Chicago Giants, 4–2. Future Hall of Famers Oscar Charleston and Ben Taylor played for Indianapolis that day.

Although the playing field at Washington Park was satisfactory, the Indians did not allow the ABCs and their visiting black opponents to use the locker rooms. This prompted Taylor to build changing facilities in the back of his pool hall on Indiana Avenue. After 1920, the Indians also became increasingly restrictive about when and how the ABCs could use the park. Then with the rise of the Ku Klux Klan in 1922–1924, Washington Park no longer allowed black teams to lease the field.

Washington Park saw its first night game on June 9, 1930. The field was lit by six steel light towers positioned around the field, generating 75 million candle-power. This was a major event and drew several luminaries, including Kennesaw Mountain Landis, first commissioner of Major League Baseball. The Indians lost the game to St. Paul, 1–0.[17]

Even with the new lights, Washington Park no longer had sufficient amenities to accommodate a top minor league team. Plus, limited space around the facility could not satisfy parking demands for the growing number of fans driving to games. The Indians started the 1931 season at Washington Park but finished the year in a more modern facility.

Perry Stadium

In 1931, the Indians constructed a new ballpark 16 blocks northwest of downtown, at the intersection of Hardy and 16th Streets, along the eastern bank of White River. At the time, this was agricultural land on the city's western edge; today it is part of the

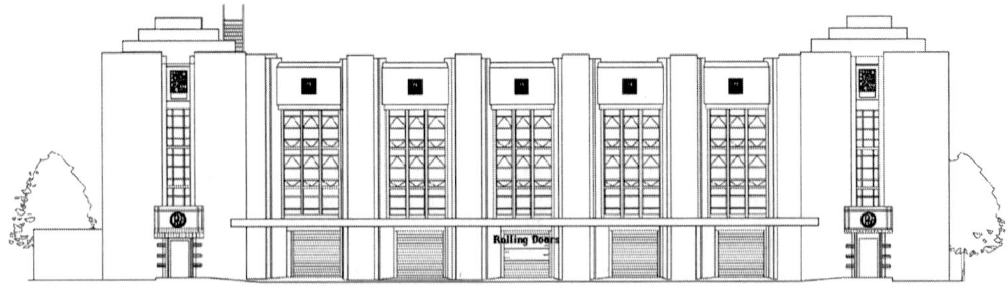

Perry Stadium's Art Deco entry pavilion.

dense urban core. Team owner Norman Perry named the new facility Perry Stadium, to honor his deceased brother. Opening day was September 5, 1931.

Architects Edward D. Pierre and George C. White of Indianapolis designed the $350,000, 14,500-seat ballpark, using reinforced concrete, steel, brick masonry, and Indiana limestone. The engineer was C. J. McCorkle of the Osborn Engineering Company of Cleveland, Ohio, and the contractor was W. P. Jungclaus of Indianapolis.[18] The park is enclosed by a 12-foot-high brick wall capped with limestone and adorned with ivy. The main entrance is located at the southwest corner, addressing the middle of the parking lot. Fans entered through a grand Art Deco gate pavilion of Indiana limestone with bas-relief carvings of Perry Stadium and Indianapolis Indians motifs.

The reinforced concrete grandstands wrapped around home plate (located at the southwest corner of the park) and ran along the first (south) and third (west) base lines. Steel posts held the steel-frame metal roof above the grandstands and supported box seats above. Additional lower-price seating was offered in concrete bleachers extending along the right field foul line. The original scoreboard was located along the left field wall, but was later replaced by an electronic board on the right field wall. Left field was 350 feet, center 395 feet, and right 350 feet. Drainage tile was installed under the field to maintain a dry playing surface. Washington Park's six steel light towers were moved to Perry Stadium in 1932.

Indians-inspired limestone bas-relief carving.

Perhaps the greatest improvements

Art Deco limestone bas-relief carving of a batter and catcher.

over Washington Park were amenities underneath the grandstand. Several concession windows and multiple restrooms made the game experience much more comfortable for spectators. Players and umpires had separate locker rooms connected to the dugouts by tunnels. Club offices with a kitchen and dining room were located on the second floor of the gate pavilion. To accommodate fans' growing dependence on personal automobiles, the ballpark had easy street access, and parking surrounded three sides, with Harding Street bordering the east side, along the left field wall.

Just one mile west of Northwestern Park, Perry Stadium also benefited from being near a thriving working-class African American neighborhood. Besides serving as the Indians' home field, Perry Stadium also hosted games for professional black teams during the 1930s, including the ABCs, the American Giants, the Athletics, and the Crawfords. The greatest player to represent a home team at Bush Stadium was Indianapolis native Oscar Charleston. The future Hall of Famer had played with the ABCs at Northwestern, Federal, and Washington Parks, then appeared at Perry Stadium in 1940 as manager and occasional first baseman for the Indianapolis Crawfords.

In 1942, former major leaguer Owen "Donie" Bush and Frank McKinney purchased the Indians and Perry Stadium. An Indianapolis native, Bush had played major league baseball for the Detroit Tigers from 1908–1920 and the Washington Senators from 1921–1923. During his playing career, he had often organized teams of major and minor leaguers to play post-season exhibition games against the Indianapolis ABCs. In the patriotic spirit of World War II, the new team owners renamed the stadium Victory Field. They also built a new ticket office just left of the main entrance, which included a "will call" window since fans were now telephoning to order tickets in advance of games.[19]

Through the mid–1940s and 1950s, the barnstorming Indianapolis Clowns, another professional African American team, also used the park for their few "home" games.

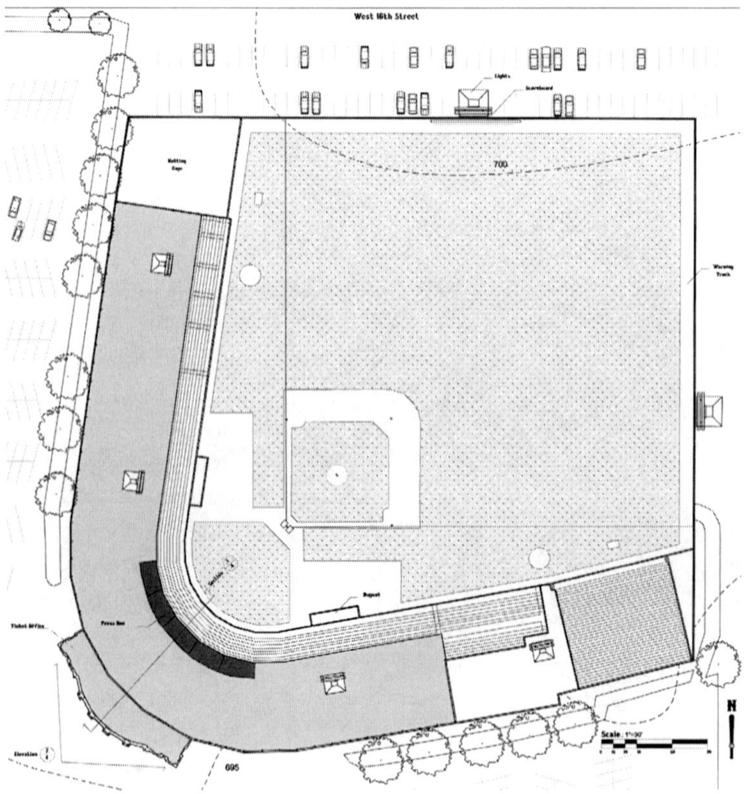

Plan view drawing of Bush Stadium (previously Perry Stadium), created by Ball State students.

The Clowns mixed baseball with comedy to provide entertainment that attracted fans during a time when integrated professional baseball was drawing attention away from the Negro Leagues. When the Clowns played at Victory Field, black fans filled the stands, but many white spectators also attended the games.

In 1952, the Indians' major league affiliation shifted from the Pittsburgh Pirates to the Cleveland Indians. While this move was not uncommon — back then the Indians changed affiliations every few years— it was noteworthy because it brought integration to professional baseball in Indianapolis. The Pirates were one of the last major league teams to integrate (in 1954), but Cleveland had signed Larry Doby in 1947, less than three months after Jackie Robinson took the field for the Dodgers. Thus, the new major league affiliation brought black players to the Indianapolis Indians, beginning with third baseman Al Smith and right fielder Dave Pope.[20] With minor league stars to follow on the home team and growing numbers of African Americans in the major leagues, interest in segregated black baseball waned.

In 1967, the Indians sold Victory Field to the city, which then renamed it Bush Stadium in honor of Indians team president Donie Bush.[21] No major changes were

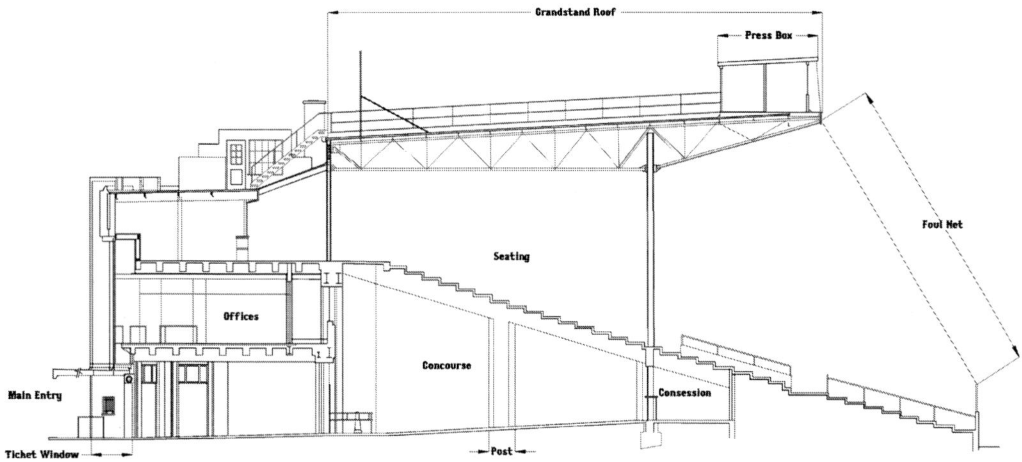

Section through Perry Stadium's entry pavilion and grandstand.

made to the park after that time, though the city briefly explored expanding the stadium to accommodate both baseball and football. Ultimately, they decided the $60 million project was not feasible.[22] However, the lack of significant architectural alteration served as an interesting advantage when director John Sayles was scouting locations for his 1988 film *Eight Men Out*. Bush Stadium emerged as a perfect choice. Still in good condition, the inside of the park could easily pass for both the Chicago and Cincinnati stadiums where the White Sox and Reds played the 1919 World Series. The only major modification required was temporarily taking down the light towers, which were painted during the filming then put back up after the movie was done.[23]

Into the late 1900s, Bush Stadium increasingly showed its age, and in 1995, the stadium was in such poor shape that the City of Indianapolis decided to build the Indians a new Victory Field on the west edge of downtown, about halfway between the former Federal League Park and Washington Park sites. No longer used for baseball, Bush Stadium was converted into the 16th Street Raceway in 1997. When that failed, the City of Indianapolis Department of Parks and Recreation took possession of the site but allowed it to remain empty for more than a decade, causing rapid deterioration throughout the park, especially as the roof began to fail and vandals broke in to strip copper wire and plumbing to sell as scrap metal. In 2009, the playing field became a vehicle storage location for the "Cash for Clunkers" federal economic stimulus program.

Baseball historians feared the fate of Bush Stadium. As one of only a handful of surviving ballparks where Negro League teams played, it has great historic value, but the city could not generate enough interest and funding to rehabilitate it into a viable 21st century ballpark. The city explored other options and in June 2011 announced plans to redevelop the stadium for commercial and residential uses. The

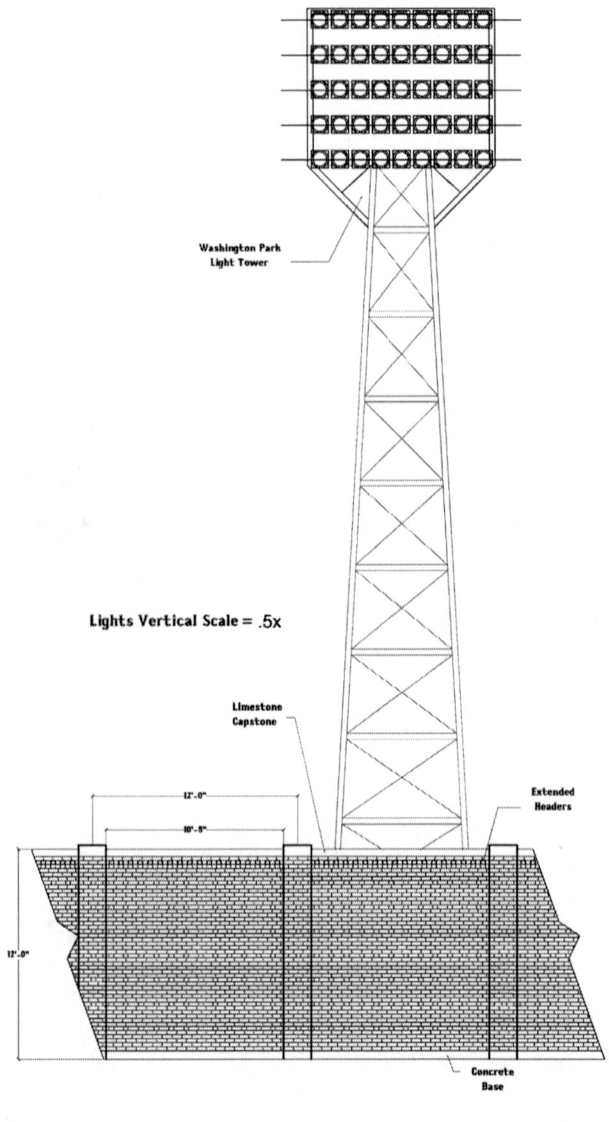

Detail of Perry Stadium's outfield wall and light tower. The light towers were moved from Washington Park.

project is preserving the ballpark's historic façade but gutting the seating to accommodate three floors of apartments. The Stadium Apartments are scheduled to open in August 2013.[24]

Completed just before this demolition and construction work began, the Bush Stadium HALS documentation captures a final snapshot of the historic ballpark before it enters its next phase.

Conclusion

Documenting these important landscapes of black baseball history certainly took copious work. However, the faculty members and students involved take pride in knowing that even though these ballparks will continue to change over time and perhaps someday even disappear, their existence and importance to the African American communities in Indianapolis has forever been recorded for future generations to study. Aside from the satisfaction of knowing that our work now resides in the Library of Congress, the group also received recognition from the American Society of Landscape Architects, which hosts an annual HALS Challenge to recognize the best documentation efforts. The Ball State group claimed second place in this professional national competition in 2011.

Through technical drawings, HALS documentation provides alternative research products to traditional written reports or journal articles. The program's graphic component allows historians an artistic outlet for interpreting significant landscapes. We encourage other baseball researchers to see this project as a model for future ways to document our ballparks. Ball State students have also completed HALS documentation of Detroit's Hamtramck Stadium. Other parks, such as New Jersey's Hinchliffe Stadium that recently achieved National Historic Landmark status, would be great candidates for connecting students to black baseball's rich history.

Notes

1. Charles A. Birnbaum and Christine Capelle Peters, *The Secretary of the Interior's Standards for the Treatment of Historic Properties with Guidelines for the Treatment of Cultural Landscapes.* (Washington, D.C.: National Park Service, 1996).
2. Adapted from the HALS Landscape of Black Baseball short form.
3. Phillip J. Lowry, *Green Cathedrals: The Ultimate Celebration of Major League and Negro League Ballpark* (New York: Walker and Company, 2006). Geri Strecker, "The Rise and Fall of Greenlee Field: Biography of a Ballpark," *Black Ball* 2 (Fall 2009): 37–67; Geri Strecker and Christopher Baas, "Batter Up: Professional Black Baseball at Indianapolis Ballparks," *Traces of Indiana and Midwestern History*, Fall 2011, 26–33; Christopher Baas and Angie Gibson, "86°10'54"W, 39°46'1"N: Using Geographic Information Systems to Document Historic Sporting Landscapes," *Journal of Sport History* 3, no. 2 (Fall 2011): 475–487.
4. National Park Service, "HALS 101: The Historic American Landscape Survey (Brochure)," No Date. *The Secretary of the Interior's Standards and Guidelines for Architectural and Engineering Documentation* (www.nps.gov/history/hdp/standards/standards.htm) describes the documentation products accepted by the Library of Congress.
5. Paul Debono, *The Indianapolis ABCs: History of a Premier Team in the Negro Leagues* (Jefferson, NC: McFarland, 1997), 5–8; Sanborn Fire Insurance Map, Indianapolis, vol. 5, 578, 1915–1950.
6. Debono, *Indianapolis ABCs*, 5–8.
7. Indianapolis Sanborn Map, 1914–1915, vol.4 (1915), sheet 375.
8. Eddie Ash, "Hoosiers' New Park," *Indianapolis Sunday Star*, January 18, 1914.
9. Ibid.
10. Ibid.
11. "Fine Opening Even If Home Boys Did Lose," *Indianapolis Star*, April 24, 1914, 13.
12. Information about the park welcoming African Americans was gathered from the *Indianapolis Star, Indianapolis Ledger*, and *Indianapolis Freeman* during the early months of the 1914 baseball season.

13. Debono, *Indianapolis ABCs*, 53; "Federals Have a Modern Park," *Indianapolis Star*, April 20, 1914; "Traction Lines Buy Federal Ball Park," *Indianapolis Star*, November 30, 1916.

14. *The Indianapolis Star* covered the Washington Park expansion project in the weeks leading up to the 1909 season.

15. Multiple accounts of the Washington Park opening appeared in the *Indianapolis Star* throughout April 1905.

16. The flood and ensuing repairs were a major topic in the *Indianapolis Star* from March 26, 1913, into May.

17. David B. Reddick and Kim M. Rogers, *The Magic of Indians Baseball: 1887–1987* (Indianapolis: Indians, 1988), 37.

18. W.C. Madden, *P.S. Remembering Bush Stadium: Home of the Indianapolis Indians* (Noblesville, IN: Madden Publishing, 1995), 1.

19. Information taken from a 1942 Indianapolis Indians game program. The cover features a red, white, and blue image of Uncle Sam ready to swing his bat and straddling the capital V of Victory Field.

20. Richard Ian Kimball discusses the integration of the Indianapolis Indians in "Beyond the 'Great Experiment': Integrated Baseball Comes to Indianapolis," *Journal of Sport History* 26, no.1 (Spring 1999): 142–162.

21. Debono, *Indianapolis ABCs*, 56; Madden, *Bush Stadium*; "Evolution of Baseball in Indianapolis," Indianapolis Star, April 9, 1932.

22. Madden, *Bush Stadium*, 14.

23. Indians owner Max Schumacher shared this information about the light towers with Geri Strecker during a game in April 2011.

24. "Evolution of Baseball in Indianapolis," *Indianapolis Star*, April 9, 1932; "$22 Million Development on Deck for Bush Stadium," *Indianapolis Star*, June 16, 2011.

A Fine Line Between Admiration and Animosity

Ed Bolden's Philadelphia Stars, the Negro National League, and the Philadelphia Tribune, *1933–1938*

COURTNEY SMITH

Abstract

This article examines the Philadelphia Tribune*'s supportive and critical coverage of Negro League baseball from 1933 through 1938. That period spans the first five seasons of Ed Bolden's Philadelphia Stars, the local Negro National League franchise. As this article shows, the* Tribune*'s sportswriters consistently praised Bolden, the Stars' African American owner, while frequently criticizing other owners and officials in the Negro National League. Several key events triggered that critical coverage: the Stars' controversial 1934 league championship, secrecy surrounding league meetings, the denial of the first-half title to the Stars in 1936, and the spate of contract-jumping in 1937. As this article shows, the* Tribune*'s sportswriters demonstrated an utter lack of concern about the Negro National League's financial troubles. The negative coverage represented yet another problem for the Negro National League in the 1930s and foreshadowed the successful integration campaigns of the 1940s.*

Introduction

ON FEBRUARY 9, 1933, A LEADING STORY in the *Philadelphia Tribune* focused on bank failures in southern New Jersey and their ramifications for many African American–owned institutions in the region. In that same issue, a headline announcing the expansion of the Negro National League (NNL) splashed across the top of the *Philadelphia Tribune*'s sports page. As the accompanying article explained, a group of owners met in Ed Gottlieb's office to finalize plans to add a division of eastern teams to the league.

Black Ball / DOI: 10.3172/BLB.6.37 / Volume 6 / 2013 / pp. 37–50 /
ISSN 1939-8484 (Print) / ISSN 1939-8379 (Online) / © 2013 McFarland & Company, Inc.

In an acknowledgement of the troubles facing black professional baseball in recent years, the article's author commented that the owners met "without any undue bickering and unhampered by irrelevant preliminaries."[1] The article listed a brand new team, the Philadelphia Stars, as one of the franchises under consideration for the Negro National League's new eastern division. Other pertinent information reported in the article included plans for a split-season schedule and a revival of the once-popular Negro World Series. Near the end of the article, the author revealed the names of the two individuals leading the new Philadelphia Stars franchise — Ed Bolden and Dick Lundy.[2]

Five weeks later, Randy Dixon, the *Tribune*'s sports editor, authored an article providing details on the "choice coterie of diamond laborers" who had joined the new franchise.[3] Dixon mentioned names familiar to the Philadelphia area's black baseball fans: shortstop Lundy, who would also manage the team; pitcher Webster McDonald; catcher Raleigh "Biz" Mackey; third baseman Jud Wilson; infielder Jake Stevens; and outfielder Chaney White. Dixon's article conveyed Bolden's satisfaction with his roster and his confidence that he would add more players who would "make this city forget its baseball headaches of recent seasons."[4] The article also states that Bolden had begun to secure a home ballpark for the Stars in West Philadelphia, further emphasizing his role in leading and operating the new franchise.[5]

Approximately two years later, the *Tribune*'s Ed Harris wrote a column contrasting the NNL's offseason with that of the National League and the American League. Harris noted that teams in both the National League and American League had publicized their personnel moves and created a sense of anticipation for the upcoming 1935 season. He compared the leagues' publicity to the offseason secrecy surrounding teams in the NNL. Harris's column appeared in February 1935; during the previous month, the NNL's owners met in New York City. The league's secretary, however, never sent an official statement concerning important decisions the owners made at their meeting. Harris positioned black newspapers as a key conduit between the NNL and its fans, thereby implying that the league's secrecy undermined its relationship with its key supporters. He offered a biting summary of the league's attitude: "They sit at the conference tables and beef about the lack of space they get in the newspapers, but ask them to use a little energy and money to get that space and you would think they had all been stricken dumb."[6] He sarcastically welcomed the league's owners to find a way to reach their fans and generate publicity without the support of black newspapers. Harris concluded that the sooner the league's owners realized that they needed the support of black newspapers and fans, "the sooner things will start to brighten up for them."[7]

Those *Tribune* articles encapsulate the key issues analyzed in this article. The *Tribune*'s coverage of the Stars consistently praised Bolden's efforts to build a winning team and his work as a NNL official. Simultaneously, the paper's coverage of the NNL frequently contained an undercurrent of negativity, most often directed at league officials and team owners other than Bolden.

During the period analyzed in this article, several events in particular drew the sportswriters' ire: the controversial 1934 NNL championship series between the Stars and the Chicago American Giants; secrecy surrounding NNL meetings; the denial of the first-half NNL title to the Stars in 1936; and the spate of contract-jumping in 1937. Not surprisingly, the Stars stood in the middle of two of those controversial events. From 1933–1938, the Stars and the rest of the NNL operated against a backdrop of the on-going Great Depression. The dire economic climate probably limited what the NNL could reasonably accomplish and shaped the owners' actions. In their critical columns, however, Harris and other *Tribune* sportswriters never considered the dire economic climate as a mitigating factor in the NNL owners' actions. The coverage represented yet another problem the NNL faced in the 1930s, and it foreshadowed the deep divisions between the black press and the NNL that appeared during the successful integration campaigns of the 1940s.

Ed Bolden, owner of the Philadelphia Stars, relaxing with a copy of *Esquire Magazine* (courtesy NoirTech Research, Inc.).

Neil Lanctot's *Negro League Baseball: The Rise and Ruin of a Black Institution* provides a valuable context for this article. Lanctot extensively details the stark economic realities facing NNL and Negro American League (NAL) teams during the 1930s. The Great Depression limited the ability of teams and leagues to generate profit, and low attendance at many NNL games further undermined the league's economic health. As owners sought to ensure their teams' survival, they pursued actions that harmed the NNL's cohesion and created an appearance of dysfunction within the league's operations. Lanctot also briefly describes the rise of a new breed of sportswriters in black newspapers—like the *Tribune*'s Harris and Randy Dixon—who demonstrated little sympathy for the league's owners since the owners seemed to exacerbate the league problems with their decision making. With its broad focus, Lanctot's work provides background and context for the issues addressed in this article. The poor economic climate played a role in the controversies that triggered negative coverage in the *Tribune*. The *Tribune*'s sportswriters, however, unsympathetically criticized the NNL owners and bemoaned the NNL's inability to resemble the more stable National and American Leagues.[8]

Other scholars have analyzed the multi-faceted relationship between the black press and Negro League baseball, and those works also provide a context for this article. Brian Carroll's "Rube Foster, C.I. Taylor, and the Great Newspaper War of 1915" argues that black newspapers played a booster-like role for black baseball in an era before the establishment of professional leagues. Carroll also examines the close working partnership between Foster and the Chicago *Defender* and Taylor and the Indianapolis *Freeman*, showing that both men used those newspapers as platforms to express their views and engage in a war of words.[9] Carroll's article helps to explain the relationship between Bolden and the *Tribune* that existed before and after the Stars' creation in 1933.

Beginning in 1911, Bolden assumed direction of the Darby-based Hilldale Daisies and transformed them into one of the top eastern black professional baseball teams. As part of his efforts to promote Hilldale, Bolden used the *Tribune* as a platform to advertise the team to the Philadelphia area's black baseball fans. The *Tribune* printed the team's press releases and box scores; the newspaper even gave the team its own column, "Hilldale Pickups." A Hilldale veteran, Otto Briggs, worked as the newspaper's circulation manager and married the daughter of the *Tribune*'s founder.[10] Bolden and the *Tribune*, therefore, enjoyed a favorable working partnership prior to the Stars' existence, and that partnership extended into coverage of the Stars during their first five seasons.

Carroll's "'A Perfect Baseball Day': Black Press Coverage of the East-West Classic" uses that annual event to analyze changes in the black press's coverage of Negro League baseball from the 1930s through the 1950s. According to him, the black press joined owners in supporting the leagues in the 1930s, distanced themselves from league owners in the 1940s, and focused on black players in the major leagues in the 1950s. Carroll correctly notes that black newspapers made the East-West Classic possible since fans used ballots in the newspapers to vote for the classic's participants.[11]

His "To Pittsburgh from Chicago: A Changing of the Guard in Black Baseball and the Black Press in the 1930s" adds another level of complexity to the multi-faceted relationship between black baseball and the black press. As Carroll notes, the 1930s witnessed the rise of a new kind of owner, symbolized by Gus Greenlee, in black professional baseball. Greenlee and other owners of his ilk differed from owners of previous eras in their connections to illegal activities. Similarly, the 1930s witnessed the arrival of younger and more aggressive black sportswriters, such as the Pittsburgh *Courier*'s Wendell Smith, who openly campaigned for integration. Those trends set the stage for the *Courier*'s and other newspapers' well publicized integration campaigns of the 1940s.[12]

The integration era of the 1940s and 1950s represents the focus of the bulk of other works on the black press and black baseball.[13] Of those works, two stand out: Carroll's *When to Stop the Cheering: The Black Press, the Black Community, and the Integration of Professional Baseball* and David K. Wiggins' "Wendell Smith, the *Pittsburgh Courier-Journal* and the Campaign to Include Blacks in Organized Baseball, 1933–1945."

Carroll makes observations about the black press in the 1930s that are particularly relevant to this article. He notes that the black press adopted a more neutral stance toward the Negro Leagues than it had in the previous decade. Carroll also notes another change from the previous decade — black sportswriters did not regularly attend league meetings. Consequently, black sportswriters lacked access to the leagues' operations and failed to develop a familiarity with the leagues' officials. Carroll does not include any columns from black sportswriters expressing disgust with the leagues' secrecy and their lack of access to meetings. Instead, he concentrates on the integration campaigns that began at the end of the decade and continued into the 1940s.[14]

By examining the efforts of Wendell Smith, Wiggins offers a more concentrated analysis of the integration campaigns sustained in black newspapers. According to Wiggins, Smith's concern for integrating professional baseball took precedence over any concern for the health of the Negro Leagues. Smith, however, did believe that the integration of the major leagues would bring financial benefits to the Negro Leagues. Wiggins rightly calls that view naïve. His work provides some context for this article's analysis of the *Tribune*'s coverage during the era immediately preceding Smith's push for integration. Both of the *Tribune*'s baseball writers cared about the NNL's well-being and offered suggestions for ways the league could improve its operations. Neither writer, however, used the NNL's precarious financial health as a mitigating factor in their assessment of the league's actions. While they never expressed a lack of concern about the NNL's financial ills, they also never directly tied the league's finances to the owners' actions and to league-related controversies.[15]

This article builds upon the analyses contained in those other works by examining the *Tribune*'s coverage of the Stars and the NNL from 1933–1938, the first five seasons of the Stars' 20-season history. An examination of the *Tribune*'s coverage during that era reveals the complicated nature of the newspaper's black baseball coverage. The *Tribune*'s articles on the Stars almost always included words of praise and respect for the franchise's African American owner, Ed Bolden. By contrast, the *Tribune*'s articles on the NNL almost always included words of criticism for the other owners and league officials. In their columns, the paper's sportswriters never directly addressed the league's precarious financial health or considered it a mitigating factor in its operations. Instead, they drew unfavorable comparisons between the NNL and the more stable National and American Leagues. When combined with the Great Depression and other external threats, the negative coverage helped to make the 1930s a trying time for the NNL. Additionally, the negative coverage foretold deeper animosity between the NNL and the black press in the 1940s as sportswriters openly, and successfully, pushed for integration in the major leagues.

Ed Bolden and the *Philadelphia Tribune*

Since the Philadelphia Stars operated as an independent team during their inaugural season, the *Tribune* provided scant coverage of the NNL during the 1933 baseball season. A few stories early in the year mentioned the NNL's meetings and optimistic plans for the upcoming season.[16] Later in the year, the newspaper printed a review of

Philadelphia Stars, 1933–1934 (courtesy NoirTech Research).

the NNL's season that presaged future columns on the league. The review labeled the NNL's 1933 season as "[h]ectic" and noted that only three of the seven teams completed their full schedules.[17] It rebuked team owners and managers for their "childish pouting" and their "outrageous belief that they were members of a prejudiced and unfair group."[18] While acknowledging that the league faced obstacles beyond its control, the review sharply chided owners for "regard[ing] their own obligations to the league as a most flexible object."[19]

Stories about the Stars filled the *Tribune*'s sports pages during the 1933 season, and the newspaper acted like a booster for the new franchise. One article on a Stars preseason practice referred to the team as a "sterling outfit" and as potentially the "most colorful combination in colored baseball."[20] The newspaper faithfully printed articles on the Stars' games against local semipro and professional teams and against teams in the NNL, such as the Pittsburgh Crawfords.[21] It also promoted a budding rivalry between the Stars and the Bacharach Giants, a Philadelphia-based team owned by white businessman Harry Passon.[22] The two teams met several times during the 1933 season, and the *Tribune* provided detailed analyses of each team's roster and handicapped every contest. Prior to one of their final contests, an article proclaimed that "heated controversies are raging [throughout Philadelphia] over the respective merits of the two teams with the majority of fans surprisingly leaning towards the Bacharachs."[23] To increase anticipation for the contest, the article claimed "Bolden has ordered his chattels to be ready, and doubtless a hair-raising tilt will result."[24]

In addition to acting as a booster for the Stars, the *Tribune* also acted as a booster for team owner Ed Bolden. The franchise officially went by the name "Ed Bolden's Philadelphia Stars," and the newspaper often used Bolden's name in its coverage of the Stars. Box scores listed the team as "Bolden's Stars," not the "Philadelphia Stars." Similarly, headlines and articles referred to the new franchise as "Ed Bolden's Philadelphia Stars," "Bolden's Stars," or the "Boldenmen."[25] The *Tribune*'s identification of the Stars in that manner helped to elevate Bolden's role with the team and concealed Ed Gottlieb's connection to the franchise as well as to the NNL. Gottlieb, a white Jewish booking agent, scheduled games for the Stars and booked games for NNL teams when they traveled east of Pittsburgh. Gottlieb provided financial support for the Stars, and his connections helped the team secure leases at ballparks in West Philadelphia for their home games.[26] The *Tribune*, however, rarely mentioned Gottlieb and never mentioned the financial and logistical support he provided to the Stars. By contrast, the newspaper promoted Bolden's work with the Stars and trumpeted his elevation to the NNL's presidency in 1936. The newspaper's sportswriters also reported on Bolden's efforts to sign players and on his involvement in NNL meetings. That coverage further boosted Bolden and left Gottlieb in the shadows.[27]

The Ugly Championship

In 1934, the Stars joined the NNL and won the league championship in a controversy-filled series that prompted negative coverage in the *Tribune*. The infamous series featured the winners of the NNL's two half-seasons, the Stars and the Chicago American Giants. During game six, the Stars' third baseman Jud Wilson and catcher Emil Brooks each physically attacked an umpire in two separate incidents. The umpires, however, allowed both players to remain in the game; the Stars won the game to tie the series with the American Giants. Dave Malarcher, the American Giants' manager, unsuccessfully filed a protest with NNL Commissioner and sportswriter W. Rollo Wilson. Game seven, which ended in a tie, featured another physical altercation between an umpire and a player. In the second inning, the American Giants' left fielder "Mule" Suttles hit an umpire with his bat after he was called out on strikes. Unlike the previous game's incidents, the umpires removed Suttles from the game. Game eight, played before a mere two thousand fans at Passon Field in West Philadelphia, featured protests from both the Stars and the American Giants. The American Giants protested an umpire's call, whereas the Stars protested the American Giants' use of a player whom they claimed belonged to another NNL team. Despite those protests, the two teams played a complete game, and the Stars secured the NNL championship with a 2–0 victory over the American Giants.[28]

Instead of celebrating the Stars' triumph, the *Tribune*'s Ed Harris proclaimed that the league "took a kick in the pants" and criticized both the players as well as the umpires for the "two sorry incidents" that marred game six.[29] Harris referred to the players' actions as illegal, childish, and foolish, but he reserved his most pointed disapproval for the umpires. As he reasoned, the "job of [an] umpire is an important one" because baseball "games are in his absolute charge."[30] The bad decisions made by the two umpires in game six "set unfortunate precedents" that had the potential of undermining their authority as well as the authority of other umpires and could undermine attempts to build a solid league organization.[31]

The controversial 1934 championship series affected league operations, and those operations triggered more negative coverage in the *Tribune*. At a November 1934 meeting, American Giants owner Robert Coles refused to sign the paychecks for several league officials, including Commissioner Wilson.[32] In March 1935, league owners ousted Wilson as commissioner and replaced him with Ferdinand Q. Morton, a Civil Service Commissioner in New York City. Harris linked Wilson's removal to the decisions he made during the championship series and noted that none of the league's officers came from Philadelphia. Harris, furthermore, noted that the new league commissioner did not possess much knowledge about baseball. He mirthfully declared that what Morton "doesn't know the boys will be very glad to teach him. It's going to be fun to watch things this season."[33] Regarding Morton as little more than a puppet for the league's most powerful owners, Harris predicted a one-year reign for the new commissioner and lamented the lack of a commissioner in the mold of Kenesaw Mountain Landis. While Harris hoped for a strong season for the NNL, he correctly observed that "the league is working for the owners and not the owners for the league."[34]

Secrecy and a Denied Title

Harris's criticism of the NNL's owners and operations persisted throughout the 1935 season, but his criticism never included Bolden. As an example, a controversy arose over the fact that players in the annual East-West Game received only $5.00 apiece. That controversy came in the midst of other questions about the league's financial health and distribution of revenue among all league teams. The *Tribune* printed a lengthy statement from Bolden that included his determination to quit the NNL because of monetary disputes and internal politics. In the statement, Bolden complained about lengthy unprofitable trips to Chicago and Pittsburgh and suggested eliminating western clubs from the NNL. He also called for moving the East-West Game to Philadelphia and berated other league owners for flouting the rules.[35] Harris never commented upon Bolden's statement, but the fact that the newspaper printed it showed some degree of sympathy for the Stars' owner. Harris expressed skepticism about the distribution of only $5.00 to players in the East-West Game, showing that he also possessed doubts about the league's operations.[36]

Another example of Harris's deft avoidance of criticizing Bolden appeared in September 1935. In response to a disappointing season, Bolden released six players, including popular second baseman Dick Seay, before the season officially ended. Harris carefully addressed the situation and declared that it "would be an idle impertinence" to criticize Bolden's actions.[37] Harris expressed some mild surprise at Seay's release, but acknowledged that baseball operated as a business and that owners should release under-performing players. He also reminded his readers that Bolden warned his players he would take such action if they failed to produce for the Stars. Calling Bolden the "veteran baseball impresario," Harris concluded that the release of the six players kept the Stars' owner focused on his goal of producing a championship-contending team.[38]

In January 1936, Harris launched a fierce assault against the NNL, first for canceling a meeting and then for blocking press access to a meeting. Following the cancelled meeting, Harris expressed amazement "that those who operate the association do not realize the immense benefit that would accrue if some effort was made to show the doubters that the loop was a legitimate organization that operated in an intelligent manner."[39] Once the NNL had held its meeting, the owners asked the seven black sportswriters present at the meeting to leave, reneging on an earlier invitation. Harris, one of the seven sportswriters asked to leave, decried the league's action and issued warnings about the larger implications of blocking press access to NNL meetings. He saw himself and his fellow sportswriters as the representatives of black baseball fans whose money supported the league and its teams. Denying the press access to league meetings meant

The 1934 Philadelphia Stars (courtesy NoirTech Research).

denying fans information about the league's operations. As he explained, "the man who spurns an agency that reaches thousands of people regularly, is a fool," and "it is a mighty stupid person who throws money on an inferior article."[40]

Later in the season, a dispute over the winner of the first-half title prompted more critical columns from Harris. The Baltimore Elite Giants claimed the first-half title; the Stars pointed out that the two teams needed to play rained-out games in order to complete the first half of the season and to determine the first-half winner. Commissioner Morton initially agreed with the Stars and ordered the two teams to play two games. The Stars and the Elite Giants, however, never played those games, and the latter team met the second-half winners— the Pittsburgh Crawfords—for the league championship.[41]

When the dispute first flared, Harris dispiritedly called the NNL a flop and compared it to a married couple who neglect to adhere to their marriage vows. He also lamented that the team owners constantly engaged in petty feuds and, therefore, missed golden opportunities to build a stable and successful organization. Harris used the dispute to complain about other problems besetting the NNL and to issue another warning about the league's failure to cultivate continued fan support:

> Postponed games, exhibition games suddenly listed as league games and vice versa have done much to give the fan a jaundiced eye as far as the organization is concerned.... Another thing [the owners] have to learn is that they can't do anything they want and expect the public to swallow it without gulping. Brother, the bleacherites don't do it and when are dissatisfied they show it in the most hurtful way, by boycotting the box office.[42]

The start of the Elite Giants–Crawfords championship series sparked even more vitriol from Harris. The Stars and Elite Giants never played the two re-scheduled rain outs because the Elite Giants had allowed some of their best players to participate in a tournament sponsored by the Denver *Post*. That tournament team also included players from the Crawfords and Homestead Grays. Harris pointed out the impossibility of such a situation happening in the major leagues, indirectly taking a swipe at the NNL's legitimacy.[43] To make the situation even worse, the Elite Giants and Crawfords played only one game in the championship series. In a press release, NNL Secretary John L. Clarke denied that the two teams had abandoned the championship series and insisted that the teams would resume the series prior to the start of the 1937 season. Harris decried the plan as the "essence of asininity" and wryly joked, "I wonder why some of the club owners do not open a metal foundry, they have so much brass."[44] He proclaimed the season dead and advised the league to simply forget about the aborted championship series and move on to the next season.[45]

Jumping to the Caribbean and More Secrecy

Throughout the 1937 and 1938 seasons, coverage in the *Tribune* from Harris and Randy Dixon followed the same pattern apparent in previous seasons. Both writers praised Bolden's efforts to build a winning team and even expressed excitement when the Stars showed promise. Both writers also offered biting critiques of the NNL's operations, particularly its continued secrecy and its botched response to players who jumped their contracts. In his preview of the 1937 season, Harris showed sympathy for Bolden as he tried to build a successful team. He lamented that the Stars and the A's, a rare mention of one of Philadelphia's major league teams, seemed destined to finish in last place.[46] Later in the season, the Stars' bus crashed during a trip to Cleveland; while the wreck injured several players, the Stars responded by playing better than they had previously. Dixon joked that the team needed more bus crashes and predicted higher attendance at future home games.[47]

At the start of the 1938 season, Dixon praised the additions Bolden had made to the Stars' roster and predicted a strong season for the team. As the Stars played winning baseball, Dixon lauded the team's top players, giving credit to Bolden for assembling the roster, and noted the increased attendance at home games.[48]

In the midst of those laudatory columns, Harris and Dixon continued to direct anger and frustration at the NNL. When players jumped their contracts to play in the Dominican Republic, Harris correctly predicted that the owners would forget about punishments and cut each other's throats rushing to sign the players.[49] In early 1938, Dixon complained about the NNL's continued secrecy and wondered if the league had decided to operate without a commissioner. He seemed to expect the league's secrecy, noting that "ace sports men have worn out plenty of shoe leather pacing up and down the corridors outside the meeting rooms that were barred to them by league edict."[50] While the NNL muddled through another season with on-field and off-field problems, Harris again warned that fans would stay away from games and bemoaned the lack of organization within the league. He urged NNL owners to emulate their "older and more experienced brothers in the big leagues" and adhere to a more structured league organization with a commissioner and other officers.[51] As he reasoned, the major league owners employed men like Kenesaw Mountain Landis and Ford Frick not "because they are in love with them," but "because it is good and profitable for their business of selling baseball."[52]

Conclusion

Overall, analysis of sports coverage in the *Philadelphia Tribune* from 1933–1938 reveals two divergent tendencies: praise for the owner of the local NNL franchise and criticism for both the NNL and its other owners. Ed Harris and Randy Dixon, the *Tribune*'s primary baseball reporters, used their columns to laud Bolden's decisions and to express excitement about the Stars when the team enjoyed some success. Their columns, as well as other coverage given to the Stars in the *Tribune*, showed a close affinity between the newspaper and Bolden. That affinity stemmed from the *Tribune*'s boosterism of Bolden's earlier team, Hilldale, and from the connection between Bolden,

Otto Briggs, and the newspaper. That affinity also seems remarkable given the presence of the second tendency in the *Tribune*'s coverage, the vitriol directed at the NNL from Harris and Dixon. Even though Harris and Dixon freely criticized the NNL, they spared Bolden and focused their ire at other NNL owners whom they felt acted against the league's best interests.

As this article shows, Harris and Dixon held the NNL to a high standard. They never considered the league's financial situation as a mitigating factor in their critical columns on the NNL's operations. The controversy-filled 1934 NNL championship series, and the effects that series had upon the league's operations provoked biting commentary from Harris. Harris, along with his counterpart Dixon, reported on the secrecy surrounding the NNL owners' meetings and expressed doubts about league commissioner Ferdinand Morton's credibility. Of the two sportswriters, Harris provided the more critical commentary. He used his columns to issue dire warnings about fans staying away from games because of their disgust over the league's operations. Harris also used his columns to question the NNL's legitimacy, particularly after the denial of the 1936 first-half title to the Stars and the subsequent abandonment of the championship series. In addition to questioning the NNL's legitimacy, Harris directed his ire at the league's owners who appeared to lack a shared commitment to building and sustaining a stable league organization. He directed their attention to the major leagues, a more stable and successful organization with a powerful commissioner and other officials.

The coverage of the NNL found in the *Tribune* from 1933–1938 shows the existence of deep tensions between the newspaper's sportswriters and the NNL. While the newspaper acted as a booster for the Stars and Bolden, it did not act in the same manner for the NNL during an era when the league needed boosterism. When combined with the dire economic climate of the 1930s, the critical coverage found in the *Tribune* added to the NNL's woes. In the years following the time period covered in this article, black newspapers launched campaigns to integrate the major leagues. As other scholars noted, the baseball integration campaigns launched in black newspapers regarded the health of the NNL and the NAL as secondary to the goal of having black players in the major leagues. Wendell Smith and other sportswriters, not Negro League owners or officials, touted the talents of black players to major league officials and arranged for black players to have tryouts with major league teams. Calls to support the Negro Leagues came later, once the Brooklyn Dodgers and other major league teams began to sign black players. Those calls came too late to save the Negro Leagues.[53]

Notes

1. *Philadelphia Tribune*, February 9, 1933.
2. Ibid.
3. Ibid., March 16, 1933.
4. Quoted in ibid.
5. Ibid.

6. Ibid., February 14, 1935.
7. Ibid.
8. Neil Lanctot, *Negro League Baseball: The Rise and Ruin of a Black Institution* (Philadelphia: University of Pennsylvania Press, 2004).
9. Brian Carroll, "Rube Foster, C.I. Taylor, and the Great Newspaper War of 1915," *Black Ball* 4, No. 2 (Fall 2011): 36–54. http://dx.doi.org/10.3172/BLB.4.2.36
10. Neil Lanctot, *Fair Dealing and Clean Playing: The Hilldale Club and the Development of Black Professional Baseball 1910–1932* (Jefferson, NC: McFarland, 1994), 11–23, 40.
11. Brian Carroll, "'A Perfect Baseball Day': Black Press Coverage of the East-West Classic," *Black Ball* 1, No. 1 (Spring 2008): 14–28. http://dx.doi.org/10.3172/BLB.1.1.14
12. Brian Carroll, "To Pittsburgh from Chicago: A Changing of the Guard in Black Baseball and the Black Press in the 1930s," *Black Ball* 2, No. 2 (Fall 2009): 86–05. http://dx.doi.org/10.3172/BLB.2.2.86
13. Ryan Rynzer, "The Black Press and Negro League Baseball in 1940s Cleveland," *Black Ball* 2 No. 2 (Fall 2009): 68–85; Brian Carroll, "North vs. South: Chicago *Defender* Coverage of the Integration of Professional Baseball in the City," *Journalism History* 33, No. 3 (Fall 2007): 163–172; Brian Carroll, "'Praising My People': Newspaper Sports Coverage and the Integration of Baseball in Wichita, Kansas," *Kansas History* 33 (Winter 2010-2011): 240–255; Chris Lamb, "L'Affaire Jake Powell: The Minority Press Goes to Bat against Segregated Baseball," *Journalism and Mass Communication Quarterly* 76, No. 1 (Spring 1999): 21–34; Chris Lamb, "What's Wrong with Baseball': The Pittsburgh *Courier* and the Beginnings of Its Campaign to Integrate the National Pastime," *The Western Journal of Black Studies* 20, No. 4 (2002): 189–192.
14. Brian Carroll, *When to Stop the Cheering: The Black Press, the Black Community, and the Integration of Professional Baseball* (New York: Routeledge, 2007), 72–87.
15. David K. Wiggins, "Wendell Smith, the Pittsburgh *Courier-Journal*, and the Campaign to Include Blacks in Organized Baseball, 1933–1945," *Journal of Sport History* 10, No. 2 (Summer 1983): 5–29.
16. *Philadelphia Tribune*, February 9, 1933, and February 23, 1933.
17. Ibid., October 5, 1933.
18. Ibid.
19. Ibid.
20. Ibid., April 13, 1933.
21. Ibid., May 4, 1933, and May 18, 1933.
22. Harry Passon and Ed Gottlieb were friends and business partners. For a full overview of Passon's and Gottlieb's partnership, see Rich Westcott, *The Mogul: Eddie Gottlieb, Philadelphia Sports Legend and Pro Basketball Pioneer* (Philadelphia: Temple University Press, 2008).
23. *Philadelphia Tribune*, August 24, 1933.
24. Ibid.
25. Ibid., April 20,1933; April 27, 1933; May 4, 1933; May 18,1933; June 22, 1933; July 20, 1933; August 17, 1933; August 24, 1933; and September 14, 1933.
26. Westcott, *The Mogul*, 77, 84, 94–95.
27. *Philadelphia Tribune*, March 14, 1935; April 11, 1935; and March 12, 1936.
28. Ibid., October 4, 1934.
29. Ibid.; E. R. Harris, "To Be or Not To Be."
30. Ibid.
31. Ibid.
32. Ibid., November 8, 1934.
33. Ibid., E. Harris, "Now The Fun Begins," March 14, 1935.
34. Ibid.
35. *Philadelphia Tribune*, August 29, 1935.
36. Ibid., E. Harris, "The Chiseling Brigade," September 5, 1935.
37. Ibid., E. Harris, "Hoping I'm Right," September 26, 1935.
38. Ibid.
39. Ibid., E. Harris, "Don't Come After Us!," January 16, 1936.
40. Ibid., "It Comes Out Here," January 30, 1936.
41. *Philadelphia Tribune*, September 3, 1936, and September 10, 1936.
42. Ibid., E. Harris, "The League A Flop?,"July 30, 1936.

43. Ibid., "Why Don't You Quit?," September 10, 1936.
44. Ibid., "This Is A Killer," October 29, 1936.
45. Ibid.
46. Ibid., "An Amazing Parallel," April 22, 1937.
47. Randy Dixon, "Sports Bugle," July 11, 1937.
48. Ibid., May 5, 1938; June 23, 1938.
49. Ibid., E. Harris, "Dog Eat Dog," June 3, 1937.
50. Randy Dixon, "Sports Bugle," *Philadelphia Tribune*, February 3, 1938.
51. Ibid., E. Harris, "Three Strikes And Out!!!," July 21, 1938.
52. Ibid.
53. Carroll, *When to Stop Cheering*, 175–193.

The Puzzling History of the Tate Stars

SHAWN MORRIS

Abstract

The history of Negro League Baseball is riddled with teams that lasted only a short time before folding and becoming a forgotten part of the past. Some of these clubs, however, left their mark on Negro Leagues history. The Cleveland Tate Stars provide one good example of such teams. In 1922, the Tate Stars became Cleveland's first professional entry into Rube Foster's Negro National League. The club was owned by George Jennings Tate, who created the Tate Baseball Company and constructed Tate Field, which was hailed by many as one of the finest black-owned ballparks in the country. By the end of that inaugural season, however, the team was near the bottom of the standings, and Tate was entangled in multiple legal disputes. The following year saw the Tate Stars return to Negro League baseball midway through the season, but George Tate's increasing legal troubles would lead to the club's demise. While the Tate Stars lasted less than two full seasons as a professional outfit, they serve as the foundation upon which the rest of the city's association with professional black baseball is built.

NEGRO LEAGUE BASEBALL IN CLEVELAND HAS AN INTRIGUING, yet largely overlooked history. The city was home to 10 professional black teams from 1922–1940, few of which lasted more than a year before they folded. When one team disbanded, there was an ownership group ready to put another in its place. Tracing the history of these teams, much like the rest of the Negro Leagues, is difficult. In his groundbreaking book *Only the Ball Was White*, Robert Peterson summed up the task best when he wrote: "Tracing the course of the organized Negro Leagues is rather like trying to follow a single black strand through a ton of spaghetti. The footing is infirm, and the strand has a tendency to break off in one's hand and slither back into the amorphous mass."[1]

The 1922 Cleveland Tate Stars were the city's first entry into Rube Foster's Negro National League (NNL). The team was started by George Jennings Tate, a native of Tennessee who arrived in Ohio before the Great Migration brought thousands of

Black Ball / DOI: 10.3172/BLB.6.51 / Volume 6 / 2013 / pp. 51–69 /
ISSN 1939-8484 (Print) / ISSN 1939-8379 (Online) /

African Americans north in search of industrial employment. By his early thirties, Tate had proven successful in his retail enterprises, and he began funding a black baseball team. The Tate Stars got their start as a semipro team that played on the city's sandlots as early as 1917. In 1921 the team accepted a position as an "affiliate" of the NNL, and in 1922 they were invited to join the league full-time after paying the required $1000 league entry fee.[2] They had a brand new ballpark that was christened Tate Field, built with funds raised by a public stock sale in the Tate Baseball Company, and the support of the local black press. There was a positive buzz surrounding the team, and many in the community expected big things from George Tate and his baseball team. The Tate Stars would get off to a great start during their inaugural year in the league, but by the end of the season the team was dismal on the field and mired in financial problems off it.

George Tate was in and out of the local courts after being sued numerous times for repeatedly failing to pay outstanding debts. Many did not expect the club to return for the 1923 season, and in fact the Tate Stars spent the first part of that season playing as an independent team; but when the Toledo entry in the NNL folded halfway through the season, the Tate Stars replaced them. The resurrection of the club during that season was short lived, as by the end of the year the Tate Stars would be gone forever. Examining the history of the team, and focusing largely on the one-and-a-half seasons the team was a member of the NNL, researchers find that many questions arise, but none larger than the question of why the club lasted such a short time. It appears that the organization was poised for success, yet its story ends in failure.

The historiography of the 1922-1923 Cleveland Tate Stars is best described as shallow at best, with only a handful of works even approaching the topic. Peterson's was the first highly regarded book on Negro league history, but he mentions the Tate Stars only once in the text, in a brief biographical entry of Negro Leaguer Vic Harris. The appendices add a partial roster, and list the team in the final standings for 1922 and 1923. Much of this same information can be found in other scholarly Negro League books. Leslie Heaphy's general history, *The Negro Leagues, 1869–1960*,[3] is another work that briefly touches upon the Tate Stars and contains the same appendix statistics as Peterson's effort. The years after Heaphy's book was published, *Shades of Glory* appeared. The product of years of digging by the Negro Leagues Researchers and Authors Group (NLRAG), this wide-ranging book never touches on the Cleveland Tate Stars.[4] It is not until Stephanie Liscio's 2010 work, *Integrating Cleveland Baseball*,[5] that the Cleveland Tate Stars receive more than a brief mention. Over the course of a few pages she gives a general historical overview of the team and its owner, as well as the Tate Baseball Company. Liscio's account of the Tate Stars may not be as in-depth as some of her work on the other Cleveland teams, but she encourages further scholarship on the subject. Overall, the amount of information on Cleveland's first Negro National League club in secondary sources is limited, and the listings of the team's record, statistics, and roster change little throughout the respective appendices.

To examine the historiography on a "larger" scale, one must look at scholarly works that focus upon a specific team or city in more depth. Rob Ruck's *Sandlot Seasons:*

Sport in Black Pittsburgh focuses almost exclusively upon the numerous professional black baseball teams that grew from various neighborhoods within the city. While the Pittsburgh Crawfords and Homestead Grays are rightly at the center of the book, Ruck writes thoughtfully about the other professional teams that grew from the city's various neighborhoods.[6] The histories of these teams are interwoven almost seamlessly with the roles they played in the city's African American community. No one has taken Ruck's sociocultural approach to writing about Negro League baseball and applied it to another city or team. *Black Baseball and Chicago* focuses on a single city, but does not attempt to integrate the various strands of Chicago's Negro League history into a cohesive story.[7] Several teams that called Chicago home are discussed, including those that began play as early as the mid–19th century. Other essays in the work examine various players and managers, as well as influential owners. Coverage of the Chicago Giants and their owner, Rube Foster, is especially thorough. Janet Bruce's *The Kansas City Monarchs: Champions of Black Baseball* is concerned with the Monarchs and their long, storied tenure within Negro League baseball.[8] The Monarchs survived the entire 35-year span that professional black baseball was in existence, and the team is among the most dominant Negro clubs in history. Bruce analyzes the team's relationship with the urban black experience in Kansas City and shows how they often go hand in hand.

These works represent a variety of different approaches to the topic of black baseball. All of them employ different methodologies, but the results are similar in that they shed new light upon "old" subjects. An examination of Web-based sources for information on the Cleveland Tate Stars finds only a few credible entries, all written by Stephanie Liscio. The information contained in these sources also appears in *Integrating Cleveland Baseball*.

The overwhelming majority of the information gathered for this article was drawn from primary sources. Both the white-owned *Cleveland Plain Dealer* and the African American *Cleveland Gazette* provided coverage of the Tate Stars on a semi-regular basis, although the *Plain Dealer*'s coverage of the team was far more sporadic than that of its black counterpart, and the articles that appeared in its pages dealt mainly with the outcomes of games. Over the course of the five years from 1919 to 1923, the *Plain Dealer* wrote well over one hundred articles related to the team, all of which are available in an electronic archive through the Cleveland Public Library. However, the *Cleveland Gazette* provided far superior coverage throughout the existence of the Tate Stars, from its earliest sandlot years through its demise following the 1923 season. Many of the articles on the team appear to be written by Alan H. Dorsey, and they ran in the *Gazette* under the "Prime Sports News" heading. These articles are available on microfilm at the Western Reserve Research Library in Cleveland.

The *Chicago Defender* also provided limited coverage of the team, but the articles that appear are often very similar to those in the *Gazette*. Here again it seems that any detailed history of the Tate Stars, and any understanding of its abrupt end, will have to rely heavily on the Cleveland newspapers that reported on the team, although they are not without their drawbacks. Often the coverage of the Tate Stars that appeared in both the *Plain Dealer* and *Gazette* was from a week before and was sometimes limited. The *Plain Dealer* provided limited coverage of the team's play on the field but offered miniscule insight and information on the Tate Stars Baseball Company, and nothing on the organization's legal issues. The *Gazette* provided more regular coverage on the team, the owner, the company, and the financial issues. However, the articles in both local papers were routinely short, maybe only a paragraph or two long, and they often only referred to a player by his last name in accompanying box scores, which can lead to confusion when players share a common surname. Attendance statistics were not regularly given and the crowd size often went unmentioned, making it difficult to gauge the extent to which the local black community supported the team at the gate. Another common problem with relying so heavily on newspaper articles is that they are often inconclusive. The papers would frequently allude to various topics relating to the Tate Stars being covered in the following week's edition, yet the stories never appeared. During the Tates' final days in 1922, and again in 1923, the coverage in the papers was sporadic, leaving parts of the Tate Stars history unanswered. Despite these drawbacks, the city's newspapers of the time still serve as the most reliable and credible source of information on the team and the man responsible for it, George Tate.

George Tate

If a great deal of mystery surrounds the history of the Cleveland Tate Stars, the same can be said for the man responsible for the team. George Jennings Tate was from Morganton, Tennessee, and may have been born around 1890. The exact date and year are unclear. He was in Ohio for the first time by 1905 and attended Oberlin's preparatory academy (similar to a modern-day high school) from 1905 to 1906. From his entry in the 1908 General Catalogue of Oberlin College, it appears he entered the "mid" academy, around a sophomore level, which would put his age in the 14–16 range.[9] His file states that he was an African American student, and contains nothing else except for a note stating he was from Morganton. The fact that the Oberlin College archive contains such minimal information on Tate contradicts the claims that other historians have made regarding his storied athletic career at the institution. As early as 1922 the "myth" of his athletic abilities at Oberlin appeared in print in the *Gazette*, which states: "He showed an interest in athletics at Oberlin and was prominent in sports, where he was a clever pitcher."[10] Kenneth Kusmer notes in *A Ghetto Takes Shape* that Tate was "a black baseball star who had attended Oberlin College."[11] Kusmer's source for this information was an interview with Dr. William Saunders, in addition to the *Gazette* article. Stephanie Liscio reiterates in her work *Integrating Cleveland Baseball* that Tate was "a clever pitcher" with Oberlin.[12]

If George Tate was indeed the standout athlete at Oberlin as first claimed in print in 1922, one would expect the college to have some record of his accomplishments. Yet they do not have a single one, nor do they have any record of him even attending Oberlin College — only the preparatory academy for two years.[13] No research has yet been uncovered that can disprove Oberlin's own archival records and prove that Tate achieved anything or even attended the collegiate institution. Little reliable information can be found on Tate after his short tenure at Oberlin, until he appears in Cleveland's City Directory in 1920. The *Gazette* reported that Tate made his way up to Detroit for a number of years before coming to Cleveland by late 1917,[14] but one cannot say with certainty.

It is apparent that Tate was in Cleveland by the spring of 1918, but he may have come to the city earlier. He had formed the semipro Tate Stars and some of the results of their baseball games on the city's various sandlots would sporadically appear in the *Cleveland Gazette* beginning in 1920 and the *Plain Dealer* in 1921. An article that appeared in the *Cleveland Gazette* in October 1920 notes Tate was a "quiet, modest, unassuming sportsman who has backed Tate's Stars from the beginning, several years ago, and is 'still at it.'"[15] This article proves that he may have been in the city as early as 1916. Regardless of the exact year of his arrival, it is apparent that he was in for Cleveland over a year before he appeared in the 1919/1920 city directory, where he is listed as being in the "men's furnishings" business, with two locations given, one on Central Ave. and the other on E. 28th.[16] Advertisements for his Central Shirt Shop in the *Gazette* list the Central Ave. location. However, the following year Tate appears in the directory again as being involved in men's furnishings, but the address that appears is on E. 90th, completely different from those listed in the previous directory.[17] It was also during the first half of 1921 that advertisements for the Central Shirt Shop go from stating "G.J. Tate, Proprietor" to "Under New Management."[18] It is evident that Tate's focus was turning away from his retail enterprises to his baseball team, as 1921 marked the first year the Tate Stars organization would be aligned with Rube Foster's Negro National League as one of two "affiliate" teams that would play games against the other eight "fully fledged" teams in the NNL. He also started the Tate Stars Baseball Company around this time, offering potential investors a chance to buy stock for as little as ten dollars. Instead of selling men's furnishings, George Tate was now trying to sell his team to the black citizens of Cleveland.

By the early spring of 1922, Tate's new baseball field had been constructed. His team was now a full member of the Negro National League, and Tate was elected to serve as the league's vice president. The local black press praised the man who gave Cleveland "a team in our 'big time' baseball league."[19] The 1922 city directory reflects Tate's change in occupation for the previous year, as he is listed as being a salesman, and the accompanying address is the E. 90th location as listed in the 1921 directory.[20] Only after the Tate Stars were granted full admission into the NNL in 1922 did George Tate's listed occupation in the directory change from salesman to Tate Stars Base Ball Club at 4306 Cedar Ave. in 1923.[21] As the team struggled on the field and financially throughout the 1923 season, it was apparent that the end of the Tate Stars was imminent.

The 1924 listing for George Tate hints at his downfall: he is listed at the same address, but this time without an occupation.[22] Soon afterward, he took a job as a manager at the Majestic Hotel and was working there in 1925.[23] By the following year he had left the city. It is not clear when exactly he left or where his destination was, but by 1930 he had not returned, and it is uncertain whether he ever did. Other than city directory listings or what was recorded in various newspaper articles of the time, there is little known about George Tate.

Sandlot Years and 1921

The first time Tate Stars game recaps and box scores appear with regularity in the *Gazette* is during the spring of 1920, although it can be inferred from articles in the paper that the team may have been in existence as early as 1917.[24] If there are records of Tate Stars games prior to the 1920 season, they have yet to be uncovered. The team was without a home park and played their home games at various fields in the area that season, including League Park. The Tate Stars played numerous opposing clubs, both white and black. Some of those teams included Dille Roads, Gilmour K of Cs, and Stroud Awnings, but far and away the club's biggest rival that year was the Naco Giants. Numerous articles in the *Gazette* report on the large and enthusiastic crowds that gathered to watch every time the two teams squared off. One of those games on August 12 drew the largest number of spectators that ever attended Naco Field.[25] As the 1920 campaign came to a close, George Tate had ambitious plans for the following season; in December he announced plans for the construction of Tate Field to serve as the club's home park, as well as the formation of the Tate Baseball Company.[26]

Accompanying his other substantial previous announcements was one to the effect that the Tate Stars had been assured a franchise spot in the Western Colored National League by president Rube Foster and the board of directors.[27] Playing in the professional league meant the Tates would face much tougher opponents that season, instead of the local sandlot teams they had played the previous season. During the 1921 season both local papers reported on Tate Star games in which the home team faced off against teams such as the Bacharach Giants, Pittsburgh Keystones, Indianapolis A.B.C.s, Dayton Marcos, Chicago Giants, Homestead Greys, and Cuban Stars. The team played well at times during that season, including an impressive winning streak in June attributable to the team's remarkable pitching,[28] and they managed to defeat mainstays like the Chicago Giants, the Indianapolis A.B.C.s, and the Cuban Stars during different points of the season. The final record of the team that year is unknown, however. The *Gazette* reported on October 29 that the rest of the NNL schedule had been suspended as of October 2 because of an unexpected fall in attendance during weekday and Sunday games.[29] The Tate Stars played well enough during the abbreviated season, and drew large enough crowds to Tate Field that many believed they would be successful the following season, when they would fully join the Negro National League as one of the circuit's main eight teams.

The Tate Baseball Company and Tate Field

On Christmas Day 1920 the *Gazette* proclaimed: "A Big Undertaking! Cleveland to Have Fine Ball Park in 1921."[30] George Tate and a number of local men announced their plans to construct a new home ballpark for his team at the site of Forest City Park, located 15 minutes from Central Ave. and E. 55th. The plans called for the park to be one of the finest of the time, complete with a large grandstand and bleacher seating as well. In order to fund this enormous undertaking, Tate also announced the incorporation of the Tate Stars Baseball Company, with a capital stock of $25,000. Joining president George Tate on the company's board of directors were secretary/treasurer Coleman A. Lewis, vice president "Honest Jim" Pitts, company attorney George A. Mundy, and associates Lem R. Williams, J.R. DeVoe, and Dell Williams.[31] To secure the additional necessary capital to obtain the land and construct the park, the men behind the Tate Baseball Co. came up with a unique idea for the time.

The company offered the public an opportunity to purchase shares of common, non-preferred stock for $10 apiece.[32] (The amount would later increase to $15 a share.[33]) In a large advertisement that appeared on the same day as the article announcing the new ballpark, the company outlined their proposition. They hoped to obtain enough funding to go from holding the option on Forest City Park, nearly five acres at E. 55th and Sykora Avenue, to securing the title on the property. They placed the value of the future site of Tate Field at $20,000. They also planned and proposed the erection of a large grandstand and bleachers at a cost of $20,000. The ad claimed that this would make the actual potential value of the property "that you can acquire interest in" easily $40,000.[34] It goes on to detail how clubs playing in the Western Colored National League had been making "big" money and reasoned that with the Tate Stars playing many games in that league in the upcoming season, the team was sure to prove to be a solid and profitable investment.

Two weeks after George Tate's substantial announcements, A.H. Dorsey reported in the *Gazette* that "the campaign of the Tate Baseball Company to buy and erect a fine park and grandstand has already started a fever of baseball talk. Looks like it will be the greatest season in Cleveland history."[35] The excitement over the upcoming season must not have translated into an overwhelming urgency from the city's 35,000 African American residents to purchase stock. Only a little over a month into his stock-selling campaign, Tate grew impatient waiting for the necessary capital to accumulate to procure the title on the property. One day in early February Tate left "his office and after several hours absence returned with well over $3,000 for his business deal." Soon afterward, the Tate Company held the title to the land and the officers were finalizing the plans on the grandstand that would accommodate five thousand.[36] It has never been made clear how Tate obtained the money that day, but it was enough to get his project underway. By the end of March construction on the new park had begun. The *Gazette* also reported that well-known and successful Central Avenue businessman A.C. Roberson had joined the Tate Stars Baseball Company as a very large stockholder and member of the board of directors. As the stock-selling campaign was rapidly drawing to a close, the local paper was proclaiming that success was assured and that Tate's long-pursued plans would soon become a reality.[37]

On Saturday, June 4, 1921, Tate Field opened amid much celebration. Enthusiasm ran rampant. A grand parade down the "avonoo" led to the park, where the festivities were headed by a 20-piece band.[38] During the dedication of the new park, Coleman Lewis received hearty applause when he was presented to the crowd. It was noted that a great amount of the success the Tate Baseball Company had achieved was due to the hard-working young secretary-treasurer.[39] From the archives of the local city papers it appeared that all went well for the Tate Baseball Company for the rest of the 1921 season, but 1922 would be radically different. The start of the following year brought about rumors of the team's increasing financial troubles, which were confirmed when Negro National League president Rube Foster visited the city in January. He rectified some of the team's more pressing economic concerns, paying the players their remaining salary for the previous year and signing them all to new contracts.[40] Coleman Lewis was replaced as secretary-treasurer. The reasons why he severed ties with the company were never reported.

Months before the Tate Stars would learn if they would be granted admission into Rube Foster's Negro National League for the 1922 campaign, the board of directors appointed Col. J.E. Reed as the new treasurer of the Tate Baseball Company.[41] Reed was a successful local fishmonger, with a great deal of business experience. Within months of assuming his new position, the first mention of legal action being taken against the Tate Baseball Company appeared in the local press. On May 18, 1922, Alger C. Roberson filed a petition in common pleas court, claiming the baseball outfit owed him $4,302.41.[42] This is the same A.C. Roberson who heavily invested in the company the previous year and had served on the board of directors. Three weeks later it was reported that Roberson's case against the company had been resolved as a result of some agreement on the part of the plaintiff and defendants.[43]

Roberson's legal action, however, had inspired others to follow his lead. According to the *Gazette* "Several of the other more or less numerous creditors of the company are now arranging to force the appointment of a receiver, or change the management of The Tate Baseball Co. against which many and varied complaints are being made by stock-holders and creditors of the company and others."[44] The following week the *Gazette* reported that new treasurer J.E. Reed acknowledged that the company's business affairs were not being handled in a regular and proper way and that it is why "the affairs of the company are to be thoroughly threshed out in the courts at an early date to secure the regularity and stability" that had eluded the company for months.[45] He also made it clear that he had not been permitted by Tate to see the company's financial records, and in fact no one had other than Tate himself.[46] With one man having complete control of the books and electing which debts to pay and which ones to ignore, the Tate Stars would unfortunately never find the stability they required to ensure continued, lasting success.

As the financial-based legal troubles continued,[47] the board of directors responded by appointing treasurer Reed an assistant who would help handle the money that Reed should have been handling. After doing so it was reported that the board "patted themselves on the back," believing they had smoothed over all of their financial troubles.[48] E.J. Reed's public allegation concerning Tate's persistent refusal to let any other company officials see the financial records or handle any money did not sit well with stockholders and creditors. To others outside the board of directors, the appointment of an assistant treasurer was a counterproductive assignment, and nothing more than a halfhearted attempt to ease growing concerns. It also came out in the local press that neither Tate nor Reed was bonded, an incredible fact when it is considered that thousands of dollars were handled almost every week.[49] The fact that neither was bonded is a contradiction to the large advertisement the company had taken out in the *Gazette* on Christmas Day 1920, which claimed the company was fully bonded and insured. As the summer progressed the legal troubles of the company only seemed to blossom. The off-field financial issues of the organization, combined with the increasingly poor play of the team, were making it apparent that the future of the Tate Stars was in danger and their time in the NNL could be coming to a close.

As the season progressed there was more coverage in the *Gazette* about the Tate Baseball Company's financial problems than about the baseball team itself. By midseason the team had fallen apart on the field and was losing much more than they were winning, so the legal dramas of George Tate took center stage in the Prime Sport News columns. Dissatisfied stockholders and creditors had now retained prominent white attorneys who had begun legal proceedings against Tate and his company.[50] S.I. Dorsey, another stockholder, filed suit against Tate for $250 due for labor performed over a year previously and which Tate had steadily refused to pay. By this time stockholders, as well as many others, including local black journalists, had repeatedly speculated about "what has happened to the thousands of dollars the team has taken in at Tate Field, since the 1922 season had begun, and the previous year too."[51] That question in itself is an essential part of the Tate Stars history, and it is one that can never be answered with certainty—only with educated guesses and speculation. President Tate's stranglehold on the finances was evident, with both the local press and stockholders alike calling for financial control of the company to be pried loose.[52] It was becoming obvious that the organization would be ruined otherwise, and the thousands of dollars invested in it by many would be forever lost. Tate would continue to maintain his steadfast grip on the team's finances despite the increasing outcry from the stockholders and reports of the company's tangled affairs in the press. It was reported that the team was $20,000 "in the hole" and that its creditors would be lucky to get 25 percent of what they felt they were due. It was also made known that a portion of the grandstand was on leased ground that had a large second mortgage on it and that Tate was still trying to purchase the mortgage. The mortgage holder was a white man named Anthony Strunko, who was also a large stockholder in the Tate Baseball Company and a director with the outfit.[53] At the end of November 1922, Tate still owed his ballplayers more than $1,000 in back salary, and courts began awarding the plaintiffs judgments in their favor in the legal suits against Tate. One was reported to be for "either three or five thousand dollars."[54] Another obstacle facing Tate at this time was that he was unable to secure insurance on the grandstand of Tate Field or the fence on the property, because they were constructed of wood. Members of the board of directors as well as stockholders were fed up with Tate and his financial dictatorship, and they set in motion plans to seize control from their president.

The Players and Managers

While teams like the Chicago Giants, Kansas City Monarchs, and Homestead Grays were willing, and able, to spend large sums to acquire the services of talented players outside of their respective locations, the Tate Stars were not. Instead, the Tate Stars relied on homegrown talent, fresh from the numerous sandlots that dotted Cleveland's landscape. Before they joined the ranks of the NNL, the club was led by manager and catcher Josh R. DeVoe, a hustling, never-say-quit player who infected his team with the same spirit during the 1920 season.[55] In 1921, the team made perhaps its biggest acquisition ever when Tate secured "Candy" Jim Taylor to serve as manager. Taylor was well respected within the game before he signed on with the Tate Stars and was thought of as a brainy leader who could also hold down the third base.[56]

Taylor would play for and act as manager of the club through the 1922 season. He would go onto have a long career in the Negro Leagues and spend a great deal of time on various teams in both Cleveland and Pittsburgh. Josh DeVoe returned to act as skipper for the 1923 season, and that would be his last stint with the club. Claude Johnson was chosen to lead the Tate Stars in 1924. Numerous articles in both the *Plain Dealer* and *Gazette* mentioned Johnson's exceptional play as a second baseman and prowess at the plate since 1921. He was one of the men who had a "long" tenure with the team. Rosters for both the 1922 and 1923 teams can be found in *Integrating Cleveland Baseball*.[57] Joining Johnson as a member of the Tate Stars for both years were John "Fat" Barnes, Finis Branahan, Slim Branham, George "Rube" Henderson, James "Bobo" Leonard, and Bob McClure. Many other players joined these men on the field throughout the existence of the team, but none was of the quality that wins championships. The fact that Tate spent little money on acquiring players that would make his team one of the more competitive in the NNL is surprising, given the way he liked to flash his money in baseball. It is curious that the same man who spared little expense in assuring Tate Field was one of the finest black-owned ballparks in the country would assemble a team not on par with the venue they would play in.

1922

The start of a new year came with promise for George Tate and his baseball team. The Negro National Baseball League was holding its annual meetings in Chicago from January 26 to 28. There were persistent rumors coming out of the Windy City that there were going to be a couple of significant changes within the league for the upcoming season. One was concerned with changes on the boards of directors and the other focused on several new magnates being invited into the league. Tate had expectations that his team would be one of the new invitees. It was thought that "the circuit, which is composed of eight clubs with two affiliated clubs, will probably remain the same. Cleveland would likely go into the circuit in place of the Cincinnati Cuban Stars who will not return as members of the league."[58] Tate planned on attending the meetings to make sure Cleveland's interest in joining the league was well represented. The new ballpark that the Tate Stars called home had drawn praise from visiting teams the previous season, and Tate was hoping that was enough to outweigh the financial difficulties plaguing the Tate Stars Base Ball Company.

A week and a half before the NNL meetings in Chicago, league president Rube Foster came to Cleveland with the intention of straightening out the tangled affairs of the Tate Stars. The club was still heavily in debt and the players' refusal to conclude a series against the Cardinals the previous fall had put them, and the team in general, in disfavor with the fans. Foster paid the players the remaining salaries they were due for the 1921 season, and then he proceeded to sign them all to new contracts for the upcoming campaign.[59] Foster was not the only important league figurehead to visit Cleveland that week; C.I. Taylor, the leader of the Indianapolis A.B.C. ballclub, came to hold a conference with Tate. Taylor let his displeasure with the financial state of the club be well known and threatened "to do some plain talking at the upcoming league meetings."[60] When the Tate Stars Base Ball Company's board of directors gathered after Foster's and Taylor's visits, they decided to make a change in hopes of resolving some of the financial problems: "J.E. Reed, a well-known fish merchant, was elected treasurer, succeeding Coleman A. Lewis, who was secretary and treasurer."[61]

On the 25th of January president George Tate and team manager "Candy Jim" Taylor left for the league meetings in Chicago. The meetings went well for the duo from Cleveland, well enough that on February 11, 1922, the *Gazette* broke the news to the city's African American populace that the Tate Stars had officially entered "our national baseball league."[62] At the meetings, Rube Foster pointed out that Cleveland had one of the finest baseball stadiums in the country, and it was owned by African Americans. The *Gazette* used Foster's remarks to drum up support from the local community: "This is something to be proud of and our local fan-flock should rally in increasing multitudes to the support of the local team and park."[63]

The Tate Stars Base Ball Company was also increasing its efforts to become more profitable. The company began making a large push to sell \$3,000–\$4,000 in advance tickets. They hoped to use the revenue these advance sales would provide to make improvements to the ballpark for the upcoming season. Tate Field was becoming well known throughout Negro League Baseball; it was already being hailed as one of the best ballparks in the country and played a large part in the city's being awarded its first league franchise. With all of the excitement surrounding the team's inaugural year in the league, and "when it is remembered the management of the Cleveland Indians sold seventy thousand dollars worth of tickets, two months before the season opened last spring, the Tates should have no difficulty in securing the modest sum they desire."[64] The team also began booking games for the upcoming season, and the first practice game, against a fast white semipro team, had already been lined up for April 16.

The first game results from the Tate Stars' 1922 season appeared toward the end of April. On April 22, the *Plain Dealer* mentions that the Tates won the first game of spring against the Telling Ice Creams the previous week, 4–0.[65] The *Cleveland Gazette* contained the results of the second game of the series, a 6–4 Stars victory, in front of a reported crowd of more than six thousand fans despite the chilly, breezy weather.[66] The final spring practice series was held on the weekend of April 29 against the Massillon Agathons, a white semipro team that featured ex–big-league pitcher Earl Mosely. On Saturday, a crowd of about two thousand fans watched Massillon trim the Tates, 10–3.[67] The Sunday game drew a much larger crowd and saw the Tate Stars drive Mosely from the game as they went on to an 8–6 win.[68] The training games had shown that the Tates were capable of performing well on the field and that the local community would come out to support the team. Drawing almost eight thousand fans to the final spring practice games gave hope to the Tate Base Ball Company that the 1922 season could bring great success.

The *Gazette* noted: "The Tate Stars easily won their first official league game here, last Saturday [May 6, 1922] at Tate field, by a score of 6 to 0 from the Pittsburg Keystones, Sunday's score, 11 to 4, in the Tate's favor."[69] The Tate Stars' quality play during spring practice games had continued into the first two games of the five-game series with the Keystones. However, the third game belonged to the Pittsburgh team from the start; by the second inning they held a seven-run lead on the Tates and would go on to win, 15–2.[70] Tuesday's contest between the two was closer, but the victory belonged to the Keystones by a score of 4–2.[71] The final game of the series saw the Keystones knock out the Tates' starting pitcher, Keaton, in the third inning and go on to win, 10–2.[72] The first series of the season against another Negro League ballclub might not have turned out as Tate and manager Jim Taylor would have preferred, but it was an overall positive start to the young season. The team had proved capable of playing very well, and the attendance at the games was encouraging. There were high expectations for the next series, which would bring the Cuban Stars to town for a five-game set.

George Tate hoped to capitalize on the popularity of the visiting Cuban Stars ballclub by drawing large crowds to watch the series beginning on Saturday, May 13, and concluding on Wednesday the 17th. He advertised heavily for the series in both the *Gazette* and *Plain Dealer*, and his efforts proved not to be in vain. Saturday and Sunday's games drew enormous crowds to Tate Field, with the latter being the largest yet that season.[73] The Tates held the Cuban Stars to only five hits and took the opening game of the series on Saturday, 7–1. The Cubans held off a ninth-inning rally by the Tates on Sunday to pull off a 7–5 victory. That would be the visitors' only win of the series, however, as the Tate Stars took the third game on Monday, 5–2, the fourth game on Tuesday, 5–1, and Wednesday's finale, 6–5 (in 11 innings).[74] The Tate Stars were off to a successful start of the 1922 season. Their first home stand resulted in a winning record and large crowds at the park. Their next matchup would take them to Detroit, where they would face the Detroit Stars in their first road series of the season.

In Detroit, the Tates ruined the opening celebrations at Mack Park, beating the hometown Stars, 5–1.[75] However, Detroit would go on an offensive tear over the next two games and win both, 8–2 and 7–6. On Wednesday's series finale the Tates held on to win, 4–2, resulting in the clubs splitting the series two games apiece.[76] The Tate Stars would return to Cleveland to finish out the month of May with a couple of non-league contests at Tate Field. On the weekend of the 27th and 28th they faced off against the Detroit Cowper All-Stars and won both games.[77] On Monday the 29th several thousand fans made their way to Tate Field, where the hometown squad was hosting the Bacharach Giants of New York for a single game. The fans in attendance were treated to a 9–5 Tate Stars victory that was driven by the stellar play of the center fielder, Leonard, with "his home run being one of the longest drives ever made on Tate field."[78] The next day was Dedication Day, and while the Lincoln Memorial was being dedicated in Washington, D.C., the Tate Stars were set to host the Pittsburgh Keystones for a doubleheader. The Tates took the first game, but fell to the Keystones in the second when they failed to score a single run.[79] As the Cleveland Tate Stars' first full month in the Negro National League came to a close, the team was playing over .500 and was performing well on the field. There were high expectations that the team could remain competitive heading into the summer.

The first mention of the Tate Stars' on-field activity in June appeared on the 8th when a headline in the *Plain Dealer* proclaimed "Agathons Whip Tates."[80] The previous day in Massillon, the home team defeated the Tate Stars in a close game, 6–5.[81] Immediately after their defeat at the hands of the Agathons, the Tates traveled to New Philadelphia, Ohio, to take on a local club calling themselves the "Sweepers" the next day. The game lasted only five innings and saw the Tate Stars lose a second straight game.[82] The team would return to Cleveland to host the talented Indianapolis A.B.C.s for a five-game series that would commence on Sunday, June 10. The promising play the Tate Stars had displayed in May had all but disappeared by the time the A.B.C.s left town. In the first game the Tates were decisively defeated, 12–5.[83] Things did not improve for the home team the following day when the A.B.C.s delivered another drubbing.[84] As the *Gazette* put it: "The Indianapolis A.B.C.'s 'mopped up the ground' again with the Tate Stars, Tuesday afternoon beating them 10 to 5."[85] Alan H. Dorsey, writer for the *Gazette*, summed up the next game of the series when he wrote, "The A.B.C.'s killed the Tates Sunday, Monday, and Tuesday and buried them Wednesday afternoon at Tate Field. The sermon topic was 9 to 2."[86] The fifth and final game of the set was closer than any of the four previous contests, but the result was the same, with the A.B.C.s emerging victorious.[87] The optimism that had surrounded the team only weeks before was quickly disappearing.

The correlation can be made between the team's poor play and the Tate Baseball Company's increasing off-field issues. Through mid–June, the local black press was giving more attention to the organization's legal troubles and board of directors meetings than to the team's on-field affairs. As the month progressed, George Tate could only hope to put an end to the disappointment that followed his company and players.

The Tate Stars enjoyed their first Sunday win of the season on June 17 against a white club calling itself the Lorain Holley Krohns. The locals defeated the white squad by the decisive score of 19–2, by far their largest margin of victory so far that season.[88] The victory would be short-lived, as the team was solidly defeated 11–5 the following day by the Massillon Agathons.[89] On the following Saturday an aggregation wearing baseball uniforms with the insignia "Buffalo Stars" on the jerseys invaded the city to play the Tate Stars for three games. The Tates took all of the contests by lopsided scores.[90] The series against Buffalo would be the last time that Tate Stars game coverage would appear in the city's press in the month of June, but more articles concerning the Tate Baseball Company's legal misfortunes appear in the *Gazette* at the end of the month. George Tate was unable to turn the fortunes of his company and players around. Going into July it was apparent that both off and on the field, the organization was heading in a negative direction.

The first series in July was a Tate Stars home stand against fellow Negro National League member the Pittsburgh Keystones. The Tates, able to maintain the momentum they had gained from sweeping Buffalo, defeated the Keystones in the series opener on Sunday, July 2.[91] The following day, the Tate Stars come out on top in a lopsided game, 7–1.[92] The third and fourth games of the series were to be played on Tuesday, July 4, as a doubleheader. The Keystones took the first game, while the second ended in a 6–6 tie because the visitors had to catch an early train out of town.[93] The following weekend, the Massillon Agathons came to Tate field on Saturday and defeated the Tates. Sunday, the New York City Bacharachs and Tates faced off for a doubleheader in what would be the first two games of a five-game series. The Tate Stars won both of the games in close matchups. The third game, on Monday, ended in another win for the Tates, but the real story of the game came after the final out, when "street contentions" between adherents of both teams compelled a squad of police to make several trips to Woodland, Scoville, and Central Aves., in the 11th and 12th wards, resulting in about forty being jailed.[94] "Several members of both clubs were reported by police as included in the clean-up,"[95] according to the *Gazette*.

After the problems of the preceding night, tensions were high when the teams took the field for the fourth game of the set, which would end in a tie because of inclement weather. When the series finale concluded on Wednesday, the Tate Stars were victorious, and the city's safety forces relaxed as the large contingent of New York fans left town without further incident.[96] However, the actions on Monday night were serious enough to elicit a response from the black press. The *Gazette* urged its readers to remember that "such occurrences that require the services of the police only serve to lower the status of baseball among our good people of the city."[97]

As the season progressed it was evident that the Tate Stars' situation was in disarray. The team was near the bottom of the standings in the eight-team league, and anything occurring on the field was being overshadowed by the organization's increasing legal troubles. When the 1922 season finally drew to a close, the team saw itself finish tied for seventh place with an overall record of 17 wins and 29 losses.[98] Tate hoped to have his team return to the NNL for the 1923 season, but his hopes were dashed when the Tate Stars were dropped from membership at the annual league meeting in November. Even though the club had brought in around $8,000 during the 1922 campaign, it was not enough to save the Tate Stars, who were reportedly $20,000 in debt.[99] But George Tate would not be deterred. He was determined to field a team for the following season.

1923

The first mention of a game played by the post–NNL Tate Stars is on April 21 when the *Gazette* reported a Tate Stars victory over Cleveland's reigning class AAA champions the Tellings Ice Creams the previous week.[100] Following the victory against the Tellings, the Tate Stars' performance on the field was unremarkable, as the club played roughly .500 baseball against teams such as the Akron General Tires, Canton Terminals, Washington, D.C., Potomacs, and Harrisburg Giants. So it came as a surprise in the end of June when it was announced that George Tate had traveled to Chicago to meet with NNL president Rube Foster in order to resolve their differences. The result of the sit-down between the two men was that the Tate Stars would rejoin the NNL for the remainder of the 1923 season as a replacement for the Toledo Tigers which had disbanded.[101]

In addition to rejoining the league, the Tate Stars were also going to be "strengthened" in order to make them more competitive, but the local press failed to mention which players were added to the roster. The team was going to play most of its remaining games that season on the road; however, Foster and Tate arranged for the club to play a doubleheader at Tate Field on the Fourth of July, providing the team with a much-needed holiday attendance boost.[102] The team played well in front of the home crowd that day, defeating the visiting Youngstown squad decisively in both contests.[103]

Whatever positive momentum the holiday sweep may have provided was soon lost. When the team was not on the road, their attendance numbers were down at Tate Field, where the Stars continually struggled to fill the seats.[104] One game was called off when the manager of the opposing Rochester Terminals refused to let his club play the scheduled doubleheader unless George Tate guaranteed the visiting Pennsylvania team an undisclosed amount of money.[105] According to Stephanie Liscio, "The visiting team likely required a minimum sum in order to pay their players and cover transportation costs to Cleveland." While this particular situation was likely frustrating to the players involved, it caused the small crowd to lose faith in their home town team."[106] The Tate Stars struggled through the remainder of the season, playing well below the .500 mark and watching as the financial situation worsened. As the season drew to a close the team's final record after rejoining the NNL was a dismal 7–14.[107] It was apparent through articles in the black press that Tate had every intention to see the Tate Stars return for the 1924 season, contrary to the persistent rumors circulating in the community that he planned to sell the club.

Conclusion

In early February 1923 Rube Foster stopped in the city to attend a banquet in his honor. At the gathering, Tate Stars board members J.E. Reed and Anthony Strunko spoke openly about the financial difficulties of the company and its bleak outlook.[108] Dissatisfied stockholders began to rebel and hold meetings trying to figure out how to get some of their money back. They demanded Tate turn over a complete list of the stockholders so that all of them could be notified of what was occurring. They also secured the services of an attorney to represent their interests in case Tate sold the team without notification.[109] They believed that if the team was sold, the stockholders would lose all of their money. A month later it was reported that Reed and Strunko were on the verge of wresting control of Tate Field away from George Tate.

Tate could no longer hide from his legal issues. His club's 1923 resurrection back into the NNL was his last shot at being profitable enough to retain the team and park, and it had fallen short. Now Reed and Strunko were "looking forward to taking over Tate Field, at an early date, when the receivership, under which the Tate Baseball Co. has been operating, has terminated."[110] By the end of the 1923 season it was apparent that the Tate Stars would cease to exist but the formal announcement would not come until March 1924 when the *Gazette* ran a short story under the title, "The Tate Stars Are No More."[111] The piece fails to answer any questions of the legal issues of the Tate Stars and only relates that the club was now under new ownership and the name had been changed to the Cleveland Browns.[112] The Tate Stars were finally gone.

Tate never gave up control over the organization's finances and it is unclear what he did with the money the team made over the years. By 1924 he was out of the baseball business for good; the last mention of him in the city comes in 1925 when he appears in the City Directory as being employed as a manager at the Majestic Hotel.[113] It can be inferred that this was also his residence, as no other address appears in the listing. By 1926 he vanishes from the city records. The history of the Tate Stars is one that is full of rich stories and unanswered questions. It will never be known what Tate did with the company's earnings or why he kept such tight control over the finances. Just like his life prior to his arrival and departure from Cleveland, much of the history that surrounds the team will never be able to be fully and accurately retold. Questions that arise through the Tate Stars story simply cannot be answered with certainty, only with educated speculation. The history that has survived in the archives of the city is invaluable and the story contained within the stacks of records and microfilm is one that deserves appreciation. The Tate Stars were the first in a long line of Negro League teams that would call the fifth city home. George Tate and his players showed that it was possible for the fifth city to support professional black baseball. Following the Tate Stars, nine other Cleveland teams would join the ranks of Negro League baseball and only survive for a single season or maybe two. It was not until the Cleveland Buckeyes of the 1940s that the city would be represented by a Negro League team that would enjoy continued success for a number of years. The Tate Stars began a rich tradition of black baseball within the city, and their history is one that should be remembered for its contribution to Cleveland's baseball legacy.

Notes

1. Robert Peterson, *Only the Ball Was White* (New York: Oxford University Press, 1970), 80.
2. *Cleveland Gazette*, February 4, 1922.
3. Leslie Heaphy, *The Negro Leagues, 1869–1960* (Jefferson, NC: McFarland, 2003).
4. Lawrence D. Hogan et al., *Shades of Glory: The Negro Leagues and the Story of African-American Baseball* (Washington, DC: National Geographic Society, 2006).
5. Stephanie Liscio, *Integrating Cleveland Baseball* (Jefferson, NC: McFarland, 2011).
6. Rob Ruck, *Sandlot Seasons: Sport in Black Pittsburgh* (Chicago: University of Illinois Press, 1979).
7. Leslie Heaphy, ed., *Black Baseball and Chicago* (Jefferson, NC: McFarland, 2006).
8. Janet Bruce, *The Kansas City Monarchs: Champions of Black Baseball.* (Lawrence, KS:University of Kansas Press, 1985).
9. Sarah McLusky, pers. comm., *Electronic Correspondence with Oberlin College Archivists*, March 5, 2013. Unpublished Source.
10. "The League's New Vice President," *Cleveland Gazette*, March 18, 1922.
11. Kenneth Kusmer, *A Ghetto Takes Shape: Black Cleveland, 1870–1930* (Chicago, IL: University of Illinois Press, 1976), 195.
12. Liscio, *Integrating Cleveland Baseball*, 13.
13. Sarah McLusky, pers. comm., Mar. 5, 2013.
14. "The League's New Vice President," *Gazette*, March 18, 1922.
15. *Gazette*, October 2, 1920.
16. City Directories of the United States, Segment IV 1902–1935, Cleveland, OH 1919–1920.
17. Ibid., 1921.
18. Advertisement, *Gazette*, May 28, 1921.
19. "The League's New Vice President," *Gazette*, March 18, 1922.
20. City Directories of the United States, Segment IV 1902–1935, Cleveland, OH, 1922.
21. Ibid., 1923.
22. Ibid., 1924.
23. Ibid, 1925.
24. *Gazette*, October 2, 1920.
25. "Tates are Victors," *Gazette*, September 18, 1920.
26. "A Big Undertaking!" *Gazette*, December 25, 1920.
27. "A Good Investment," Advertisement, *Gazette*, December 25, 1920.
28. Photograph, *Cleveland Plain Dealer*, June 20, 1921, 14.

29. "Prime Sports News," *Gazette*, October 29, 1921.
30. "A Big Undertaking!" *Gazette*, December 25, 1920.
31. Ibid.
32. Ibid.
33. Stephanie Liscio, "Cleveland's Negro League History, Part 1 of 11: The Cleveland Tate Stars," It's Pronounced "Lajaway" (blog); http://itspronouncedlajaway.com/?p=4129.
34. "A Good Investment," advertisement, *Gazette*, December 25, 1920.
35. A.H. Dorsey, "Prime Sports News," *Gazette*, January 15, 1921.
36. "Some Money Raiser!" *Gazette*, February 12, 1921.
37. "Work Starts on the New Tate Field," *Gazette*, April 2, 1921.
38. A.H. Dorsey, "Prime Sports News," *Gazette*, June 11, 1921.
39. Ibid.
40. *Gazette*, Jan. 21, 1922.
41. *Gazette*, Jan. 28, 1922.
42. "Asks Receiver for Tates," *Gazette*, May 27, 1922.
43. "Facing a Crisis!" *Gazette*, June 10, 1922.
44. Ibid.
45. "Col. E.J. Reed's Alleged Demand," *Gazette*, June 17, 1922.
46. Ibid.
47. "Facing a Crisis," *Gazette*, June 10, 1922.
48. "Tate Baseball Co. Troubles," *Gazette*, July 1, 1922.
49. "Another Tate Baseball Co. Meeting," *Gazette*, June 24, 1922.
50. "Tate Baseball Co. Troubles," *Gazette*, July 1, 1922.
51. "Big Trouble Looms for the Tate Stars," *Gazette*, August 26, 1922.
52. Ibid.
53. "Tate Baseball Co. Affairs a Mess," *Gazette*, November 25, 1922.
54. Ibid.
55. A. H. Dorsey, "Prime Sports News," *Gazette*, August 24, 1920.
56. A.H. Dorsey, "Prime Sports News," *Gazette*, September 10, 1921.
57. Liscio, *Integrating Cleveland Baseball*, 191–192.
58. *Gazette*, Jan. 14, 1922.
59. *Gazette*, Jan. 21, 1922.
60. Ibid.
61. Ibid.
62. *Gazette*, Feb. 11, 1922.
63. Ibid.
64. Ibid.
65. *Plain Dealer*, April 22, 1922, 15.
66. *Gazette*, April 29, 1922.
67. *Plain Dealer*, April30, 1922, 29.
68. *Gazette*, May 6, 1922.
69. *Gazette*, May 13, 1922.
70. Ibid.
71. Ibid.
72. *Plain Dealer*, May 11, 1922, 22.
73. *Gazette*, May 20, 1922.
74. Ibid.
75. *Gazette*, May 27, 1922.
76. Ibid.
77. *Gazette*, June 3, 1922.
78. "Tate Stars Beat Bacharach Nine," *Plain Dealer*, May 30, 1922, 15.
79. *Gazette*, June 3, 1922.
80. *Plain Dealer*, June 8, 1922
81. Ibid.
82. *Gazette*, June 17, 1922.
83. Ibid.

84. Ibid.
85. Ibid.
86. Ibid.
87. "Tates Blanked in Closing Tilt," *Plain Dealer*, June 16, 1922, 21.
88. "'Whitewash' Was Not Sufficient," *Gazette*, June 24, 1922.
89 Ibid.
90. "The Buffalo Team a 'Joke,'" *Gazette*, July 1, 1922.
91. "Pittsburg Keystones Stop Tates," *Gazette*, July 8, 1922.
92. Ibid.
93. Ibid.
94. "Beat the Tates," *Gazette*, July 17, 1922.
95. Ibid.
96. Ibid.
97. Ibid.
98. Peterson, *Only the Ball Was White*, 258.
99. "Tates Out of the League," *Gazette*, December 30, 1922.
100. "Prime Sports News," *Gazette*, April 21, 1923.
101. "Prime Sports News," *Gazette*, June 30, 1923.
102. Liscio, *Integrating Cleveland Baseball*, 16.
103. "Prime Sports News," *Gazette*, July 7, 1923.
104. Liscio, *Integrating Cleveland Baseball*, 16.
105. "Refused to Play Before Small Crowd," *Gazette*, July 23, 1923.
106. Liscio, *Integrating Cleveland Baseball*, 17.
107. Ibid.
108. Prime Sports News, "Fireworks at Foster Banquet," *Gazette*, February 17, 1923.
109. Prime Sports News, "Tate Baseball Co. Stockholders Rebel," *Gazette*, May 5, 1923.
110. Prime Sports News, *Gazette*, June 2, 1923.
111. Prime Sports News, "The Tate Stars Are No More," *Gazette*, March 23, 1924.
112. Ibid.
113. City Directories of the United States, Segment IV 1902–1935, Cleveland, OH, 1925.

The Color of Baseball

Race and Boston's Sporting Community

ROBERT CVORNYEK

Abstract

The story of black baseball in Boston reveals an added dimension to the game's history. Boston never hosted a professional team in the traditional Negro Leagues, but the city produced several of the finest amateur and semi-professional teams and players in New England. For too long, scholars have overlooked the players, owners, and promoters who developed the local game and ensured its intimate social and cultural presence in the community. African Americans in Boston resisted the indignities of segregation during the Jim Crow Era by creating and supporting successful baseball teams that reflected the strength and vitality of their neighborhoods. Boston fans found a dignity and consistency in their black players that shaped racial identity and reinforced the notion that the struggle for racial equality can be found in several different arenas, including the baseball stadium.

> "Oh for the good ole Boston Tigers days when ole Carter Field was the haven of many a baseball classic. The field where the Tigers were kings!"—William "Sheep" Jackson, *Boston Chronicle*, July 11, 1942

ON MAY 29, 1993, THE BOSTON RED SOX celebrated the history of Negro League baseball in a pre-game ceremony at Fenway Park. The Sox invited Mabry "Doc" Kountze, former sports editor for the *Boston Guardian*, and Fran Matthews, a local Cambridge star who played for the Kansas City Monarchs and Newark Eagles of the Negro National League, to participate.[1] As Kountze caught the ceremonial first pitch tossed by Matthews, all thoughts should have turned to the legendary Negro League players and teams of the past. Instead, both men rekindled memories of Boston's amateur and semi-professional teams. Although Boston never hosted a team in the modern professional black leagues, it did showcase the finest amateur black players throughout all New England. Kountze recognized the significance of the local game and published the only book on black sports in Boston.[2] Matthews played longer in the city's hub

Black Ball / DOI: 10.3172/BLB.6.70 / Volume 6 / 2013 / pp. 70–106 /
ISSN 1939-8484 (Print) / ISSN 1939-8379 (Online) /

leagues and for the well-known Boston Colored Giants than he did for the Eagles. When Matthews's career finally ended, he enjoyed recognition as a member of the Boston Park League Hall of Fame's class of 1987.[3] The story of black baseball in Boston is truly a local one.

African Americans participated at all levels of the local game. Black churches and fraternal organizations fielded makeshift nines to promote recreation and enhance brotherhood among their members. These teams played a casual schedule and oftentimes competed at weekend picnics, holiday celebrations, and other social gatherings during the summer. At the next level, the city's independent amateur black teams played fixed schedules usually carded against white teams that belonged to the city's segregated amateur leagues. Black amateur clubs operated on a neighborhood level and rarely traveled beyond Greater Boston. The semi-professional teams represented Boston's baseball aristocracy. Semipro players were paid for their efforts and this remains the critical distinction between them and their amateur counterparts. These teams traveled extensively throughout New England and frequently into Canada. Semipro baseball was a money making operation and, as such, represents one of the earliest forms of black entrepreneurship. Semipro teams supported a front office which commonly included the owner and promoter; both responsible for a payroll that needed to be met each week. Players could not survive solely on their baseball salaries so most played the game to supplement their incomes. College students who spent their summers at home could find good money playing on these teams as well.

Charlie Lloyd, who played ball for the Highland Colored Giants, provided a rare and intimate glimpse of semiprofessional life. Lloyd, a hard-hitting outfielder who played between 1927 and 1935, stated that "life for a black baseball player was not an easy one. There was no official league and the team played wherever it could book an opponent which meant hours and sometimes days of traveling in parked cars and sleeping in cheap, sometimes segregated motels for just one game." Lloyd recalled that he received between $32.00 and $37.00 per game, just enough to keep a bachelor going.[4]

Boston holds a long and proud tradition of amateur and semi-professional blackball. In the years following the American Civil War, baseball grew in popularity in Boston and around the nation.[5] Unfortunately, opportunities for black players to participate in the city's amateur leagues narrowed, and in 1870 Boston outfitted its first "colored" team, the Resolutes. During the late 19th and early 20th century, a colored team included anyone considered non-white and these clubs often included African Americans, Native Americans, Cubans, and Cape Verdeans. Black or "colored," Boston's non-white teams distinguished themselves as premier baseball clubs throughout New England.

For the most part, these teams and the men who played the game remain unnoticed; so whenever we break the silence of the past there is cause for joy and celebration. For too long, the history of black baseball in Boston has focused on racism at the major league level and overlooked the players who represented the local game and their significant presence in the community. Boston, like most northern cities, was not exempt from the indignities of segregation during the Jim Crow Era, but the success of its black baseball teams provided a constant reminder of the strength and accomplishment that accompanied the skill and determination of the city's ballplayers. Boston fans found a dignity and consistency in their black players that shaped and reinforced racial identity and reinforce the notion that the struggle for racial equality can be found in several different arenas including the baseball stadium.

The Resolutes and the Origins of Boston Black Baseball, 1870–1900

During the late 19th century, the Boston Resolutes successfully represented the city's African American baseball fraternity. The team dates back to 1870, but little is known of the Resolutes' history during its inaugural decade. Like most black ballclubs in the immediate post–Civil War era, the Resolutes were a local or "stay at home team" and did not schedule traveling games beyond greater Boston. The team played other black clubs, most likely representing fraternal organizations and churches, but also scheduled games against established white semi-professional teams. Games staged between the Resolutes and well-known white clubs offered baseball fans of both races an opportunity to see the city's best players and gate receipts provided club owners with needed funds to keep the teams financially sound. Both teams shared a percentage of ticket revenue and it is reasonable to conclude that local rivalries developed between black and white ballclubs to stimulate sales. Rivalries fueled gate receipts, but interracial play before an integrated crowd also strengthened racial pride and identity during a time when African Americans struggled to achieve recognition and racial equality.[6]

According to historian Leslie Heaphy, the team procured its name in a most unusual way. The black Resolutes scheduled a game with a local white team also known as the Resolutes. Both teams agreed that the winner of the game reserved the right to use the name. The black team won by the score of 25–12 and retained the Resolutes name. Despite the number of runs scored, Gregory, the winning pitcher, received accolades from fans and the press.[7] High scoring affairs were typical in the 19th century amateur game and pitchers with strength and stamina ruled the day.

> *"This, readers, is the one real fight we must win. Baseball is a well-established sport and a big business. As such we must fight to include ourselves in it. At present it would appear as a "lost cause" but it isn't and it is our task to keep at it until we are given the same opportunity others have."*—**Boston Chronicle,** *July 6, 1940*

At the end of the decade, the

renowned Mutuals of Washington toured New England on their way to Rochester, New York, but did not play the Resolutes. At the time the Resolutes may not yet have had the drawing power that the Mutuals were looking for in their opponents. The Mutuals were made up of young black players, most of whom worked for the Freemen's Bureau in Washington, D.C., and featured Charles R. Douglass, son of abolitionist Frederick Douglass. Historian Ryan Swanson notes that Charles and Frederick frequently corresponded about the team and about black baseball in the District of Columbia. Frederick also donated money to help outfit the team and lent his name and support to several fundraising events to keep it afloat. The Mutuals scheduled games throughout the greater Boston area with white teams representing the newly established New England Association, and eventually played three of them. On August 10, 1877, the Mutuals lost to Lowell, 6–0, before a crowd of 600 fans at the city's fairgrounds, and on August 20, they lost to the Live Oaks from Lynn, 10–2. The Rhode Islands met and defeated the Mutuals in two games played in Providence's Adelaide Park. Prior to the games, the *Providence Journal* reported that the Mutuals had "unsuccessfully competed with seven New England clubs for the victory" and now "pitched their tents" in Providence to take on the Rhode Islands. On August 17 and 19, the Mutuals lost by scores of 6–0 and 10–2 respectively. Despite the losses, the *Journal* characterized the black players as "a strong, hardy set of fellows" with several of the players "displaying remarkable skill and agility in handling the leather." In particular, Talbot, the Mutuals second baseman, turned a double play that "met with prolonged applause from the 400 spectators."[8]

Our knowledge of the Resolutes expands considerably during the 1880s. By then, the club emerged as the best-organized and most skillful black team in Greater Boston. According to the New York *Freeman*, the leading African American newspaper in the nation, the Resolutes were the "only colored team in the state which has demonstrated ability of no mean order" and has "aroused interest in the white baseball public." The paper concluded in 1887 that "there should be a corresponding interest and pride taken in the nine by all the colored people in the city."[9]

By the late 1880s, several other independent black ballclubs of professional caliber existed throughout the country, and in an attempt to consolidate these teams into a viable professional league, Walter S. Brown, a Pittsburgh newspaper dealer, announced his intention to establish the National Colored League (NCL).[10] The popular magazine *Sporting Life* reported that "there have been prominent colored baseball clubs throughout the country for many years past, but this [1887] is their initiative year in launching forth on a league scale by forming a league ... representing ... leading cities in the country. Boston, one of the nation's leading cities ... fielded one of the best black teams in the country."[11] On February 3, 1887, Marshall Thompson, manager and promoter of the Resolutes, accepted Brown's invitation and his team joined the newly created NCL. Thompson immersed himself in local politics and served as one of the few African Americans who worked at the Massachusetts State House. This position allowed him to function as a link between the state's politicians and Boston's black community. He earned enough political clout to be named a featured guest at Boston's 1887 St. Patrick's Day Parade and garnered sufficient popularity to run the black community's cherished cakewalk contest.[12] As one of his many responsibilities, Thompson's leadership of the Resolutes would prove his most difficult challenge.

During the NCL's preseason, organizational phase, Brown announced that the League's Eastern Division would include New York, Boston, and Philadelphia, and the Western Division would have teams in Pittsburgh, Baltimore, and Louisville. The Resolutes competed in a few warm-up games in anticipation of their professional debut. They easily defeated the region's other major black team, the Providence Grays, in a game played at Union Grounds in Boston, by the lopsided score of 20–5. The NCL opened on May 5, 1887, but only a few games into the season, storm clouds gathered and it appeared as if the league was headed for disaster. Scheduling snafus and inadequate financial backing left the Resolutes out of money and stranded in Louisville on May 8. The team folded two days later when it became evident that the club failed to meet its financial obligation to travel and play in Pittsburgh. The *Louisville Courier Journal* ran the following description of the team's opening game in the new league: "The National Colored League season was formally opened yesterday at the Louisville Base Ball Park. The Falls City team comprised of the best ball-tossers of the city were defeated with ease by the Boston Resolutes. The game was witnessed by about 500 people. The Resolutes are all fine players, especially the dusky little twirler Selden. He struck out thirteen men, and held the Falls Citys down to six hits, two of which were bases on balls. Selden has a most deceptive drop curve, and a most perfect control over the ball. But there are no flies on the other Boston players. Smith is an excellent left-hand throwing catcher, and hits the ball hard enough to burst the cover. Penno, Walker and Williams are all good infielders, and understand thoroughly the fine points of the game."[13]

Boston Resolutes	***AB***	***R***	***1B***	***PO***	***A***	***E***
Cross, 1b	5	2	2	10	0	0
Brown, RF	5	2	4	0	0	0
Penno, SS	5	2	3	0	3	0
Selden, P	4	1	3	0	6	0
Williams, 2B	5	0	1	2	2	0
Walker, 3B	5	1	1	1	2	1
Taylor, Lf	5	1	3	1	0	1
Terrill, Cf	5	1	2	0	0	0
Smith, C	5	0	3	13	0	1
TOTALS	44	10	22	27	13	3

Louisville Courier-Journal, May 8, 1887

In spite of the club's stellar performance, insufficient financing, bad luck, and ineffective leadership by the league's front office contributed to the demise of the NCL on May 28. Some teams, like New York, Baltimore, and Pittsburgh remained on the road and barnstormed the country for most of the summer. Others, like Boston, returned home and continued their season playing games against local teams. "At last accounts," noted the *Sporting News*, "most of the Colored Leaguers were working their way home doing little turns in barbershops and waiting on tables in hotels."[14]

Not all of the Resolutes made it back to Boston. Several notable players joined professional black teams operating in the New York metropolitan area. Dan Penno, a Cape Verdean from East Greenwich, Rhode Island, left the Resolutes to play for the Cuban Giants, the nation's first truly professional black baseball club. The team originated in 1885 under the leadership of Frank P. Thompson, a hotelman and head waiter by profession, who masterfully combined two accomplished ballclubs from Philadelphia, the Keystone Athletics and the Orions, and another from Washington, D.C., the Manhattans, into the Cuban Giants. The team played its opening season at the luxurious Argyle Hotel in Babylon, a town on Long Island, and later moved to Trenton, New Jersey. During the late 19th and early 20th century the team traveled extensively throughout New England engaging in single-game contests and extended "championship" series with notable white clubs. There were, however, no Cubans on the Giants. The waiters agreed to adopt the name as a way of scheduling games with white teams who refused to play against African Americans. According to one observer, "If Cuban in the team name was part subterfuge, Giants was pure tribute." Another Resolutes player, William H. Selden, joined Penno to help bolster the Giants starting pitching rotation. Others, like Windsor W. Terrill, found a home with the Cuban X Giants, a team comprised mostly of defecting Cuban Giants.[15]

The loss of such key players weakened the Resolutes, and the team struggled to thrive in later years. In 1889, Marshall Thompson reported that he was "hard at work towards reorganizing the Resolutes" and had been "offered backing by several prominent men," but Thompson's efforts failed to fortify the team. Instead, he orchestrated a merger of his team with a rival West End club, the Seasides. The Seasides played excellent ball and openly challenged the Resolutes for the city's blackball bragging rights. Both teams, however, scrambled for funds. Hoping to resolve financial woes, the teams officially consolidated in May 1889 and thereafter were known simply as the Seasides. The new team fell under the control of Theodore E. Roberts, who moved the front office to 93 Union Street and appointed William James, one of his own, as team manager. He reported that he intended to schedule home games at Presumpscot Park.[16]

The Seasides lasted only one year, and the former Resolute players, now playing under the name of the Resolute Reserves struggled through the 1890s. Midway through 1890, the defection of several key players, including the team's crack battery of pitcher Windsor Terrell and catcher Davis, to the original Cuban Giants left the team without top-notch gate attractions. Recurring financial difficulties, most notably a lack of travel money, resulted in forfeited games. When opponents began labeling the Resolute Reserves as unreliable, word spread and the team experienced greater difficulty in scheduling games. Charges of financial mismanagement also hounded the team. The club hit rock bottom following an incident involving W.W. Walker, manager of the

Reserves, and E.J. Ellis, manager of the Beverly Athletic Association, who nearly came to blows over absent advanced payments, lost gate receipts and a history of forfeited games.[17]

Growth and Expansion, 1900–1920

As the nineteenth century turned into the twentieth, several new "colored" ballclubs emerged to fill the void left by the legendary Resolutes. The number of teams steadily increased and the level of competition intensified. Moreover, an old-fashioned rivalry developed between teams representing Boston and Cambridge. Fans witnessed firsthand the convergence of these trends in the opening game of the 1901 season, staged between the Mentors of Cambridge and the Windsors of Boston. Promoters billed the game as a showdown between rival communities, one destined to ignite local fervor. As an added attraction, the contest featured celebrity George Dixon, ex-featherweight champion of the world, as home-plate umpire. The Mentors, established in 1900, drew players from the black employees of Harvard University's Memorial Hall. According to the *Boston Daily Globe*, the Mentors fielded one of the classiest, best-organized, and well-financed black teams in the state.[18]

By 1903, the requisite number of teams and talented ballplayers allowed for the creation of Boston's first organized race league, called the Greater Boston Colored League (GBCL). Robert Teamoh, an African American journalist, organized the association and served as its president. Teamoh, a dynamic figure in the black community, displayed a passion for politics and sports. In 1894, he was elected on the Republican ticket to the Massachusetts State Legislature representing Boston's upscale Ninth District. The Ninth's constituency included both black and white residents, and Teamoh moved comfortably between both races. At 30 years old, he became the youngest African American to hold elective office in the State House. Teamoh knew the city well. He was born and raised in Boston, where he attended Boston Latin High School and later the Boston Industrial Drawing School. As a young man, he developed an interest in newspaper writing and landed a position with the *Boston Globe*. At the *Globe*, his success and ambition led to his notoriety as the first black reporter chosen as a member of the Boston Press Club. He also served as director of the *Globe* Athletic Club.[19]

Teamoh scouted the region's best ballclubs and invited the West Medford Independents, Boston Royal Giants, Cambridge Washingtons, Malden Riversides, West Newton Athletics, and the Allstons to join the League. Each team enthusiastically agreed. Upon completion of the first season, the Independents won the championship and the Royal Giants placed second. Years later, Joel Lewis, a pitcher for the Allstons, recalled that "the type of ball played was high grade, and the players, themselves, were as fine a bunch of fellows [as] I have ever played with. I am sorry the League is not going today, as I believe players trained in it would have, by now, won wide recog-

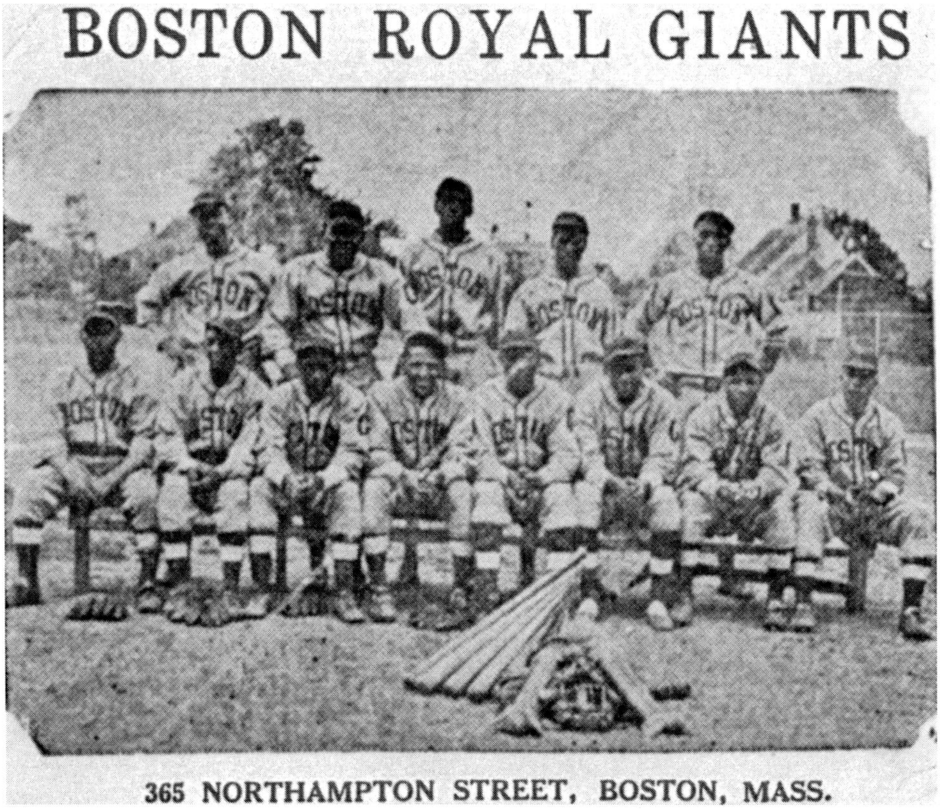

The Boston Royal Giants, who had participated in the Greater Boston Colored League, posing for a publicity shot in 1935. That year there was talk of a new league for area teams (courtesy Layton Revel).

nition and helped considerably in the recognition of Colored players."[20] Lewis would never see another league like the GBCL, although word did circulate in April 1935 that a similar Greater Boston League had been planned by local African American promoters.[21]

Following their championship season in 1903, the West Medford Independents continued to have great success. Originating in 1902 and outlasting any of its league opponents, the team included a combination of local talent and players recently arrived from the South as part of the Great Migration. The Independents drew the largest crowds recorded at the town's Playstead Park and attracted large numbers of fans when they played in nearby Boston. The original Independents had thrived from 1902 to 1912; reorganized in 1912 and lasted until 1917, when most of the players enlisted to fight in World War I; and after the end of the War, regrouped, adding more players and lasting until the early 1920s.[22]

The first incarnation of the team, mostly because of its championship season in the GBCL, evokes the strongest memories and connection to the community. Local resident Hilton Parnham, whose family members either played for the team or demonstrated their support from the bleachers, stated that the "first Independents, the original team, well it was really great." He recalled the players with a bit of exaggeration when he concluded that

> all of them were of Major League caliber. Roy Campanella was a great catcher, we all know. But I'd say [Jim] Gabriel was his equal; especially in throwing. Gabriel threw from the rocking chair crouch. He had a powerful arm. Art Ransome was another great star and first baseman.... He could hit, field with that stretch, and he was a brilliant baserunner with that slide.... Otis Parham Sr. was one of the best right-handers in the state, bar none.... His pitching team-mate, Dick Banks of Arlington, was right up there with him. So his fast ball was partly a knuckle ball that did tricks to enemy batters. The early outfield of Waldron Furr, Arnold Benjamin and Branch Russell, was a good one, all sluggers.... The club beat the Boston Tigers regularly, and the Tigers were among the best in the country.... Other players replaced the oldtimers later to keep the club strong.... But I'd say that Art Ransome and, later, the club left hander pitching star, your brother, Hillard Kountze, were the two best first basemen the club ever had.... You know that Medford Mayor Lewis Lovering, had a lot to do with the success, and progress, of the Independent Baseball Club. He helped to get the first uniforms for the team and was the team "Number One" fan.... Mayor Lovering let people know that this Afro-American athletic group was bringing honor and prestige to the city, and this is what the club did as long as it existed and represented Medford.[23]

By 1905, fan attention shifted to the Dartmouth Athletic Giants, a powerhouse club listed as the precursors of the legendary Boston Giants of the 1920s and 1930s. The Athletic Giants carded games against teams in Greater Boston, including Boston, Cambridge, Malden, Winchester, Everett, Lynn, and Medford. Teams from these cities reportedly played "mostly among themselves" but not in an organized league structure.[24]

In the heart of Boston's South Side, another team began its rise to prominence during the early decades of the 20th century. The history of the Boston Tigers reads like a storybook tale. The ballclub started as a sandlot team of grammar-school boys who managed to stay together over the years and develop into the region's most admired ballclub. Bob Russell and Arthur "Fat" Johnson were the two men most responsible for the success of the Tigers. Russell, an excellent ballplayer and manager, combined his talent with Johnson, a money man and enthusiastic promoter, to create the team.[25]

The two met in 1912 and shortly thereafter helped a struggling sandlot ballclub aptly named the Progress Team to become the renowned Tigers. The Progress players attended and represented Robert Gould Shaw House, a community home for African American boys, located on Hammond Street. As a youngster, Russell reportedly spent a great deal of time at the Shaw House and played for the Progress club. In 1910, he entered English High School, where he became a stellar athlete, and later attended

Colby Academy in Maine. Russell's reputation as a power pitcher earned him a spot in the East Coast "Hotel Circuit," playing each summer for resort teams in Rhode Island and each winter for hotel teams in Florida. He finally settled back in Boston, and by 1915, he and Johnson had succeeded in transforming the Progress club to the Tigers.[26]

When Johnson met Russell, he worked for the 20th Century Limited Railroad and spent most of his free time playing ball at the Columbus Avenue Park. Johnson later partnered with Bertie Davis and operated a successful laundry business in the heart of Harvard Square, where he became a popular figure and cultivated friendships with the neighborhood's wealthy clientele. Johnson's business experience and connections made him the perfect spokesman and promoter for the up-and-coming Tigers.[27]

Prior to World War I, the team had come into its own and possessed enough moxie to challenge the St. John's team from Cambridge, an aggregation regarded as the "toast of the colored baseball fans and top attraction of this area." A spirited rivalry developed between the teams, but the onset of war interrupted the contests. On August 1, 1918, several members of the Tigers—including Arthur Carrington, William "Bullet" Campbell, James Moore, John "Southy" Thomas, and owner "Fats" Johnson—reported for military service at Fort Devans in Georgia.[28] When the Tigers ballplayers returned at war's end, they re-established themselves, dominating blackball in the Greater Boston area throughout the 1920s. Russell and Johnson had rejuvenated the team, which now enjoyed unparalleled success and admiration.[29]

The Pilgrims and the Tigers: Black Baseball in the 1920s

In the years preceding and during World War I, African Americans left the South and relocated in the North as part of the nation's Great Migration. Black communities flourished and so did baseball. Ballparks that serviced black neighborhoods—including Carter Field and Lincoln Park in Boston's South End, Russell Field and Hoyt Field in Cambridge, Playstead Park in Medford, and Dorchester's Town Field—remained busy with games through the 1920s and 1930s.[30] The Tigers opened the 1920s in glorious fashion and prompted the *Boston Globe* to report that they were "one of the best semi-professional teams in the state," regardless of color, and the club easily claimed the title as the "champion colored nine of New England." All season long, William "Bullet" Campbell provided excellent pitching while John "Southy" Thomas and Mose Sisco added the fine fielding and clutch hitting that defined a well-balanced team. Given the ballclub's success, the *Globe* expected the Tigers to eventually "travel over the country and play the strongest teams they could book."[31]

The paper's prediction came true but with an interesting twist when several Tiger players were asked to join a newly formed professional baseball league in 1921. On

December 31, 1920, George Herman "Andy" Lawson, a Boston area sports promoter announced the creation of the new league as a rival to Major League Baseball's American and National Leagues. Lawson's "Continental League," sometimes referred to as the Continental Baseball Association, captured the attention of the African American community after Lawson hinted that his new league intended to include black ballclubs. This was a bold move on Lawson's part since the gentlemen's agreement to ban blacks from professional baseball was still in effect. Lawson sought to include a black team from Boston, and the obvious choice was the city's champion Tigers.[32] The Tigers changed their name to the Pilgrims for the move to pro baseball, highlighting the team's regional identity. But the ill-fated Continental League lasted only a few weeks, and the Pilgrims changed their name back to the Tigers before returning to the ranks of semipro ball. Years later, in 1943, William "Sheep" Jackson, sportswriter for the *Boston Chronicle* reminded his readers that in 1921, the Pilgrims were the "best negro baseball team that ever put on a pair of spikes in this community ... a club that compared favorably with any A.A. minor league club." Jackson recalled that the team "played its home games at the Everett High School Filed on Chelsea Street. It played weekdays and Saturday afternoons and I am glad to report played before several thousands at all times."[33]

> *"The new Continental Baseball League contemplates invading Chicago, it was learned today, when a letter was received from Secretary George M. Riley, inviting the American Giants, a colored professional team, to join the new circuit. The letter stated that two strong colored teams hand joined, the Boston Tigers and the Knoxville Giants, and two more colored teams were sought by the organization."*—New York Times, *January 26, 1921*

Before the Pilgrims again became the Tigers, they played in a Continental League game against an opponent that significantly impacted the landscape of black baseball in New England. The Pilgrims met the Cleveland Colored Giants in a doubleheader at Everett High School Park to open the season. The Pilgrims defeated the Colored Giants by scores of 10–2 and 12–2.[34] Not long after these games, the league folded and the Colored Giants found themselves stranded in New England without scheduled games and a guaranteed income. Fortunately, James Gibbons, owner of the Gibbons Express Trucking Company in Providence, Rhode Island, rescued the team. Gibbons financed the team and promoted games with regional semi-professional clubs. In doing so, he turned the Cleveland Giants into one of the premiere traveling ballclubs in Greater Boston and throughout southern New England.[35]

As fate would have it, the Pilgrims, now once more the Tigers, and the Cleveland Colored Giants clashed again, this time in 1923, to determine the regional black baseball championship. The black press touted the game as the principal athletic event of the Emancipation Day celebration held at Rocky Point Park in Rhode Island. African Americans in Rhode Island and throughout New England celebrated West Indian emancipation on August 1 instead of the traditional January 1 festival honoring President Lincoln's Emancipation Proclamation.[36] Emancipation Day drew thousands of celebrants and the game served as the principal entertainment for all in attendance. The Colored Giants defeated the Tigers by a score of 4–3 in a 10 inning thriller. Southy Thomas, Mose Sisco, and Zeke Crudup played, receiving special praise for their efforts in a losing cause.[37]

Throughout the 1920s, the Tigers continued to play outstanding baseball. The team engaged in several championship games with ballclubs like the Philadelphia Giants and the Colored All-Stars from Providence, Rhode Island. The team even made sports history when it took part in the first baseball-football doubleheader. In the opening game, the Tigers played the Providence Colored All-Stars for the "colored baseball title" of New England, and later that day the Providence Steam Roller football team met the Newport Torpedo Station in a gridiron classic.[38] But the Tigers remained fixed in the hearts of their fans for other reasons. They played most of their games nearby at the Columbus Avenue Park, and most of the players hailed from places like Boston, Cambridge, Everett, Malden, and West Newton. Boston fans identified with these local men, knowing that the ballplayers experienced the same challenges and hardships off the field that they did. The fans also knew that baseball provided an opportunity to demonstrate black talent and identity, especially in contests against white opponents.

Long after their careers ended, many former Tigers participated in a series of memorable old-timer's games that reunited them with their fans and reaffirmed their standing in the community. Billed as the "must-see game of the year," these contests featured former stars representing Boston and Cambridge. The tradition originated in 1937 under the sponsorship of the Cambridge Works Progress Administration (WPA) Recreation Committee and the guiding hand of its supervisor, ex–Tiger Ralph "Stody" Ward. The initial exhibition game quickly turned into a sizzling inter-city rivalry that became a best-of-seven series between the teams. Games scheduled in Cambridge were played at the Russell E. Hoyt Playground field located on Western Avenue, and games held in Boston were at William E. Carter Playground on Columbus Avenue. In 1938, the opening contest between the teams played at Carter Field attracted over 10,000 fans, the most to attend a game in over a decade. The ensuing game, played in Cambridge, featured the town's mayor, John W. Lyons, who tossed the ceremonial first pitch, and the WPA Band of Medford, whose musicians entertained the crowd at Hoyt Field before and during the game.[39]

By 1940, the *Boston Chronicle* reported that the old-timer's games had become a "magnet that draws people who, at one time, were rabid, dyed-in-wool fans" of the Tigers. The 1941 game, for example, featured most of the past Tigers. According to one observer, "the Boston Old-Timer's club will stir rosy memories as veteran ball fans gaze ... on Big Jim Moore, the veteran and ex–Tiger first baseman; the famed pitcher "Bullet" Campbell; and the popular player and pilot, Bob Russell, all ex–Boston Tigers, who need no introduction anywhere in New England." Fans attended the games to recall an important time in their lives when the Tigers showcased their talent and proved that they were the best semipro team, black or white, in New England. They also attended to support the community, beginning in 1939. The financial proceeds of that year's game were donated to cover the medical expenses for beloved former Tiger centerfielder Mose Sisco, and throughout subsequent years gate receipts were collected for the North Cambridge Community Club.[40]

> ***"The bitter struggle of baseball supremacy in-so-far as the Old Timers of Boston and Cambridge are concerned will be staged at the Russell E. Hoyt Playground next Sunday, Sept 11, 1938 at 2:00 o'clock. This baseball game that promises to offer thrills galore, between the ex-stars of Cambridge and Boston, will go down in history as an event of local significance. As an added attraction, the W.P.A. Band of Medford will render selections before the game and during the innings."*—Boston Chronicle, *September 10, 1938***

William "Sheep" Jackson and the Lore of the Tigers

"I have always believed, very firmly, that Boston colored athletes of yesteryear are forgotten too easily."—William "Sheep" Jackson, *Boston Chronicle*, July 22, 1944

Before the opening of the 1945 baseball season, William "Sheep" Jackson, sports editor for the *Boston Chronicle*, found himself caught somewhere between memory and history as he recounted the triumphs and achievements of several ballplayers on the city's own Boston Tigers. Black fans enthusiastically supported the national pastime through the local men who played the game. During the 1920s, the Tigers emerged as the black community's most beloved and successful semi-professional ballclub. Decades later, Jackson insured that the team's memory would never linger in the shadows. He passionately reminded his readers how their neighborhood ballplayers once illuminated the diamonds situated at Carter Park and Columbus Avenue Playground. Jackson made every effort to recognize and recount the history of Boston's Tigers to keep the team's memories flourishing.

Jackson enjoyed a lifelong relationship with amateur sport in greater Boston. Born and raised in Malden, he excelled in baseball, football, basketball and track at Malden High School. He later attended Cushing Academy on a football scholarship and Lincoln University in Pennsylvania, where he displayed athletic versatility and demonstrated academic talent. He accepted a part-time sports-reporter position at the *Boston Chronicle* while still a student at Lincoln. Upon graduation from college, he married his girlfriend Lydia and relocated to a home on Broadway in Cambridge. In 1934, he served as athletic director of the Cambridge Community Center and began his graduate studies at the Boston University School of Social Service and Religious Education. Despite his busy schedule, he managed to continue writing his sports column Sports Shots for the *Chronicle*. In 1940, he became the paper's sports editor and strengthened his broader community connections as a field representative for the National Youth Association. Jackson answered his country's call for duty in July 1943 when he entered the United States Army. After a distinguished career in the military, he returned home where he and his wife became the proud parents of a son, William Daniel Jackson. By 1945, Jackson had returned to his familiar role as sportswriter. One of his first tasks was to launch a series of biographical sketches that reconnected the Boston Tigers to their fans and the community they both shared.[41]

Jackson epitomized the capacity of sportswriters to connect events from sports history to the social and cultural outlook of the present. In the years between the publication of Sol White's monumental *History of Colored Baseball* in 1907 and Mabry "Doc" Kountze's *50 Sports Years Along Memory Lane* in 1979, the history and significance of Boston's race teams fell mainly to local black sportswriters who kept the public memory of the game intact.

During the first half of the 20th century, these chroniclers approached their subject in numerous ways, but always in an effort to make baseball's past part of a public transcript that clearly defined the black community's collective memory. Sportswriters who recalled and interpreted the long history of colored baseball occupied the ambiguous and oftentimes conflicted position of writing "between memory and history."

Scholars have recently focused their attention on the relationship between the black press and the integration of professional major league baseball during and immediately after World War II. Jackson elected to examine the sportswriter's role in explicating the proud heritage of local black baseball, identifying neighborhood heroes to emulate and celebrating the game's contributions to black cultural expression. Jackson, with his potential to reach broad segments of Boston's African American population, provides a strong example of how black sportswriters exercised their right to interpret and make use of their community's baseball past.

Sports reporters enjoyed their widest readership in city newspapers, and in Boston the *Chronicle* was the place for black sports. The paper served as a lifeline to the city's baseball enthusiasts, often capturing the personalities and highlights of past years and their impact on black cultural identity. In Jackson's series, he entwined the game's history with feature stories on former players' careers. He covered special occasions like retirements, managerial and front-office appointments, and neighborhood commemorations of local sports heroes to familiarize his readers with players whose past accomplishments proved worthy of consideration. Sometimes, newspaper coverage of the death of black ballplayers evoked an outpouring of stories and memories that turned otherwise private mourning ceremonies into public expressions of the history and meaning of black baseball. Jackson operated as a middle man somewhere between history and memory and fashioned a usable baseball past, albeit selective and incomplete.

Jackson also examined traditions-in-progress to further influence the community's collective identity. One such tradition, Old-Timer's Days, made the game's historic past, and racial identity, part of contemporary social life. During the mid–1930s and early 1940s, long after most of the Tigers had retired from baseball, the community clamored for their return in a series of old-timer's games that often pitted former players who hailed from Cambridge against their teammates from Boston. These contests, often benefiting local charities, were played at Hoyt Field in front of fans where "everybody knows everybody else." Children accompanied parents and grandparents to get their first look at the men whom their elders considered legends in the community. As one observer noted, "Baseball is the game we love," and the old-timer's game "will present a galaxy of some of the greatest diamond stars in New England's progressive history even though many of the boys will be long past their prime." Jackson and any other sportswriter in the city would agree but add that in their prime a number of these men were good enough to play in the major leagues. These celebrations encouraged Jackson to reflect on the game's history and the accomplishments of former players.[42]

Boston's Golden Age of Black Baseball, 1931–1946

As the 1920s ended, no one could have predicted the economic devastation that awaited most Americans during the Great Depression. The duration and severity of this economic collapse affected most aspects of life including black baseball. By 1931, the professional Negro National League crumbled under the weight of the Depression and the recent death of its founder, Andrew "Rube" Foster. Many players found themselves without a team and a paycheck. This unfortunate situation led many players to seek tryouts with local semi-professional teams. Boston, like many other cities, benefited from this influx of talent.

In 1932, the black press reported that "Lincoln Park and the William E. Carter Playground ought to be scenes of a large number of good baseball games ... since there are three exceptionally good colored ballclubs with enough talent and ability to make games interesting anywhere." The Boston Tigers, the Philadelphia Giants, and the Boston Royal Giants contained comparable talent and remained competitive with each other and the strongest semipro white teams in the state.[43] The Providence Colored Giants, another regional team that included exceptional talent, petitioned to play in Boston's Twilight League, becoming the fourth powerhouse semipro team playing in Boston.

In addition to the Philly Giants, the Tigers, and the Colored Giants, numerous other ballclubs represented Boston's black neighborhoods. Clem Mack's Boston ABC team attracted many professional black barnstorming teams to Boston's Lincoln Park. Prior to his arrival in Boston in 1935, Mack managed the Colored House of David and scheduled games with teams around the country. He used his contacts to card games in Boston with teams like the New York Colored Giants and Homestead Grays. The ABCs probably traveled further than any Boston-based team as evidenced by its preseason trip to the South during its inaugural season in 1935. Reports from Henderson, North Carolina, affirmed that the "Boston ABC baseball club which gained national publicity in its first trip here in southern training quarters is now ready to pack up and depart for New England. The new team has been here since the middle of March whipping into shape for what is expected to be the most strenuous baseball season in Boston and which may result in that city securing a franchise in the Negro National League by next year." Mack's efforts, however, did not result in a professional franchise and his tenure in the city lasted only one year.[44]

Black teams also participated in the city's amateur leagues. The city's Park League, for instance, hosted several African American teams in the late 1930s. These teams included the Rangers, Mohawks, and Wolverines. Ike Bailey's Rangers included a mix of veterans and youngsters, and manager Edward Hill of the Mohawks joined the Park League in 1938 after winning the championship of the Sunset League the year before. Fans, however, favored the Wolverines and their star player Eugene Wood, a former outstanding athlete at Memorial High School.[45] The Wolverines originated in 1934 and served as the athletic counterpart to the civic-minded Wolverine Club located on 558 Massachusetts Avenue.[46]

> *"Next Tuesday, Boston will pack up and head North. And the grand opening at Lincoln Park in a few weeks will be eagerly awaited by white and colored ball fans of New England. Manager Clem Mack will be content to enter all 1935 games as the underdog because of his first year aggregation. But all Boston will witness one of the hardest fighting ballclubs ever seen here before. And they can expect real baseball."*—Boston Chronicle, *April 27, 1935*

West Newton fielded one of the most competitive teams in Greater Boston during the 1920s and 1930s. The team originated as the Colored Town Nine and came from an area known as the Colored Village. Since the turn of the 20th century, African American families had established a community there centered in the Myrtle Baptist Church. Baseball quickly became a passion among the residents. The Colored Town Nine operated in the 1920s, sometimes under the name of the Galloping Dominoes, and played an informal and independent schedule with nearby white teams. In 1932, a former star with the Boston Tigers, Earl Lomax, reorganized that team as the West Newton Colored Tigers and coaxed several of his Tiger teammates to join the club. Former Tigers who accepted Lomax's invitation included Gus Gadsen, Fleet Taylor, Zing Rice, and Stody Ward. The addition of these "outsiders" helped transform the club into a truly semi-professional outfit. In 1932, the team emerged as a strong regional contender with a record of 18 games won against 12 losses. The following year, the West Newton Tigers held a 22–12 record and in 1934 the team reached a high point by going 34–5. The Tigers grew in popularity as it continued to excel on the field. According to one observer, the fans "hustled through their suppers, converged on the local ballpark, filled up the small grandstands, stood two and three-deep along the sidelines, and around the fifth inning tossed their nickels, dimes, and (sometimes) quarters into the baseball caps that were passed around." In 1935, the team ceased playing as a semipro team and joined the Newton Twilight League. A year later, the seasoned veterans disbanded the team and ended a memorable era in West Newton sports history.[47]

The 1930s and 1940s, however, belonged to the Philly Giants, Boston Colored Giants, and the Providence Giants. By the early 1930s, the Boston Tigers no longer stood atop the city's black baseball world. The team opened the 1932 season by defeating a strong opponent in the Lincoln Athletic Club of Harlem. Yet, the Tigers, which included former Providence Giants standouts Oliver Marcelle at third base and Tubby Johnson in the outfield, failed to perform as expected.

This was the last year the team would remain competitive, and the press declared that the end of the Tigers represented both "confusion and possibilities" for Boston's black baseball future. Confusion in that the familiar Tigers had lost their combative edge and possibility in the form of the Boston Giants, a new team destined to capture the attention and support of the former Tiger fans.[48]

The Tigers did maintain their presence in the following years. In 1934, the team defeated the Harvard All-Stars, a team composed of current and past Harvard baseball players, by a score of 9–4 in a benefit game for St. Monica's Home. An aging Jim Moore hit a grand slam home run to win the game. Baseball legend George Herman "Babe" Ruth had agreed to toss the ceremonial first pitch of the game, but was unable to attend because he experienced a hard afternoon against the Red Sox and wasn't feeling well. More important than the presence of the "Bambino" was the meaning behind the game, expressed eloquently in the *Boston Chronicle*: "The contest was simply another example of the inter-racial friendship bond which is slowly being revealed at Harvard and also to the ability of 'Fats' Johnson as a promoter." By 1935, the Tigers rarely played in the city, but in subsequent years many of the players returned to thrill their followers in a series of old-timers games played at Carter Playground.[49]

"The Wolverine baseball club, one of the best amateur teams in the State, is giving the old dyed in the wool baseball fans some great Sunday afternoons. For it is on these Sunday afternoons that the Wolverines put on their best baseball manners and give the visitors a run for their money. The team is young, aggressive and full of fight. They play head up baseball and are never beaten until the final out is made in the ninth."—Boston Chronicle, *August 8, 1942*

For a brief moment, the Providence Giants helped fill the void left by the Tigers. The Giants name had been popular among black teams since the 19th century and all three Greater Boston teams adopted the same title. The Providence Giants opened the 1930s in strong fashion. Arthur "Daddy" Black, the owner, assembled a championship team in 1931 that included several professional players looking for work after the demise of the Negro National League. Black, an African American, had been involved in owning and promoting sports teams since the mid–1920s when he managed the all-white Boston Monarchs Baseball Club. Black made his livelihood as the "numbers king" of black Providence. He operated his illegal numbers racket from his home on Cranston Street in Providence's Hoyle Square neighborhood. His operation took in an estimated $5,000.00 a day during the height of the Depression in 1932.[50]

In 1931, Black acquired the Providence Colored Giants from Daniel Whitehead, his friend and fellow sports promoter. Black had the financial resources and sports connections to acquire the finest black players to play for his team. He acquired, for example, Oliver "Ghost" Marcelle, an outstanding third baseman who previously played for the championship Baltimore Black Sox. Marcelle was approaching the end of his career when he signed with Providence, but Black managed to attract younger players on their way up. Pitchers Luther Farrell and Jesse Hubbard, both former Providence Giants, played for the Bacharach Giants and between them defeated the mighty Pittsburgh Crawfords twice in a doubleheader in 1934. Likewise, outfielder "Tubby" Johnson joined the New York Black Yankees after departing Providence. Other players with professional experience included Elmore "Scrappy" Brown and Robert "Highpockets" Hudspeth.[51]

> *"Whitehead, unquestionably the czar of Negro baseball around New England, can be given direct credit for bringing these leading attractions to Providence. Capitalizing on the fact that Sunday baseball was prohibited in Massachusetts, big Dan would negotiate with either the Braves or any of the visiting teams during their Sunday in Boston, to play in Providence. The big leaguers grasping the opportunity of killing an afternoon by making some easy money."*—**Boston Chronicle**, *May 9, 1936*

Rhode Island's semi-professional and amateur leagues refused admission to the powerhouse Giants and local clubs declined to play them. Black took his team to Boston and found a home in the city's Twilight League, where his team captured the league title in 1931. Black's Giants opened the season in grand fashion by assisting in the dedication of Boston's newest ballpark, Lincoln Park, located at Massachusetts Avenue and Island Street. The stadium operated as the Hub's first sports venue owned and operated by an African American, John H. Prioleau.[52] During the season, Black arranged for his team to travel to New York to play the Harlem Stars, owned by entertainer Bill "Bojangles" Robinson. Robinson's Stars, later to become the New York Black Yankees, defeated the Giants in a doubleheader played at the Polo Grounds by scores of 6–4 and 8–1.[53] In the postseason, Providence challenged the Philadelphia Giants for New England's "Grand Title." The Providence Giants entered the contest as heavy favorites, but lost to the Philly Giants in a hotly contested nine-game contest.[54]

Black believed the team failed to play professional-level ball. The Providence Giants never achieved its full potential or merited its hefty payroll. Black's financial investment did not produce a favorable return and his interest in blackball decreased. Moreover, the likelihood of the team becoming an independent and professional traveling team diminished as players weighed their options for the upcoming year. Black turned the team back over to Whitehead, with disastrous results. During the opening game of the 1932 season, several players on the team mutinied and left the field under rumor that Whitehead did not have the money to pay them. Whitehead replaced his high-priced talent with local players and managed to complete the season. Black, however, met a disastrous fate. He was murdered, gangland style, at his home in Providence by rival mobsters looking to muscle in on his territory.[55]

Following the demise of the Providence ballclub, the Philly Giants and the Boston Colored Giants became the city's major black baseball attractions. There has been some confusion, mostly because of inconsistent reporting in the press, over both the history and names of both these clubs. As sport historian Dick Thompson correctly explained, the name Philadelphia Giants had been used by many squads over the years, but the team originated in 1902 under the leadership of Sol White, a member of the Baseball Hall of Fame for his playing and managing accomplishments. In 1905, the team toured New England where it generated excitement and enjoyed an enthusiastic following. The New England bookings, especially Boston, were so successful that the team returned each summer. The city's supportive fans made an impression on one of the Giants, pitcher Danny McClellan. He recalled the loyal fans in Boston when he took control of the team in 1923, and he relocated the historic franchise there each summer. McClellan's Phillies made an impressive showing in their first Boston-based year by defeating several of the region's most talented white teams, including the Providence Steam Roller, ballclubs from Salem, North Cambridge, Dilboy, Fitchburg, and additional teams from the Bay State Twilight League.[56]

When the Giants made their customary entrance into Greater Boston in June, 1925, baseball authorities rated them as one of the best black semi-professional teams in the nation. The team satisfied these expectations by defeating the Pennsylvania Red Caps of New York in a thrilling six-game series played in ballparks throughout Greater Boston. The series, billed as the "Colored World Championship," was really a semi-professional championship that pitted two East Coast traveling teams in their quest for regional supremacy. The Red Caps hailed from New York City and derived their name from Pennsylvania Station in Manhattan. The Boston press described the Red Caps as "thumpers" capable of hitting the long ball and more serious than the Philly Giants in their desire to win. William Reavis managed and promoted the Red Caps and Julius Thomas served as team captain.[57]

The Philadelphia Giants prevailed in the series defeating the Red Caps in four games, losing one, and tying another. The first game, played at Fore River Stadium in Quincy before a crowd that "packed every part of the field," featured the Giants premier pitcher Will Jackman. The Giants won behind Jackman's shutout performance, 1–0.

BIGGEST COLORED ATTRACTION IN BASEBALL

BOSTON ROYAL GIANTS

Sensational Performers

Comedians—Entertainers

Booked Through:

BURLIN WHITE
365 NORTHAMPTON STREET,
BOSTON, MASS.
Phone: Commonwealth 7683

BURLIN WHITE
MANAGER

Outstanding Attraction for
Fairs and Holiday Celebrations

PLAY DAILY

Publicity Available
(See Footnote)

Mr George Quinn
5788 Woodrow ave.
Detroit
Mich.

Mar. 18-1935.

Dear Sir.

Some time during the early winter I noticed your article in the paper, & I am now in quest of information concerning the situation of the Nashville club being in Detroit, & the status of the Detroit Mohawks, in regard to booking games with outside teams. The Boston Royal Giants, will be on tour in that section during August, & would like to play in Detroit on or about Aug. 13-14. Any

For Royal Giants Special Printed Posters, Flyers, Window Cards, Hand Bills and other Publicity, write direct or telegraph to Printing Office: 410 Maxfield St., New Bedford, Mass. Telephone New Bedford 1630.

A 1935 letter from Boston manager Burlin White to George Quinn of the Detroit Mohawks (courtesy Layton Revel).

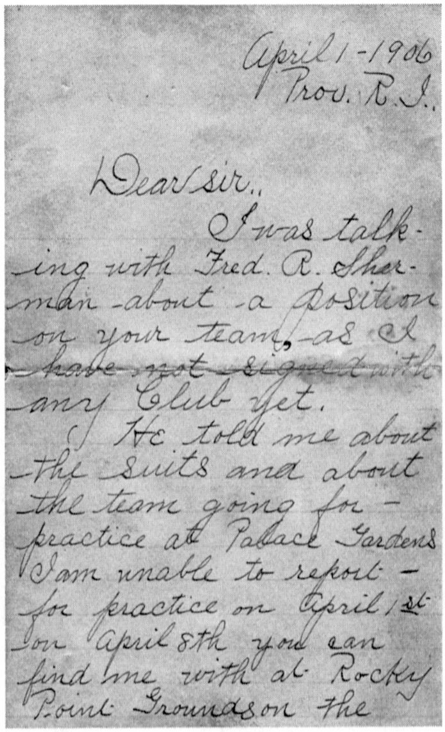

April 1-1906
Prov. R.I..

Dear sir..

I was talking with Fred. R. Sherman about a position on your team, as I have not signed with any Club yet.

He told me about the suits and about the team going for practice at Palace Gardens I am unable to report for practice on April 1st. On April 8th you can find me with at Rocky Point Grounds on the

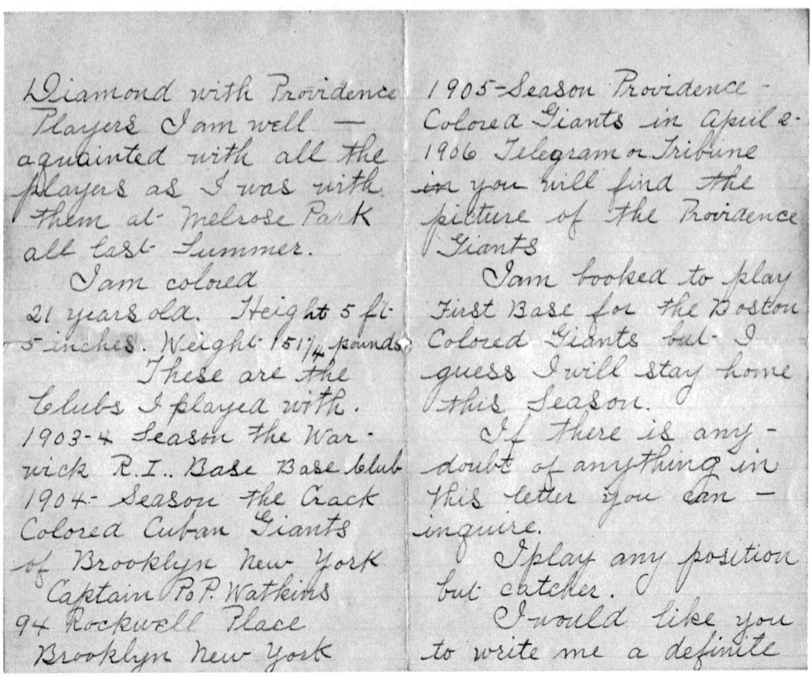

Diamond with Providence Players I am well aquainted with all the players as I was with them at Melrose Park all last Summer.

I am colored
21 years old. Height 5 ft 5 inches. Weight 151¼ pounds.

These are the Clubs I played with.
1903-4 Season the Warwick R.I.. Base Base club
1904- Season the Crack Colored Cuban Giants of Brooklyn New York
Captain P.P. Watkins
94 Rockwell Place
Brooklyn New York
1905-Season Providence Colored Giants in April 2. 1906 Telegram or Tribune in you will find the picture of the Providence Giants

I am booked to play First Base for the Boston Colored Giants but I guess I will stay home this Season.

If there is any doubt of anything in this letter you can inquire.

I play any position but catcher.

I would like you to write me a definite

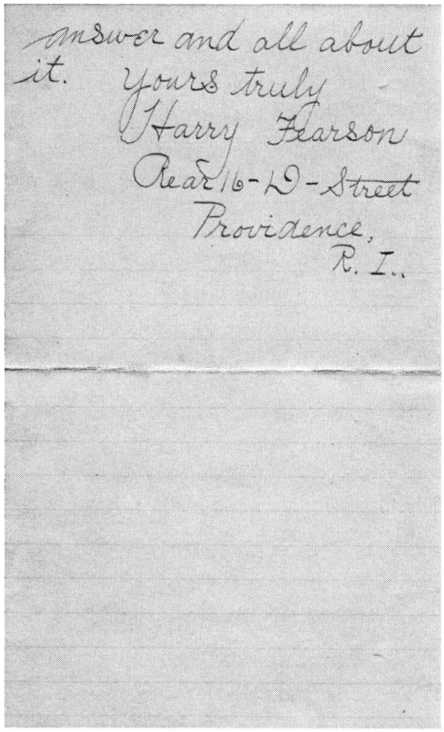

answer and all about
it. Yours truly
Harry Fearson
Rear 16-LD-Street
Providence,
R. I.

***Opposite and above:* A 1906 letter to an unknown owner or manager from former Providence player Harry Fearson (author's collection).**

The Giants triumphed in their second game, played at Walk-Over Park in Brocton, by a score of 4–2, but experienced their only defeat a day later at Ridge Hill Grove, 7–2. Jackman picked up another win in game 4 at the Walpole Grounds in Boston, 4–2, but the Giants ended up tying their rivals in game five at Memorial Park in Rockland, 4–4. In the sixth and deciding game, with Jackman resting, the Giants won an impressive victory behind the stellar pitching of Bill Pierce, 7–0. The games provided a "tonic" of excitement for Philly supporters who recorded an average attendance of 2,500 fans at each game. In Brocton, the women's Charitable Club held a celebratory dinner for both clubs which featured dancing until midnight and musical selections from "Tootsie" Jackman, "playboy of the diamond.[58]

The series featured several of the finest black players in baseball. The Giants fielded New England's most potent African American battery in Will Jackman and Burlin White. The team also acquired the talented Bill Yancy for the 1925 season. Yancy would later move to a successful professional baseball career, playing 14 seasons in the Negro Leagues. He ended his career as a manager in Latin America, where he helped introduce baseball to Panama. Yancy also played for New York's legendary Harlem Renaissance basketball team and was later inducted into the National Basketball Hall of Fame in

Springfield, Massachusetts, in 1963. The Red Caps featured a young and rising star in Dick Seay. He, too, would enjoy a long career as a player and manager in the Negro Leagues, especially with the Newark Eagles where he played shortstop and second base for the team's "million dollar" infield.[59]

The series delighted local fans and prompted one enthusiast to pen the following poem after the final game:

Just a game at twilight.
On the park Schwab built,
I saw the Philly Giants
Win a little tilt.
They beat the Pennsy Red Caps
Seven runs to none.
Then the gathering gloom
On the horizon did loom.
And the day's work was done.
[*Philadelphia Tribune*, 26 September 1925]

In 1926, the Phillies enjoyed another successful season and, in the midst of a ten-game winning streak, defeated their New England rivals, the Providence Giants, in the first game of a three-team doubleheader at Providence's Kinsley Park. In the second game, the Providence Giants were to play their major competition in the state's Suburban League, the Cromptons. Both the Giants and the Cromptons were vying for first place in the league. What made this afternoon particularly interesting was the fact that the Phillies substituted themselves for the Providence Giants and "played under their colors." According to Providence's owner and promoter Daniel Whitehead, "the Quakers [Philadelphia Giants] are to represent his club, the Providence Giants, in the nightcap and the result will count in the Suburban standing." At a time when free agency ran wild among the players and owners and players wore the uniforms of several clubs during the same season, this is the first time a team completely transformed itself into another. The Providence Giants secured a 7–3 victory over Crompton, but all the players were Philly Giants.[60]

Although based in Boston, the team toured extensively throughout New England, upstate New York, and Canada. McClellan's Phillies did, however, enter into an agreement with the town of New Bedford to play an increased number of home games at the town's Sargent Field. The team secured permission to use the field and it became their base of operations. By 1931, the press reported that John H. Prioleau, a young businessman from Roxbury, intended to purchase the Giants from McClellan and rename the team the Boston Giants. Prioleau promised Boston a team that would rank with the best semi-professional teams in the country and the chance to see his team play against the strongest black teams and leading white teams.

McClellan refused to relinquish control of the team and remained a Philly Giant until the team disbanded in 1935. In fact, 1934 proved a transitional year as "Smilin" Dan McCllelan attempted to pull a Connie Mack maneuver, bringing in new, younger players to replace the old. The pivotal transition failed to materialize and the team ended its historic run in Boston the following year.[61]

The Boston Giants entered the fray in 1932 and joined the Phillies and Tigers as one of the city's top three black teams. The local newspapers remarked that the team had "not been organized long" and had been "placed in the field by the owner of Lincoln Park," namely John Prioleau. Oliver Marcelle served as the team's first manager. The Boston Giants were soon replaced by Burlin White's Greater Boston Royal Giants. White had starred with the Philadelphia Giants for over a decade before he and owner Danny McClellan had a falling out in 1934 over McClellan's decision to restructure the team with younger players. Baseball enthusiasts touted White's Royal Giants as the city's leading team and intended to go places. Sports reporters perceived the new club as outclassing the Philly Giants and other potential African American competitors, including the Malden Giants, Rangers, and Cleveland Colored Giants, but not as formidable as the old Tigers or Providence Giants. A proven master promoter of his team, White booked games as far away as Ohio. He purchased the team its own bus and outfitted them in the finest uniforms. According to one report, "the Royal Giants have their own bus, and attired in neat blue-grey uniforms with dark caps and red, white, and blue stockings, they make a very attractive appearance on the field."[62]

During the late 1930s, the press referred to the team by a few different names. Some reports listed the team as the Boston Giants, others as the Royal Giants, and still others as the Royal Colored Giants. Regardless of the name, the team became the only black club to represent the city by the early 1940s. With the Philadelphia Giants losing momentum in Boston, the Boston Giants' White sensed that black baseball competition "may become a thing of the past." In response, White issued a "challenge to the Philadelphia Giants to play a grand baseball fest" at Lincoln Park to start the 1936 baseball season. The Boston Giants had dominated area play by compiling a record of 87 wins, 22 losses, and 5 ties. The Phillies had been on a steady slide and could not match their nearby rivals. The Phillies declined the offer and headed for the road. White was surely disappointed in the outcome since he hoped that the city's support of the contest with the Phillies would "encourage the players and tend to keep good teams in Boston instead of on the road."[63] With the Philadelphia Giants out of town for most of the season and the Boston Giants making their customary trips throughout New England and Canada, the Wolverines and Rangers supplied local fans a steady diet of baseball.[64]

In an attempt to stimulate broader interest in local black baseball, Lefty Brown and Fran Matthews, both local youngsters who made it to the professional Negro Leagues, exhorted their amateur and semipro counterparts to "get in line and stack their talent against that of boys from other sections." By the early 1940s, sportswriters lamented the black community's loss of attention to baseball and labeled it the "low point" in the city's rich historical tradition of black ball. Veteran reporter Mabe Kountze sadly observed that blackball was "dead as a door-knob," adding that "the oldtimers take their tattered uniforms out of moth balls again, sepia Boston will dream of the once famous Boston Tigers." For Kountze the answer to the dilemma rested in the hands of those former players, who should "take off their coats, grab a ball and bat, and show the kids how the game should be played and from there on from teams and Hub baseball leagues."[65]

Fortunately, in 1942, the Boston Royal Giants made an impressive comeback and insured that black baseball remained alive and well in the city. Team manager Burlin White enlisted the services of his famous battery mate, William "Cannonball" Jackman, who left the Philadelphia Giants to play for White. Jackman's reunion with White finally gave the city something to savor. In addition, the team received a request to represent the city in the ranks of professional black baseball.

According to baseball historian Todd Peterson, sports promoter Abe Saperstein decided to create a rival black professional baseball league in 1942 to keep his hand in the lucrative promotions game. Saperstein gained notoriety as the creative force behind basketball's Harlem Globetrotters, but he also played a powerful, if controversial, role as a promoter of Negro League baseball contests. Saperstein believed that Negro League owners intended to maximize their interests by restricting him from scheduling and publicizing games, especially the popular East-West All-Star Game in Chicago. In response, he formed the Negro Major Baseball League of America (NMBLA) and requested the Boston Colored Giants to join him in his venture. In addition to Burlin Whites's Giants, the league consisted of Bingo De Moss's Chicago Brown Bombers, Bunny Down's Cincinnati Clowns, Bill Casey's Baltimore Black Eagles, Charlie Henry's Detroit Red Sox, and Jimmy Brown's Minneapolis–St. Paul Gophers. League President Robert Jackson slated May 17th as Opening Day.[66] Peterson noted that despite the reported support and involvement of such notable African American figures as Jackson, who formerly served as commissioner of the Negro American League, sportswriter Russell Cowens, and professional football star Fritz Pollard, the league was little more than a shadow operation.[67]

On May 2, 1942, the *Boston Chronicle* reported that the new Negro Major Baseball League had already started spring training and that Boston was well represented by White's Boston Royal Giants.[68] Local fans supported the Giants' decision to join the new league and welcomed the chance to watch some of the nation's better black teams. Sheep Jackson, writing for the *Chronicle*, stated that "the bean town has been hungry for good Negro baseball. Not since the days of Bob Russell's Boston Tigers, the Boston Giants, and the original Lincoln Stars has the city been treated to their first sport here—baseball." Jackson believed that the black fans of Greater Boston and Providence would support the team and ask only in return that their team play aggressively and intelligently.[69]

White assembled an outstanding group of players. He mixed seasoned veterans like Cannonball Jackman with rookie stars like Boston University baseball captain Charles Thomas. His roster included former Tiger's pitching ace Elmer Munroe and Fran Matthews, who recently played professionally with the Newark Eagles. On the eve

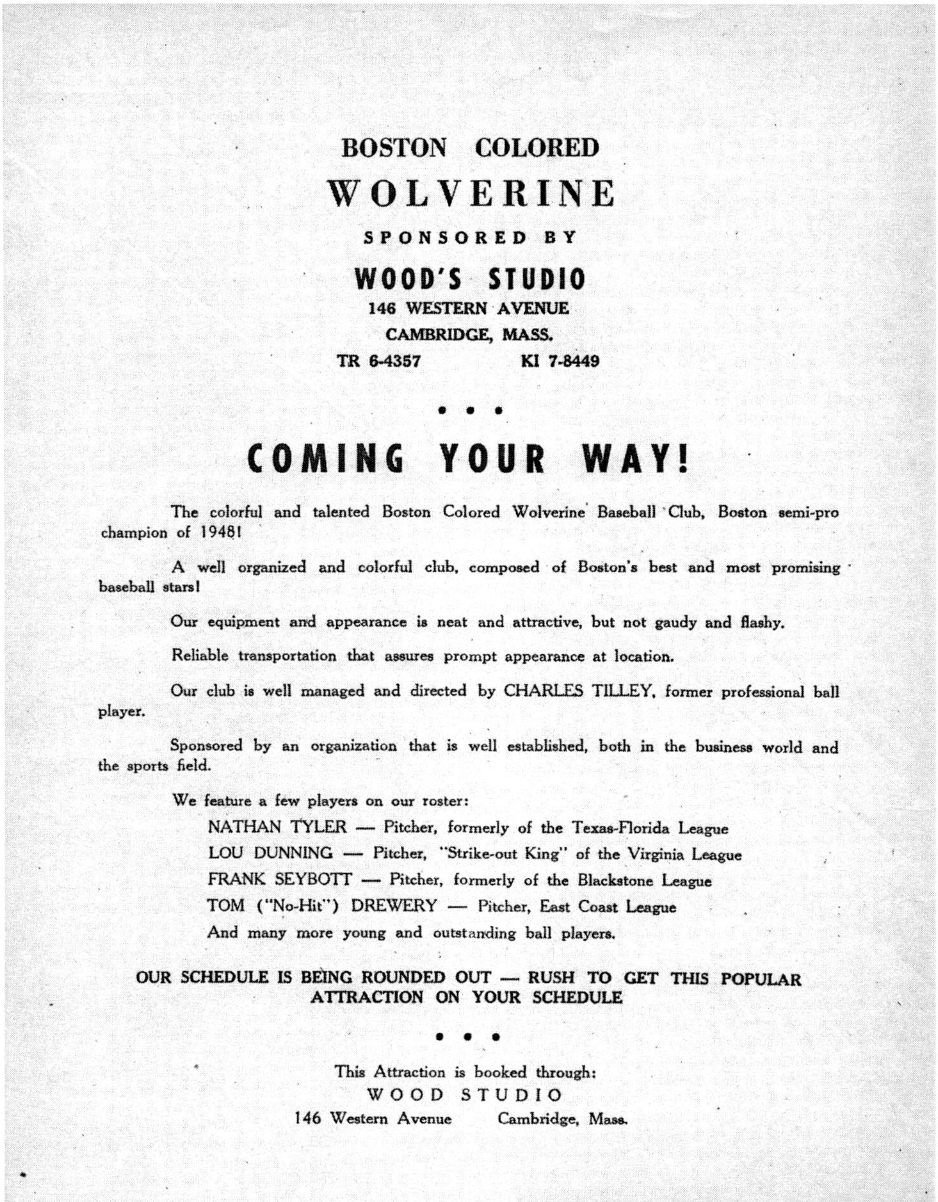

BOSTON COLORED

WOLVERINE

SPONSORED BY

WOOD'S STUDIO

146 WESTERN AVENUE

CAMBRIDGE, MASS.

TR 6-4357 KI 7-8449

• • •

COMING YOUR WAY!

The colorful and talented Boston Colored Wolverine Baseball Club, Boston semi-pro champion of 1948!

A well organized and colorful club, composed of Boston's best and most promising baseball stars!

Our equipment and appearance is neat and attractive, but not gaudy and flashy.

Reliable transportation that assures prompt appearance at location.

Our club is well managed and directed by CHARLES TILLEY, former professional ball player.

Sponsored by an organization that is well established, both in the business world and the sports field.

We feature a few players on our roster:

NATHAN TYLER — Pitcher, formerly of the Texas-Florida League

LOU DUNNING — Pitcher, "Strike-out King" of the Virginia League

FRANK SEYBOTT — Pitcher, formerly of the Blackstone League

TOM ("No-Hit") DREWERY — Pitcher, East Coast League

And many more young and outstanding ball players.

OUR SCHEDULE IS BEING ROUNDED OUT — RUSH TO GET THIS POPULAR ATTRACTION ON YOUR SCHEDULE

• • •

This Attraction is booked through:

WOOD STUDIO

146 Western Avenue Cambridge, Mass.

Broadside promoting the Boston Wolverines for the 1949 season (author's collection).

of Opening Day, White challenged the conventional wisdom that the Cincinnati Clowns had the championship wrapped up even before the season started and predicted that his team also possessed championship mettle. There is no evidence to support White's statement since there no record of the Giants playing any games in the new league. Sheep Jackson asked, "What's happened to the new Boston team, the Royal Giants?" By Opening Day, three teams, including the Giants, left the NMBL and returned to independent play. Only a few games were played under league auspices. The Royal Giants took to the road for most of the summer, leaving Jackson to wonder in July why "they seem to have dropped out of existence."[70]

During the mid–1940s the team did travel extensively, playing fewer and fewer games in the Hub. In 1944, however, the team embraced the name "Boston Colored Giants" and later maximized their presence in the city as a member of the city's Park League and City League. Under the watchful eyes of owners Bob Russell and Fats Johnson, former owners of the Boston Tigers, the team had "certainly given the fans of Bean City something to talk about." The team added professional sensation Jesse "Lefty" Brown to the pitching rotation and helped desegregate Boston's Fenway Park by playing a game there against the New York Cuban All-Stars. In the following year, 1945, the Boston Colored Giants traveled to Yankee Stadium in New York to participate in a four-team doubleheader. In the opening game, the Colored Giants defeated another African American team, the Miami Giants, by a score of 10–0. Boston's Colored Giants continued to play successful baseball in 1946, but in that year, Jackie Robinson had already broken the color line in professional baseball as a member of the Montreal Royals, the Brooklyn Dodger affiliate in the International League. Support for black baseball shifted to black players in the white professional leagues and local black teams suffered a decline in attendance. Fan support, especially financial support through ticket sales, dwindled in 1946 and 1947, leaving one sportswriter to comment that "a ballclub cannot run on cheering, it takes money to keep the club on the road." In 1947, William "Bullet" Campbell assumed the reins of team manager, but no one could replace the style and promotional expertise of Burlin White. The integration of modern major league baseball in 1947, through the persons of Jackie Robinson and Larry Doby, signaled a dream come true for most black baseball fans, but it also prefigured the end of Boston's black teams. The city's African American fans had experienced their most bittersweet moment.[71]

During the 1930s and 1940s, Boston was home to two of the most legendary players in all of New England black baseball, pitcher Will "Cannonball" Jackman and his battery mate Burlin White.

Born on October 7, 1897, in the small town of Carta, Texas, Jackman began his semi-professional baseball career in 1918 playing on teams in the Houston and San Antonio region before barnstorming his way through Oklahoma, Maryland, New Jersey, and New York. He settled in Boston sometime in 1924 when he opened the baseball season with the Boston Monarchs but finished with the city's Philadelphia Giants.[72] He spent the remainder of his career in Greater Boston, except for the year 1935 when he played professionally for the Brooklyn Eagles of the Negro National League.[73] He dominated his opponents from the mid–1920s through the late 1940s and pitched his last game in 1953 at the age of 56.[74] Although Jackman's career statistics remain incomplete, existing records indicate that he compiled a record of 200–86 in a career that included games against professional and semi-professional teams, both black and white. He struck out 1,354 batters and posted a 2.89 era.[75] Jackman recalled pitching in nearly 1,200 games during his lifetime.[76] One measure of his greatness involves a spectacular performance in one of the nation's most beloved baseball cathedrals. On July 8, 1945, Jackman took the mound at Yankee Stadium and shut down his opponent, the Miami Giants, allowing only one infield hit through seven innings and eventually winning the game on a three-hit shutout. By this time, he had perfected his underarm motion, which bewildered Miami's batters throughout the afternoon. The *Chicago Defender* captured the moment and reported, "Bill Jackman, a white-haired submarine specialist, turned in a three-hit shutout versus Miami. He struck out ten batters and aided his own cause by accounting for five runs, with four hits in five trips to the plate."[77] Sportswriter Glenn Stout reported that Jackman, at his peak, commanded a fee of $175.00 per game and an additional $10.00 for each strikeout. "If I was young today," Jackman said in 1971, "I'd probably be worth a million."[78]

The community paid its tribute to Jackman in two commemorative events. One held on August 24, 1944, at Fenway Park and the other on July 14, 1971, at Carter Field where he played many games as a member of the Philadelphia Giants and Boston Colored Giants. The 1944 tribute was not well attended and sportswriter Sheep Jackson chastised black fans by writing, "It was a sad gathering.... It was to be Will Jackman Day ... a player whose hurling has thrilled thousands in this section for the past 20 years. It was to be a tribute to Will and the colored fans were to honor this great pitcher — one of their own. But alas, Ole Joe and his friends stayed at home."[79] Prior to the game, mayor Maurice J. Tobin presented Jackman with a billfold, but the token did not provide Jackman with luck, as he lost the game.[80] The 1971 event had a much different outcome. Ralph "Stody" Ward, longtime friend and teammate, introduced Jackman and regaled the crowd with stories of the pitcher's accomplishments, but also placed the event in a broader historical context: "This affair for Will Jackman will close out an era of good baseball by black players," Ward commented. "It is amazing to note the intestinal fortitude of these black ballplayers. They continued to play day after day and year after year with the knowledge that fate had decreed that they could never enter the Big Leagues, Minor Leagues, or even Little Leagues during this particular era." Jackman, often referred to as "Baseball's Great Unknown" or the "Best Ballplayer You Have Never Heard Of" came along too soon to play in the white major leagues, but he was clearly not unknown or unappreciated by the city's black fans who regarded him as the region's greatest pitcher and top baseball attraction.[81]

In the twilight of his career, Jackman grew to depend on his battery mate, Burlin White. In 1948, Taunton's local newspaper, the *Gazette*, remarked that "Despite their age, these two timeless baseball stars are still the greatest drawing cards in New

England."[82] Burlin White was born on February 5, 1895, in Richmond, Indiana. In 1914, he began his playing days in West Baden Springs, one of Indiana's most popular mineral water resorts, with a team called the Sprudels.[83] More than thirty years later, he ended his career in Boston's Carter Field as the catcher and manager of the city's Royal Giants. Nearly 3,000 fans attended a testimonial game in his honor on July 19, 1946, recognizing the years he spent playing the game, a dozen of which he spent in the Boston City League. White enjoyed a long and fruitful baseball career alternating between independent professional black teams and semi-professional clubs between 1915 and 1942. A lifelong catcher, he played for Rube Foster's Chicago American Giants in 1916 and 1917. Foster would later establish the first professional black league, the Negro National League, in 1920 and earn the name "Father of Negro League Baseball." White also played alongside Henry "Pop" Lloyd with the Atlantic City Bacharach Giants. Lloyd, considered by many baseball historians as baseball's greatest ballplayer, black or white, mentored White in the fine points of the game and honed his leadership skills. White became the manager for two Boston-based teams, the Philadelphia Giants and the Boston Royal Giants.[84]

Known as the "Dean of Colored Baseballers," White scheduled games for his Colored Giants in cities throughout the United States and Canada, and even booked and played a Fourth of July game at Yankee Stadium.[85] Although White achieved great success as player-manager for an African American team, he consistently championed the cause of integration, especially in Boston. In an interview given in 1938, White expressed his belief "that the combined colored support of fans from Rhode Island and Massachusetts would be sufficient to show both of Boston's major league club owners that our people when once interested are quite capable of making a true major league attendance representation."[86]

At the end of the 1934 baseball season, Deedy Crosson, former stellar player for the Boston Tigers, penned a column for the *Boston Chronicle* which drew fan attention to the finest ballplayers in the region. Crosson listed Burlin White of the Boston Colored Giants as the best black catcher in New England. According to Crosson, "There are very few fast baseball players who can steal bases on the throwing arm of Whitey." More importantly, White's ability to call a game from behind the plate helped young pitchers improve their craft. Crosson credited White with developing the skills of Will "Cannonball" Jackman when both played together as members of the Philadelphia Giants. The standout pitchers included Jackman of the Philadelphia Giants and Elmer Monroe of the Boston Tigers. Both men reportedly could "make the ball hum across the plate." Moreover, they "defeated the strongest teams in New Hampshire, Vermont, Maine, and Massachusetts."[87] Several years later, in 1942, the *Boston Guardian* recalled these same men in a prophetic editorial which stated that the "probable elimination of the Major League Color Ban will serve to revive many memories of Boston players who might have made the grade ... include[ing] pitchers Big Bill Jackman and Elmer Monroe ... [and] catcher Burlin White."[88]

Ever mindful of Greater Boston's other star players, journalist William "Sheep"

Jackson reminded his readers of the local men who thrilled the city's neighborhood fans. Jackson picked an "All-Colored Team" with the following players: Elmer Monroe (Everett), Sam McCleary (Newton), and Al Dupree (Mechanics Arts) as pitchers; Buster Reddick (Rindge Tech) as catcher; Fran Matthews (Rindge Tech) at first base; Dodo Fraser (Lynn English) at second base; Reddie Hilliard (Cambridge Latin) at shortstop; Leon Furr (Medford) at third base; Zing Rice (Medford) at centerfield; Bob Russell (Boston English) at left field; and Jit Taylor (Everett) at right field. In the semi-professional ranks, Jackson selected Mose Sisco as the most gifted ballplayer.[89] Sportswriter Mabe Kountze compiled a list too. He asked Stody Ward, former Boston Tiger and keen observer of the city's black baseball scene, to list the players that had the potential to compete at the major league level. Ward responded with the following list:

> **First Base:** Pappy Ricks, Jim Moore, Fran Matthews.
> **Second Base:** Deedy Crosson, Rabbit Tucker.
> **Third Base:** Marcelle, Gus Gadsden (and the author adds the name of Stody Ward, he overlooked).
> **Center Field:** Mose Cisco, Sheriff Blake.
> **Left Field:** Zing Rice, Lem Roach, Tubby Johnson.
> **Right Field:** Ceph Cephus, Jesse Hubbard.
> **Catchers:** Burlin White, Bust Reddick, Bob Russell.
> **Pitchers:** Bill Jackman, Al Dupree, Bullet Campbell, Elmer Monroe, Lefty Brown, Windshield Willie Robinson, and others.[90]

Although Boston's top black ballplayers were denied admission to the white major leagues, several played professionally in the Negro Leagues. One team, the Newark Eagles, of the Negro National League, expressed special interest in local Boston talent. According to sportswriter Mabe Kountze, Abe and Effa Manley, co-owners of the Eagles, were "sweet" on the baseball talent in greater Boston, and their club led all others in signing New England players. Kountze reported that "the Eagles, formerly of Brooklyn, first began with Bill Jackman of Boston.... Since then Newark has given trials to Bus Reddick, catcher ... Honey Green, outfielder and pitcher ... and Frank Matthews, first baseman." In June, 1938, Koutze added the name of pitcher Jesse "Dizzy" Brown to the list of Newark players.[91]

The Boston Blues and the United States League, 1946

In 1945, the color line in modern baseball truly ended when Jackie Robinson signed a contract with the Brooklyn Dodgers baseball organization on October 23. Earlier that year, however, Branch Rickey, the same person who signed Robinson, launched one last attempt to create a segregated league of professional black ballplayers called the United States League (USL). Rickey announced the formation of the USL on May 7, 1945, and introduced its president, John Shackelford, an African American lawyer from Cleveland, Ohio. Rickey designed the league as an alternative to the Negro National and American leagues and a potential farm system for major league baseball teams that opted to eventually sign black ballplayers.[92] It was during the 1946 season, the league's second year in operation, that President Shackelford offered a franchise to the Boston Blues.[93] No one in Boston seemed familiar with the team. Allen Johnson, the team owner, ran a nightclub in Mounds, Illinois, and none of the players hailed from Boston. Sportswriter William Jackson understood the tenuous connection to the city and wondered, "In this new colored league there is an entry known as the Boston Blues. Have you heard of them?" He further noted that "the funny part of the set-up is that the club is playing all of their games in the west and New York. How come, Boston?"[94] In a recent interview with Robert Scott, a former pitcher and first-baseman for the Blues, Scott confessed that he did not remember playing a single game in Boston. The USL folded midway through the 1946 season and the Blues disbanded.[95]

Dreams Realized and Opportunities Lost: Integration, 1946

Long before Jackie Robinson signed a contract with the Brooklyn Dodgers and integrated modern professional baseball, Boston's local clubs experienced interracial baseball. Robinson's heroic accomplishment may have signaled the end and not the beginning of a process that occurred earlier at the local level. Baseball, after all, was the local pastime long before it became the national one. Unlike many places where the color line in semi-professional and amateur play had been drawn indelibly by the middle of the 20th century, Boston experienced a long history of integrated team and league play. One team, the Library Bureau of Cambridge, provides a good example of an amateur integrated team that achieved widespread acclaim during the early 1920s. Backstop Buster Williams and outfielder [first name unknown] Clarence, both African American, led the team to a championship season in 1920 and a trip to Chicago to play the Library Bureau's Midwestern champs in Chicago.[96] During the 1920s and 1930s, African American teams slowly integrated the previously all-white amateur and semi-professional leagues. These leagues usually admitted only one team composed entirely of African American players. The Providence Colored Giants achieved the distinction of being the only black team to win a league championship. In 1931, the team captured the title of Boston's Twilight League. The legendary Tigers would play in the newly established Boston City League in 1932. The City League, led by former president of the New England League Claude Davidson, promised to "give to the youth of Boston a fine chance for athletic development and to the interested baseball fan a long list of carefully scheduled baseball games."[97]

On occasion, Boston's semi-professional teams fielded an integrated roster. A few months after Jackie Robinson's ill-fated try out with the Boston Red Sox, he returned to Boston as a player for the Kansas City Monarchs. The Monarchs scheduled a game against the Boston Navy Yard Athletic Club on August 13, 1945, at Braves Field. Robinson's return captured most of the attention. Lost in the story, however, is the Naval Yard team, which included an impressive array of black and white players. The Navy Yarders were managed by Curt Fullerton, former Red Sox and Yankee pitcher, and included several of the finest white players in the city. The team also posted two African American starting players. Second baseman Billie Burke, a former standout with the Boston Tigers, and catcher Buster Reddick, who played professionally for the Newark Eagles, represented the Navy Yard Club. Both men played at Rindge Tech and were local favorites.[98]

> *"Tuesday night, August 26, over 5,000 spectators witnessed the Florida Hoboes defeat the Wolverines in a thrilling flood-light game by a score of 2 to 1 at the William E. Carter Playground. The game was sponsored by the Eastern New England Congress for Equal Opportunities, whose president. Atty. John S. R. Bourne, between innings, spoke to the hugh gathering, urging them to join the picket line and otherwise actively aid the current Congress jobs campaign in front of the McLellan store on Washington, near Ruggles street, Roxbury, the manager of which has continually refused to hire any Negro girls as clerks, though the greater volume of his trade is derived from negro customers."*—Boston Chronicle, *August 30, 1941*

The integration of major league baseball stimulated interest in eliminating the color line in Boston amateur baseball. In 1946, Jesse "Lefty" Brown, one of the top sinker pitchers in the professional Negro Leagues, having players for teams like the Newark Eagles, Baltimore Elite Giants, and New York Black Yankees, organized the New England Black and White Stars. This team, the city's first truly integrated ballclub, played its home games at Carter Playground. According to the *Boston Chronicle,* "The Stars utilized some of the best players of both races who have become famous in recent years on the local sandlots." In 1946, the team compiled an impressive record against several of New England's top semipro teams and then traveled to the South and the West to play against many professional minor league teams.[99]

The story of Brown's Black and White Stars was replicated in other cities around the region. In Providence, Rhode Island, the Circle Athletic Club, led by pitcher Charles Butler, became the city's first truly integrated team in 1949. Ernest "Biffo" Duarte, prizefighter and sports promoter from Providence's Fox Point neighborhood, acted as the inspiration behind the city's first integrated team. He personally scouted the players, black and white, because he wanted a mixed-race team of only the best players. He struggled to land his ballclub in the Tim O'Neil Amateur League, and only after relentless requests for a franchise did his dream come true. By season's end, the Circle A.C. had conquered all its divisional opponents in the Independent National League and then set its sights on the American League victors for the local amateur championship.

The Circle players subsequently won the city championship and in the process made history as the first integrated team in the city to do so.[100]

It is important to recognize that there were alternatives to the model of integration utilized by the Brooklyn Dodgers in hiring Jackie Robinson. Major league teams had several options, including signing multiple black players at once to create a genuinely integrated team, like Boston's Black and White Stars or Providence's Circle Athletic Club, or expanding the league to include the top African American professional teams. In Boston, fans gathered to watch the Black and White Stars compete against their local and regional opponents in a bid for racial equality. The baseball diamond served as a vital arena in the struggle for freedom and the game reflected the city's racial flexibility and spirit.

Postscript

In 1946, most African American baseball fans in Boston turned their attention to Jackie Robison and future Dodger teammates Roy Campanella and Don Newcombe. Both Campanella and Newcombe attracted regional attention as they helped desegregate the New England League by playing for Brooklyn's affiliate in nearby Nashua, New Hampshire. The promise of integration, accentuated by America's Cold War role as self-described leader of the Free World, was becoming a reality, and baseball played an integral role in the nation's racial transformation.

Closer to home, a former member of the city's renowned Boston Tigers affirmed the reassuring role of baseball in the local black community. William "Bullet" Campbell, no longer able to play the game, returned home to where it all started so many years before. He joined Fran Matthews and Buster Riddick of the Boston Colored Giants and Herman "Bud" Tyrance of the Philly Giants on the Robert Gould Shaw House's baseball diamond to teach the youngsters how to play the nation's pastime. These former and current players established the first annual Shaw House baseball school for youngsters aged 12–15 years old.

Thirty years earlier, Shaw House offered young men of the same age the chance to play and combine their talents as the Tigers. Campbell knew the important role baseball had played in his life. He also understood how the game created a sense of solidarity between the players and those who supported them. It was a relationship worth preserving.[101]

Notes

1. *Boston Globe*, May 30, 1993, 50 and September 30, 1994, 57.
2. Mabe Kountze, *50 Sports Years Along Memory Lane: Afro-American Sports History Hometown, Local, National* (Medford: Mystic Valley Press, 1979), *passim*.

3. *Boston Globe*, May 30, 1993, 50. Matthews played for the Boston-based Philadelphia Giants from 1934–1935 and the Boston Royal Giants from 1935–1937, 1942, and 1946–1949. He played professionally for the Newark Eagles in 1938, 1940–1942, and 1945 and with the Kansas City Monarchs in 1942 and with the Philadelphia Stars in 1945.

4. David Ortiz, "Negro Leagues Remembered," *Cambridgetab*, 29, no. 42, July 26, 2000, located in National Baseball Hall of Fame Library, Negro League File: Boston.

5. On the early game in Boston see Troy Soos, *Before the Curse: The Glory Days of New England Baseball, 1858–1918* (Jefferson, NC: McFarland, 2006), 1–100.

6. For information on the early history of black baseball see Michael E. Lomax, *Black Baseball Entrepreneurs, 1860–1901: Operating by Any Means Necessary* (Syracuse: Syracuse University Press, 2003), 14–60.

7. Leslie Heaphy, *The Negro Leagues, 1869–1960* (Jefferson, NC: McFarland, 2003), 24. The roster for the 1870 team is located in Dick Clark and Larry Lester, *The Negro Leagues Book* (Cleveland: Society for American Baseball Research, 1994), 52.

8. Charlie Bevis, *The New England League: A Baseball History, 1885–1949* (Jefferson, NC: McFarland, 2008), 20; *Providence Journal*, August 18, 1877, 1; and Ryan Swanson, "Bases Loaded: Race, Reconstruction, and Baseball in Washington, D.C., 1865–1876" in William Simons ed., *The Cooperstown Symposium on Baseball and American Culture, 2003–2004* (Jefferson, NC: McFarland, 2005), 59.

9. *New York Freeman*, February 19, 1887, accessed in www.agatetype.com. Roster for team included: A.A. Selden (manager), Marshall Thompson (manager), Robert Brown, Bunnie Cross, Ambrose Davis, Joseph Harris, ? Lewis, Dan Penno, ? Plunto, William H. Selden, Ed Smith, H.C. Taylor, Windsor W. Terrill, R.A. Walker, George Waters, and Charles Williams.

10. Lomax, *Black Baseball Entrepreneurs*, 63–70 and Heaphy, *The Negro Leagues*, 24.

11. *Sporting Life*, April 13, 1887, as quoted in Lomax, *Black Baseball Entrepreneurs*, 66.

12. *Boston Daily Globe*, March 20, 1887, 2; March 25, 1887, 4; September 5, 1896, 5; and February 5, 1904, 5.

13. "The Colored League Opening Day in Louisville," *Louisville Courier Journal*, May 8, 1887, as reprinted in Dean A. Sullivan, *Early Innings: A Documentary History of Baseball, 1825–1908* (Lincoln: University of Nebraska Press, 1997).

14. Jerry Malloy, ed., *Sol White's History of Colored Baseball with Other Documents on the Early Black Game, 1886–1936* (Lincoln: University of Nebraska Press, 1995), xxiv. For additional information see Lomax, *Black Baseball Entrepreneurs*, 63–70 and Heaphy, *The Negro Leagues*, 24.

15. Malloy, ed., *Sol White's History of Colored Baseball*, 16, 20, 143, 145, and 150; James Overmyer, "Early Days" in Lawrence Hogan, *Shades of Glory: The Negro Leagues and the Story of African American Baseball* (Washington, D.C.: National Geographic, 2006), 21–24; John Thorn, *Baseball in the Garden of Eden: The Secret History of the Early Game* (New York: Simon & Schuster, 2011), 188–189; and Clark and Lester eds., *The Negro Leagues Book*, 52–54; and Brian Carroll, *When to Stop the Cheering? The Black Press, The Black Community, and the Integration of Professional Baseball* (New York Routledge, 2007), 9.

16. *Boston Sunday Globe*, January 5, 1889, 5; and *Boston Daily Globe*, May 14, 1889, 3.

17. *Boston Daily Globe*, May 7, 1890, 6; May 13, 1891, 9; July 20, 1891, 3; April 6, 1896, 9; and *Boston Sunday Globe* August 15, 1897, 6.

18. *Boston Daily Globe*, May 27, 1901 6; June 30, 1902, 8; August 11, 1902, 6 and March 27, 1903, 2. According to the *Globe*, the following players appeared on the Windsors' roster: "Oliver, C; Belden and Eppa, P; Bankis, SS; Williams, 1B; Walker, 2B; Allen, 3B; Ray, RF; Brown, CF; and Charley Oliver, LF."

19. I am indebted to Lorenz Finison for sharing his resources on Teamoh, especially as it relates to his interest in cycling. See "Mr. Robert T. Teamoh, Reporter, *Boston Globe*," in Irvine Garland Penn, *The Afro-American Press and Its Editors* (Springfield: Willey and Company, 1891), 360–364; *Black Legislators in the Massachusetts General Court, 1867–Present* (Boston, State Library of Massachusetts, 2010), 1; and Nell Painter, "Black Journalism, The First Hundred Years," *Harvard Journal of African American Affairs* 2, no. 2 (1971): 39; and *Freeman*, June 7, 1890, 6.

20. *Boston Daily Globe*, March 6, 1903, 9; *Boston Chronicle*, March 5, 1938, 6.

21. *Boston Chronicle*, April 27, 1935, 7. The list of promoters included "From Malden, Moe Ashton; Sheep Jackson from Medford; Pat Parnham from Cambridge; Wyman Lee from Newton; the Messrs Lomax and Grey from Everett; the Messrs Collins and Taylor from Lynn; Dodo Frazier from Boston; rep of the Tigers or Highlands, from Roxbury rep of the Rangers."

22. *Boston Daily Globe*, June 21, 1915, 3; August 23, 1915, 4.

23. Mabe Kountze, *50 Sports Years Along Memory Lane: Afro-American Sports History Hometown, Local, National* (Medford: Mystic Valley Press, 1979), 28–29.
24. *Boston Globe*, August 3, 1905, 5.
25. *Boston Chronicle*, April 28, 1945, 7.
26. Ibid.
27. Ibid.
28. Ibid., April 3, 1943, 1 and 3.
29. Ibid., April 28, 1945, 7.
30. Glenn Stout, "Diamonds Aren't Forever," *Boston Magazine* (September 1986): 94–95.
31. *Boston Globe*, September 22, 1920, 9.
32. For information on Lawson and the Continental League, see Jerry Kuntz, "George H. Lawson: The Rogue Who Tried to Reform Baseball," *The Baseball Research Journal* 37 (2008): 46–48.
33. *Boston Chronicle*, January 23, 1943, 7.
34. *Boston Globe*, May 25, 1921, 4.
35. *Providence Journal*, July 19, 1921, 7 and July 24, 1921, 5
36. *Providence Evening Bulletin*, July 31, 1923, 6.
37. *Providence Journal* August 2, 1923, 7.
38. *Nashua Telegraph*, August 4, 1921; *Providence Evening Bulletin*, September 30, 1922; *Providence News* September 30, 1922 and *Providence Evening Bulletin*, July 31, 1929.
39. *Boston Chronicle*, August 27, 1938, 6; September 3, 1938, 6 and 7; September 10, 1938, 6.
40. Ibid., August 5, 1939, 6; August 19, 1939, 6 and 7; July 13, 1940, 6; July 20, 1940, 6; July 27, 1940, 6 and 7; August 3, 1940, 6 and 7; September 7, 1940, 7 and 8; July 5, 1941, 6; July 12, 1941, 7; July 19, 1941, 6; July 26, 1941, 6; August 16, 1941, 6; August 23,1941, 7; August 30, 1941, 7; September 6, 1941, 6; September 11, 1943, 7; September 18, 1943, 5 and 7.
41. For biographical information on William "Sheep" Jackson see *Boston Chronicle*, July 3, 1943, 7; July 24, 1943, 7; October 30, 1943, 7; March 11, 1944, 7; and August 27, 1944, 7.
42. On the critical role played by sportswriters in recording the history of the black baseball see, Lawrence Hogan and Robert Cvornyek, "Black Sportswriters and the (Re)construction of Negro League Baseball" in William Simons, ed., *The Cooperstown Symposium on Baseball and American Culture, 2003–2004* (Jefferson, NC: McFarland, 2005).
43. *Boston Chronicle*, June 11, 1932.
44. Ibid., April 27, 1935, 6; May 18, 1935, 6; June 8, 1935, 6; and *Lewiston Daily Sun*, June 22, 1935, 11.
45. *Boston Chronicle*, April 27, 1938, 5.
46. Ibid., April 6, 1940, 7.
47. Frank Ryan, "The Colored Village Nine: Barnstorming with a Black Ball Team from West Newton," *The Boston Herald American/Beacon*, April 3, 1977, 24–25 and 27, located in the West Newton File, National Baseball Hall of Fame Library, Cooperstown, New York.
48. *Boston Chronicle*, April 9, 1932, 7; April 23, 1932, 7; April 30, 1932, 7; May 14, 1932, 7; May 28, 1932, 7; and June 25, 1932, 7.
49. Ibid., June 2, 1934, 6; June 9, 1934, 6; and July 14, 1934, 6.
50. Ibid., October 1, 1932, 1–2; *Providence Journal*, July 12, 1926, 5.
51. *Boston Chronicle*, August 19, 1933, 6; August 18, 1934, 6; James A. Riley, *The Biographical Encyclopedia of the Negro Baseball Leagues* (New York: Carroll and Graf, 2002), 511, 274, 397–399, and 199. Located in the Dick Thompson papers is a *Philadelphia Tribune* newspaper clipping dated May 14, 1931, which lists the following players on the Providence Giants: "The P.G.'s are carrying 15 men on their squad. They are Spencer Jones (Hilldale), Tom Dixon (Philly boy), Dixie Matthews (Providence College), catchers; Luther Farrell (Bacharachs), Bullet Campbell (Hilldale), Cliff Carter (Hilldale) and Edward Dudley, pitchers. The infield consists of Highpockets Hudspeth at first; Decker (an Indiana boy) at second; Elmore "Scrappy" Brown at short; and Ollie Marcelle at third. The outfield includes Jess Hubbard, Tubby Johnson, and Babe Melton."
52. *Providence Journal*, June 18, 1931, 11; June 20, 1931, 8; June 21, 1931, 6; and *Baltimore Afro-American*, June 30, 1931, 15.
53. *New York Age*, July 25, 1931, 6; *New York Amsterdam News*, July 7, 1931, 13; and *Providence Journal*, July 16, 1931, 9.
54. *Philadelphia Tribune*, August 13, 1931, and *New Bedford Evening Standard*, August 26, 1931. Clippings located in the Thompson papers.

55. *Boston Chronicle*, April 30, 1932, 7; and October 1, 1932, 1.

56. For an early biographical sketch of McClellan see *New York Age*, June 3, 1939, 8. Dick Thompson, "Cannonball Bill Jackman: Baseball's Great Unknown," *The National Pastime: A Review of Baseball History* 27 (2007): 43. Providence *Evening Bulletin* July 2, 1923, 7; July 17, 1923, 6; July 20 1923, 4; July 23, 1923, 6; August 11, 1923, 11; August 13, 1923, 7; and August 25, 1923, 7.

57. *Philadelphia Tribune*, July 4, 1925, and *Quincy Patriot Ledger*, August 10, 1925. Newspapers located in the Thompson papers.

58. *Brockton Times Enterprise*: September 9, 1925; September 10, 1925; September 11, 1925; September 12, 1925; and September 15, 1925; *Philadelphia Tribune*: September, 26 1925; *Quincy Patriot Ledger*: September 14, 1925; September 15, 1925; and September 16, 1925. Newspapers located in the Thompson papers.

59. *Philadelphia Tribune*, July 25, 1925, and Quincy Patriot Ledger, September 15, 1925. Newspapers located in the Thompson papers. For biographical information on Yancy and Seay, see James A. Riley, The Biographical Encyclopedia of the Negro Baseball Leagues (New York: Carroll and Graf, 1994), 888–889 and 706–707. For the complete 1925 rosters of each team see Dick Clark and Larry Lester, eds., The Negro Leagues Book (Cleveland: Society for American Baseball Research, 1994), 91.

60. *Providence Journal*, August 1, 1926, Section B, 3; August 2, 1926, 7; and August 9, 1926, 7.

61. *Philadelphia Tribune*, March 19, 1931, clipping located in the Thompson Papers; and *Boston Chronicle*, April 28, 1934, 6.

62. *Boston Chronicle*, June 11, 1932, 6; May 12, 1934, 6; June 9, 1934, 6; August 24, 1935, 6; April 25, 1936, 6; and March 26, 1938, 6.

63. Ibid., April 25, 1936, 6.

64. Ibid., May 16, 1936, 6.

65. Ibid., April 6, 1940, 7; and *Boston Guardian*, March 8, 1941, 6.

66. Ibid., May 2, 1942, 7.

67. Todd Peterson, *Early Black Baseball in Minnesota* (Jefferson, NC: McFarland, 2010), 196–197; Neil Lanctot, *Negro League Baseball: The Rise and Ruin of a Black Institution* (Philadelphia: University of Pennsylvania Press, 2004), 112–114 and Rebecca Alpert, *Out of Left Field: Jews and Black Baseball* (New York: Oxford University Press, 2011), 79–81.

68. *Boston Chronicle*, May 2, 1942, 7.

69. Ibid., May 9, 1942, 7, and May 16, 1942, 7.

70. Ibid., June 27, 1942, 7, and July 11, 1942, 7

71. *New York Age*, July 14, 1945, 11; *Boston Chronicle*, July 29, 1944, 5; August 15, 1944, 7; September 2, 1944, p, 7; July 14, 1945, 11; August 11, 1945, 7; March 30, 1946, 7; April 27, 1946, 7; May 8, 1946, p 7; May 11, 1946, 7; May 25, 1946, 7; June 15, 1946, 7; August 31, 1946, 7; and May 13, 1947, 7.

72. Dick Thompson, "Cannonball Bill Jackman: Baseball's Great Unknown," *The National Pastime: A Review of Baseball History* 27 (2007): 43. One of the earliest accounts of Jackman pitching in Boston for the Monarchs is located in the *North Adams Evening Transcript*, May 16, 1924, 3. His teammates were listed as Pryor, third base; Clark, shortstop; Thompson, first base; Perry, second base; Flemming, right field; Phillips, left field; Sisco, center field; Fuller, Catcher; Ballis, Catcher; Evans, pitcher; and Dillon, pitcher.

73. Thom Loverro, *The Encyclopedia of Negro League Baseball* (New York: Checkmark Books, 2003), 149.

74. See William Jackman Application Form for the National Baseball Hall of Fame, 1972 located in the Thompson papers.

75. Thompson, "Cannonball Bill Jackman," 45.

76. "Sports in the News," *Newport Daily News*, July 14, 1971, 21.

77. *New York Age*, July 7, 1945, 11; and *Chicago Defender*, August 11, 1945.

78. Glenn Stout, "Diamonds Aren't Forever" *Boston Magazine* (September 1986): 98.

79. Quoted in Dick Thompson, "Cannonball Bill Jackman," 50.

80. *Boston Chronicle*, September 2, 1944, 7.

81. "Will Jackman Nite Program, Carter Field, July 14, 1971: Highlights and Background of Will Jackman" by Ralph "Stottie" Ward, Longtime Friend, located in the Thompson Papers and *Newport Daily News*, July 14, 1971, 21.

82. Thompson, "Cannonball Bill Jackman," 52.

83. *Boston Chronicle*, April 30, 1938, 6.

84. Riley, *The Biographical Encyclopedia of the Negro Baseball Leagues*, 833.
85. *Boston Chronicle*, July 20, 1946, 6.
86. Ibid., March 12, 1938.
87. Ibid., September, 29, 1934, 6.
88. *Boston Guardian*, August 8, 1942, 4.
89. *Boston Chronicle*, May 22, 1943, 7, and June 5, 1943, 7.
90. Kountze, *50 Sports Years Along Memory Lane*, 46–47.
91. *Boston Chronicle*, June 11, 1938, 6.
92. *New York Times*, May 8, 1945, 22.
93. Neil Lanctot, *Negro League Baseball: The Rise and Ruin of a Black Institution* (Philadelphia: University of Pennsylvania Press, 2004), 263–270 and 289–291.
94. *Boston Chronicle*, June 15, 1946, 7.
95. Interview, Robert Scott, Atlantic City, New Jersey, October, 2011.
96. *Boston Globe*, September 2, 1920, 9.
97. *Boston Chronicle*, April 2, 1932, 7.
98. Ibid., August 4, 1945, 7; August 11, 1945, 7; and August 18, 7.
99. Ibid., July 20, 1946, 7.
100. Robert Cvornyek "Integrating Providence Baseball," *Providence Journal*, July 18, 2010, 22.
101. *Boston Chronicle*, June 22, 1946, 7.

From Buckeye to Black Eye

Cleveland's 1945 Negro League Championship, Jackie Robinson, and the Beginning of the End of Black Baseball

David Krell

Abstract

When the Cleveland Buckeyes won the 1945 Negro League World Series, the club sat at the pinnacle of their baseball world. One would have expected to see them lauded and applauded when they beat the heavily favored Homestead Grays, but that did not happen. Instead it marked the beginning of the end for not only the Cleveland team but the Negro Leagues as a whole. The Buckeyes won just as the baseball world was changing with the signing of Jackie Robinson by Branch Rickey and the Cleveland Indians signing Larry Doby not long after. These events overshadowed the Buckeyes accomplishment at the time and since.

"We Could Run the Tongue Out of Anybody's Head"

Cleveland is an unsung hero of baseball.

New York City gets the glory.

Boston gets the nostalgia.

And Chicago gets the mournful optimism. At least on the North Side.

But Cleveland—city of light, city of magic—gets acknowledgment rather than applause, nods rather than cheers, and footnotes rather than stories. The city's contributions to baseball, however, are no less deserving of scrutiny, study, and celebration—particularly those of the Cleveland Buckeyes.

In 1945, the Cleveland Buckeyes won the Negro League World Series. Yet, according to Buckeyes owner Ernie Wright, the feat was underappreciated locally: "The public and media didn't get behind us the way they should have the year we won the world

Black Ball / DOI: 10.3172/BLB.6.107 / Volume 6 / 2013 / pp. 107–115 /
ISSN 1939-8484 (Print) / ISSN 1939-8379 (Online) /

championship. All we got from the city of Cleveland was a banquet. There was no parade or meeting with the mayor. The players didn't make any special appearances. It was a far cry from what the Indians got when they won the World Series in 1948."[1]

Sam Jethroe, a speedy Buckeyes outfielder, concurred: "The way the city responded, you wouldn't have thought we won anything. I was a part of bigger celebrations in the minors. Winning minor league pennants in Montreal and Toronto were much bigger events."[2] While Jethroe was tearing up the base-paths at League Park, the Buckeyes' home field, another Negro League player was on the precipice of changing baseball forever. In 1945, Jackie Robinson signed a contract with the Brooklyn Dodgers that fired the first shot in the war against segregation in baseball.

As children, we learn that Jackie Robinson played for the Kansas City Monarchs in the Negro Leagues. We also learn of the great players of the 1950s who followed Jackie Robinson by migrating from Negro League teams, for example, Hank Aaron and the Indianapolis Clowns, or Willie Mays and the Birmingham Black Barons.

Since Jackie Robinson and other Hall of Famers cast a massive shadow, other teams get lost in discussions of baseball history. Unfortunately for the Cleveland Buckeyes, the excitement of integration had a doubling shadow effect. Just three months after Robinson debuted with the Brooklyn Dodgers of the National League in 1947, Larry Doby integrated the American League with the Cleveland Indians. Suddenly, the spotlight on Cleveland baseball intensified for the Indians. Buckeyes baseball began a slow march to decline, despite its championship season, stellar ballplayers, and rich history.

The Cleveland Buckeyes' sweep of the defending champion Homestead Grays in the 1945 Negro League World Series capped a year of excellence for the team. Their 53–16 record amounted to a .768 winning percentage. But the lack of excitement, glory, or attention from the press and the fans belies the team's achievement.

Willie Grace, a switch-hitting Buckeyes outfielder, batted .313 and hit the only home run in the 1945 Negro League World Series. Fifty years later, in a 1995 interview with *Sports Collectors Digest*, he praised the talent of the best Grays player—Hall of Famers Cool Papa Bell, Josh Gibson, Judy Johnson, Buck Leonard. How could Cleveland not be hyped when they beat that line-up?

Grace said, "We were tellin' the world what a great ballclub you had.' 'Cause we beat you, but we was still tellin' the world that's the greatest thing that ever happened to me as a ballplayer was beatin' a team like this."[3]

The Buckeyes' life in Cleveland did not begin auspiciously, however. In June 1941, Ernie Wright sought the services of Wilbur Hayes, a shoeshine stand owner on Central Avenue in Cleveland, to put together a group of semipro baseball players for a game against a white team in Erie, Pennsylvania. Hayes upped the ante by persuading Wright to invest in a team with a permanent home base in Cleveland.

Al Sweeney, Sports Editor of *The Washington Tribune*, described the genesis of Wright's venture as nearly culminating in violence because of a clever turn of phrase. Sweeney commented,

> The first team that Wright bankrolled out of Cleveland was a squad picked up from a local semipro outfit named the Cleveland White Sox.
>
> The first game that they played under the Wright sponsorship saw a travesty on the great game of baseball that probably had Abner Doubleday turning over in his grave.
>
> At that time I was holding down the sports desk of the *Cleveland Call-Post* and I screamed through the *Call-Post*'s columns that Hayes was attempting to pass fifth rate baseball on an unsuspecting public at first rate prices.
>
> Hayes stormed in the office upon reading our comments back in 1941 and threatened to ram an Underwood typewriter down my throat. And only after the careful persuasion of the *Call-Post*'s city editor, did this writer leave that office without a limb or two missing.
>
> But, after cooling down, Hayes managed to take our suggestions to heart. He managed to make a deal with George Mitchell's St. Louis Stars to play out their second half schedule in the Negro American League during 1941, as the Cleveland–St. Louis Stars with Wright adding his financial blessings.[4]

Overcoming that inauspicious start the Buckeyes rose through the ranks each year. By 1945, they had climbed to the top of the Negro American League. After defeating the Chicago American Giants for the league pennant, the Buckeyes faced an opponent with deeper power. On paper, the Buckeyes could not match Josh Gibson and other

Cleveland Buckeyes in the dugout in 1949 (Negro Leagues Baseball Museum).

Grays capable of smashing home runs, seemingly at will. Cleveland relied on baseball cunning. Quincy Trouppe, the Buckeyes' catcher-manager, explained the benefits of baseball strategy against a powerful opponent in his 1977 autobiography, *20 Years Too Soon: Prelude to Major-League Integrated Baseball*:

> We weren't known as a power outfit, although we had players besides myself who could park one on you quick, but what we were doing that caught everyone by surprise and got us by them was bringing back the old brand of ball playing made famous in Rube Foster's heyday. Back then, guys like Jelly Gardner and Jimmy Lyons could drive you crazy by choking up on the bat, hitting behind the runner, and running wild stealing on the base paths. It was true the Homestead Grays could bomb you out of the park, but my team was very fast. We could run the tongue out of anybody's head.[5]

As the Cleveland Buckeyes ascended to the crown of Negro League royalty in 1945, a storm churned the waves of social change. While the Buckeyes championed excellence at League Park, the barrier separating the Negro Leagues from the major leagues showed the first signs of erosion. The Negro Leagues were about to get a black eye in favor of integration.

Robinson — and Change

Branch Rickey quietly scouted Jackie Robinson under the guise of a new Negro League called the United States League and his team — the Brooklyn Brown Dodgers. It was a smokescreen designed to distract from Rickey's true aim — scouting Robinson for the Brooklyn Dodgers of the National League. Rickey gained traction when Thomas E. Dewey, Governor of New York, signed the Ives-Quinn Anti-Discrimination Bill into law on March 12, 1945.

Though not an official edict because major league teams did not have black players on their rosters, this policy contrasted with the approach in the early years of the majors, beginning with Moses Walker as the first recognized black player. Walker was a catcher and outfielder for the Toledo Blue Stockings of the American Association in 1884. With Ives-Quinn as cover, Rickey spearheaded the breaking of the racial barrier on the baseball diamond. In his 1982 biography *Branch Rickey*, Murray Polner theorizes that Rickey's connection to Dewey yielded conversations about Ives-Quinn before Dewey signed it.

Polner wrote, "[Rickey] and Governor Thomas E. Dewey were friends and Republican Party allies who spent occasional Sundays together in Pawling, New York, where Dewey owned a farm and Rickey's close friends the Thornbergs resided. It was likely they had talked about the bill and its impact on baseball while it was still pending in Albany."[6]

Rickey selected Jackie Robinson as the player to fulfill a vision of breaking baseball's color line. Rickey's approach stemmed, in part, from the reduction of quality ballplayers caused by calls to service during World War II. Stanley Cohen, author of *Dodgers: The*

First 100 Years, wrote, "Many of their stars would be past their primes by the time the war ended. It was not too soon to plan for the future. In January 1943, Rickey took his case to George V. McLaughlin. The Brooklyn Trust Company, at the time, controlled 50 percent of the Ebbets family's stock in the team, and McLaughlin's position was stronger than ever."[7]

As McLaughlin was a man of pragmatism, Rickey argued about the inevitability of integration and its potential impact on the club's bottom line. McLaughlin gave the green light with a caveat, however: "If you're doing this to help the ballclub, go ahead," he said. "But if you're doing it for the emancipation of the Negro, then forget it."[8]

Two pioneers, Jackie Robinson and Larry Doby, enjoying a conversation in the dugout (Negro Leagues Baseball Museum).

Rickey needed a smokescreen to shield his plan. If his competitors caught a whiff of his plans, he would lose his edge in scouting players. At a press conference on May 7, 1945, Rickey announced a 100-game schedule for a new Negro League. The United States League would begin in June 1945 with six teams in Brooklyn, Chicago, Detroit, Pittsburgh, Philadelphia, and Toledo.[9]

This short-lived United States League provided a Trojan horse for Rickey's integration efforts. In August 1945, Rickey dispatched Clyde Sukeforth to evaluate Robinson, the shortstop for the Kansas City Monarchs of the Negro Leagues. 1945 was Robinson's only year in the Negro Leagues; he batted .387 in 47 games. Sukeforth was a catcher for the Cincinnati Reds and Brooklyn Dodgers between 1926 and 1934 before becoming a scout. In 1945, at the age of 44, he played in 18 games for the Dodgers because World War II had depleted major league rosters of sufficient talent.

In *Branch Rickey: Baseball's*

Ferocious Gentleman, Lee Lowenfish talked about the events leading to Jackie Robinson meeting Branch Rickey. Because Sukeforth had not yet seen Robinson play, Rickey dispatched his scout to Comiskey Park in Chicago where Sukeforth met Robinson on August 24, 1945. After introducing himself as a Brooklyn Brown Dodgers scout, Sukeforth asked Robinson to make a few underhand throws from shortstop to first base, while Sukeforth patrolled in his street clothes. Robinson obliged. What Sukeforth saw was enough to invite Robinson to meet Rickey at the Brooklyn Dodgers offices in Brooklyn Heights at 215 Montague Street.[10]

Lowenfish further explained Sukeforth's reaction to Robinson off the baseball field. The scout and prospect got further acquainted at the Stevens Hotel: "As they began to get to know each other, Sukeforth was immediately impressed by Robinson's intelligence, directness, and seriousness. The scout asked him about his army experience, and Robinson mentioned that an old football ankle injury contributed to his discharge but that it posed no problem in playing baseball."[11]

Indeed, Robinson volcanically exploded on the baseball diamond. Ability was not the only skill that inspired Rickey to sign Robinson, though. Rickey saw the Negro Leagues as a providential gold mine of baseball talent, but he needed someone with the emotional strength to withstand a cauldron of prejudice, bigotry, and intolerance in the era of separate but equal. He needed someone to react to taunts, slurs, and teases solely with sheer baseball prowess.

In *Baseball's Great Experiment: Jackie Robinson and His Legacy*, Jules Tygiel states, "He needed the self-control to avoid reacting to his tormentors without sacrificing his dignity."[12] Notwithstanding Moses Walker in the latter part of the 19th century, the first black baseball player in the 20th century would get the recognition, accolades, and hero worship commensurate with breaking the color barrier.

On August 28, 1945, Rickey revealed that the Brooklyn Brown Dodgers team was a ruse, at least as it concerned Robinson. "I want you to play for the Brooklyn Dodgers organization. Perhaps on Montreal to start with."[13] The Montreal Royals were the Brooklyn Dodgers' Triple-A team. Rickey then explained an intangible requirement concerning Robinson's emotional fortitude. According to Lowenfish,

> Branch Rickey, the dramatic actor manqué, Lionel Barrymore playing Thaddeus Stevens, began to describe vividly and act out physically the threats Robinson would endure as the first black player in twentieth-century Major League Baseball. Rickey took off his jacket and got down on the floor, imitating a base runner sliding into second, kicking Robinson in the shins, imitating the actions of a racist opponent barreling into Robinson with spikes vengefully high.
>
> He probably shouted the "'n'" word and voiced other epithets that opponents would yell at Robinson. He asked the stunned athlete how he would react when white waiters wouldn't serve him on the road, railroad conductors turned their backs on him, and other situations of discrimination in America arose that Rickey deplored but felt that he could change through the actions of a great black baseball player. The key to the success, Rickey stressed, was that Robinson could not fight back against the indignities.[14]

An astute baseball executive, Rickey assessed Robinson as a player with potential for the future, if not the moment. "He is not now major league stuff."[15] Robinson signed with the Dodgers on October 23, 1945. Rickey sent Robinson to the Montreal Royals of the International League for the 1946 season. In *Opening Day: The Story of Jackie Robinson's First Season*, Jonathan Eig wrote, "Rickey's intention was to give fans and players more time to get used to the idea of integration, and to give Robinson more time to polish his skills. And if problems arose, better to have them arise in Montreal than in Brooklyn."[16]

Robinson led the International League in batting (.349) and fielding percentage (.985). Additionally, the Royals won the 1946 International League Championship and the 1946 Junior World Series. Rickey saw the major league stuff. Jackie Robinson broke the color line of Major League Baseball on April 15, 1947. By the end of the following decade, the Negro Leagues were no more.

The Legacy of the Buckeyes

What is the legacy of the Cleveland Buckeyes? It is one of excellence that ought to be celebrated, not forgotten. For every Jackie Robinson, there was a Quincy Troupe. For every Willie Mays, a Willie Grace.

After his days as a Buckeye, Sam Jethroe played for the Boston Braves, winning Rookie of the Year honors in 1950 (Negro Leagues Baseball Museum).

The Cleveland Buckeyes disbanded in 1950, their legacy entrusted to scholars, historians, and enthusiasts of the Negro Leagues. Eclipsed by more famous Negro Leaguers, Jackie Robinson's signing to the Dodgers, and Cleveland's other team, the Indians, the Cleveland Buckeyes' place in baseball history is fragile, but no less important.

Beating the Homestead Grays in the '45 Negro League World Series was a classic tale of a scrappy team beating a more powerful team. This underdog theme echoes in baseball lore, particularly a film featuring another Cleveland team—*Major League* and the fictional Cleveland Indians of Rick Vaughn, Willie Mays Hayes, and Jake Taylor.

The Buckeyes' achievement as one of the last great Negro League teams deserves a spotlight as integration triggered a migration of the best Negro League players in the late 1940s and throughout the 1950s. Integration, while socially correct, destroyed the Cleveland Buckeyes, Homestead Grays, Newark Eagles, and the other teams of the Negro Leagues. By the end of the 1950s, they belonged to history.

Today, the League Park Society strives to protect the history of League Park, the home field for the Cleveland Buckeyes and, until 1946, the Cleveland Indians. The League Park site is a public park with only the first base grandstand wall and the ticket office building as reminders of eras passed.

The City of Cleveland is restoring League Park to its former glory as a baseball field. The ballpark that debuted on May 1, 1891, is gone, but the restoration will at least include a baseball diamond, if not the grandstands. The League Park Society web-site indicates that the romance of the game remains on a piece of land where Cy Young and Bob Feller once pitched for the Indians, Babe Ruth hit his 500th home run, and the Cleveland Buckeyes achieved the unthinkable by beating the Homestead Grays in 1945.

"You can close your eyes and just for a moment or two go back in time. Yes, the brick and mortar may largely be gone but the soul of League Park is still very much alive. The grass is still green and this field of dreams beckons baseball fans to visit, say hello and yes play again."[17]

Somewhere, Ernie Wright and Wilbur Hayes are smiling.

The 1946 Cleveland Buckeyes. Front row, from left: unknown, Al Smith, Archie Ware, Quincey Troupe, Leon Kellman, Sam Jethroe, and unknown. Middle row: Vibert Clarke, Clyde Nelson, Johnny Cowan, unknown, Gene Bremer, Jesse Williams, and Willie Grace. Back row: Gene Smith, Chet Brewer, Clyde Williams, Sam Jones, Alonzo Boone, Doc Bracken, Ross Davis, Joe Atkins, and unknown (courtesy NoirTech Research, Inc.).

Notes

1. Dwayne Cheeks, "The Cleveland Buckeyes Remembered: Played Second Fiddle to Tribe until Demise," *The Cleveland Plain Dealer*, January 18, 1982, 6-D.
2. Ibid.
3. Brent Kelley, "Willie Grace was Part of the Best Team in Cleveland History ... in 1945!" *Sports Collectors Digest* (November 10, 1995, 160).
4. Al Sweeney, *From Rags to Riches, Negro Baseball Yearbook* (Sepia Sports, 1946).
5. Quincy Trouppe, *20 Years Too Soon: Prelude to Major-League Integrated Baseball*, Revised edition (St. Louis: Missouri Historical Society Press, 1995).
6. Murray Polner, *Branch Rickey: A Biography* (New York: Atheneum, 1982), 156–157.
7. Stanley Cohen, *Dodgers! The First 100 Years* (New York: Birch Lane Press, 1990).
8. Ibid.
9. Lee Lowenfish, *Branch Rickey: Baseball's Ferocious Gentleman*, 365–366 (Lincoln: University of Nebraska Press, 2009), 365–366.
10. Ibid., 371–372.
11. Ibid., 372.
12. Jules Tygiel, *Baseball's Great Experiment: Jackie Robinson and His Legacy* (New York: Oxford University Press, 1983), 58.
13. Lowenfish, 374.
14. Ibid., 375. In Jackie Robinson's autobiography, *I Never Had It Made*, he recounts the scene similarly, but with an exchange between himself and Rickey: "Mr. Rickey, are you looking for a Negro who is afraid to fight back?" "Robinson, I'm looking for a ballplayer with guts enough not to fight back." Jackie Robinson and Alfred Ducket, *I Never Had It Made: An Autobiography* (New York: HarperCollins, 1995), 33.
15. Jonathan Eig, *Opening Day: The Story of Jackie Robinson's First Season* (New York: Simon & Schuster, 2007), 30.
16. Ibid.
17. www.leaguepark.org

Something to Cheer About

Paul Robeson, Monte Irvin, Larry Doby

Joe Dorinson

Abstract

The role of African American sports heroes continues to generate controversy. In his book Darwin's Athletes, *John Hoberman argues that the sports arena is actually a metaphorical prison that denies access to middle-class avenues of success by funneling African Americans into a narrow channel. It positions brawn over brain, forcing blacks into a state of perpetual subordination. Though well researched and forcefully written, Hoberman fails to appreciate the pivotal role black athletes have played in shoring up ethnic identity and penetrating the barriers of a once-unyielding caste system. This article examines the impact of three such athletes from New Jersey, the site of this year's Jerry Malloy Negro League Conference.*

"A life is not important except in the impact it has on other lives," wrote Jackie Robinson before his untimely death in 1972.[1] Three African American heroes from New Jersey fit this statement with the lives they lived. Though they differed in style, temperament, and career, they made a difference. Paul Robeson, Monte Irvin, and Larry Doby certainly gave us something to cheer about.

All three gained their fame initially through athletics. The role of African American sports heroes continues to generate controversy. Author John Hoberman for example insists that the emphasis on the sporting life contributes to racism. In his book, *Darwin's Athletes*, Hoberman argues that the sports arena is actually a metaphorical prison which denies access to middle class avenues of success by funneling African Americans into a narrow channel. It positions brawn over brain, forcing blacks into a state of perpetual subordination.[2] Though well researched and forcefully written, Hoberman's book is wrong-headed. What this Texas scholar fails to appreciate, I believe, is the vital, indeed role black athletes have played in shoring up ethnic identity and penetrating the barriers of a once-unyielding caste system.

Before Paul Robeson, Monte Irvin, and Larry Doby entered the mainstream, prominent blacks were typed as the inversion of America's "Protestant Ethic." They

Black Ball / DOI: 10.3172/BLB.6.116 / Volume 6 / 2013 / pp. 116–128 /
ISSN 1939-8484 (Print) / ISSN 1939-8379 (Online) /

appeared as docile or savage, faithful or tricky, pathetic or comical, childish or oversexed. This public perception perverted the black persona and reinforced segregation in sports as well as in society. In order to survive, black athletes had to conform. This meant submission to white coaches coupled with a display of moral respectability. They had to fuse individual ambition and collective action.[3]

Even in sports, the opportunity structure in the 19th century was limited to horseracing, boxing, and baseball (briefly). Success not only bolstered race pride; it also led to property ownership. Three-time Kentucky Derby–winning jockey Isaac Murphy purchased large tracts of land. The first black to enter Major League Baseball, Moses "Fleet" Walker (prior to Jackie Robinson) owned a hotel, several movie houses in Steubenville, Ohio, and an opera house. These opportunities also saved his life. In a street brawl, Fleet Walker beat a white man to death. An all-white jury acquitted him. The man who was booted out of baseball by Cap Anson did profit from his temporary fame as a ball player. Ultimately, however, Walker concluded that blacks could only survive separate from whites. In his book, *Our Home Colony*, he warned that integration might lead to a societal volcano.[4]

Explosive or not, black athletes carved out a distinctive niche in American society. Jack Jackson, the subject of a prior presentation at the "Pop" Lloyd Conference, challenged white supremacy. He appeared "ill-mannered, defiant and absolutely incorrigible." He consorted with white women, married three, and won the championship on merit. In the ring, he developed a distinctive style. Defensively, he feinted, countered, and tricked his opponents. Then, he lowered the boom. A knock-out followed. If not, Johnson retreated into a defensive pose.[5]

Larry Doby, as a member of the Cleveland Indians in the late 1940s (Negro Leagues Baseball Museum).

On the gridiron, blacks had more margin for maneuver. Earning distinction as the first national football figure, Bill Lewis entered Amherst College in 1888. He centered a fine team. After graduation, Lewis studied law at Harvard where he continued his outstanding football play. One hundred and seventy-five pounds of tempered steel, agile and fast, he played both defense and offense. Walter Camp dubbed him an All-American, the first black to be so honored. As a great student of the game, he became a coach. Success went beyond the arena. Bill Lewis became the first black to serve as U.S. Assistant Attorney General.

The next star that elicited national attention, Fritz Pollard played for Brown. A halfback with blazing speed, Pollard preferred sports to study, a trait shared with other athletes—both white and black. He led Brown to victories over favored Yale and Harvard in successive weeks in 1916. Before graduating, he turned pro, earning admiration from opponents as well as from teammates—one of whom was Paul Robeson.[6]

Robeson is probably the greatest legend that few people know. April 9, 1998, signaled the 100th birthday of this complex, brilliant Renaissance man. Athlete, singer, actor, activist, Robinson's talents transcended his first national arena, the football field. In fact, boxing champ Joe Louis said that he and baseball pioneer Jackie Robinson owed everything to Robeson. The latter's life ended in loneliness and despair. Perhaps, his tragedy was that he was born too soon. His life gives us much to ponder, to mourn, and to celebrate. Growing up in a segregated society, Robeson enjoyed a spectacular career as an athlete. Elsewhere, I have explored his illustrious life in detail. Here, I want to explore Robeson the athlete, because it sheds light on the American dilemma.

According to biographer Lloyd Brown, sports came naturally to young Paul. Born in Princeton, the youngest of four surviving children, Robeson was orphaned in 1904 when his mother Maria Louisa died as a result of an accidental fire.

"Motherless children have a hard time when mother is dead."

"Sometimes, I feel like a motherless child."

The family moved to Somerville in 1910. When Robeson entered Somerville High School, he was one of 250 students, one of three blacks and only one of eight enrolled in college preparatory work. At Somerville High School, Robeson—encouraged by his venerable father, William Drew Robeson, a runaway slave whom he affectionately called "Pops"—excelled. He played forward on the basketball team, hurled the javelin and threw the discus in track and field. In baseball, he played short-stop and caught. During inter-city games, Paul experienced racism. In one encounter, Paul whacked a tremendous triple. The High Bridge principal stormed onto the field and thundered: "That coon did not touch second base!" A major rhubarb, to echo the dulcet tones of Walter "Red" Barber, was prevented when Robeson's teammates protected him from a possible physical confrontation instigated by the incendiary principal.[7]

In high school football, Paul played fullback. On this field too he became the target of opposing players. In battling archrival Bound Brook, Paul broke his collarbone. But he held his ground, winning approval from all with his courage, tenacity, and talent. His teammate, Doug Brown, later dean and provost at Princeton University, remembered Paul as the heart of the football squad. Although sports brought young Robeson his public acclaim, he also excelled in debating, singing, and scholarship.[8]

As a result of a statewide exam, Rutgers opened its doors to this highly qualified scholar-athlete in the autumn of 1915. A private school then, Rutgers had only 500 students. Paul was only the third black to attend Rutgers since its inception in 1766. While trying out for the football team, this 6'2", 190-pound marvel incurred injury and endured pain. In the very first scrimmage, he sustained a broken nose, a smashed hand, and a dislocated shoulder. Robeson's father William and brother Ben did not let him quit. After 10 days of recuperation, Robeson recalled his ordeal by fire in an interview with *New York Times* critic, Robert Van Gelder.[9] He admitted rage—rage enough to kill. Lifting a tough running back Kelly above his head for a punishing tackle, Coach Sanford blew the whistle to prevent further mayhem. Robeson made the team. Former teammates differ on whether Paul was deliberately subjected to a brutal hazing during scrimmages. One mate, Robert Nash, recalled that Robeson "took a terrific beating."[10] Today, the truth is no less elusive than it was 85 years ago.

Coach George Foster Sanford, whom Robeson adored, taught him how to protect himself with a well-placed elbow, how to play offense. As a freshman, he served as a substitute tackle until November 20 when he earned a start against Stevens Tech. Rutgers won 39–3. Stardom loomed in 1916 as Robeson played in six of seven games at guard and tackle. The only game that Robeson missed resulted from a demand issued by Washington and Lee to "bench the nigger."

Shamefully, Rutgers capitulated. It was not the finest hour for the Scarlet Knights. Without their star player, they could manage a 13–13 tie.[11] When Robeson returned to his tackle position, *The Newark Evening News* reported, the whole line improved. In 1917, Paul gained fame as an offensive end and defensive end and tackle. Robeson wrote about this year in detail. Reprinted in Philip Foner's excellent collection, *Paul Robeson Speaks,* the retrospective offers a solid analysis of Rutgers' banner year. More important, it provides a clue to his character. Published in the *Rutgers Alumni Quarterly,* January 1918, it begins with a bang.

> The season of 1917 is over, but the memories thereof will fire the hearts of Rutgers men as long as football is football. For the team fighting as only a Rutgers team can fight, and inspired by the indomitable spirit of that greatest of football mentors, George Foster Sanford, rose to the greatest heights, and stands not only as one of the best teams of the year but as one of the greatest of all times.

Robeson mentions that only three veterans returned to the team: Rendell, Feitner, and himself, to whom he refers in the third person. In the first game, the Scarlet Knights defeated Ursinus 25–0. The next game was rout of Fort Wadsworth: 90–0. The third game was played in Syracuse. The home team capitalized on miscues to beat Rutgers 14–10. Shouldering the blame for the defeat, Robeson exonerated Coach Sanford.[12]

Redemption came against Lafayette one week later as the Scarlet Knights whipped the men of Easton 33–6. In the big game against a highly touted Fordham team led by future baseball star Frankie Frisch, the Scarlet Knights crested and Robeson excelled. You would not know this from Robeson's narrative but the *New York Times* provided ample evidence. In the 28–0 romp, the paper reported that Robeson made two important catches of 35 and 24 yards to set up two touchdowns. As a blocker at left end, he knocked three Rams out of the game. The headline read: "Fordham Crushed by Rutgers Power: Robeson, the sturdy Negro End of the Visiting Eleven, Plays a Stellar Role in the Aerial Attack." No less graphic, Charles A. Taylor wrote: "A dark cloud upset the hopes of the Fordham eleven yesterday." No silver lining appeared as Paul Robeson (evidently the "dark cloud") was all over the field.[13]

Threats against Robeson sullied the next game opposite Greasy Neale's team from West Virginia University. Unsubtly, Coach Neale warned that his southern boys would try to murder Paul. Even the biased coach had to concede that Robeson played "like a white man." Rutgers dominated the first half; but their opponents recovered a blocked punt on the 12-yard line from where they punched in a touchdown in two plays. The game ended in a 7–7 tie.[14]

Disappointed, the Scarlet vented against Springfield College with a 61–0 drubbing. They bested the U.S. Marines from Philadelphia, despite a lackluster performance, 27–0. The season's climax occurred in Brooklyn's Ebbets Field on November 24. A team of Naval Reserves composed of All-Americans under the baton of Cupid Rogers invaded Brooklyn. Robeson identified his opponents: Barrett of Cornell, Black and Callahan of Yale, Schlacter of Syracuse, Gerrish of Dartmouth. Having trounced Colgate and Dartmouth, these gridiron Goliaths faced the Davids of Rutgers minus a slingshot. Led by Robeson, the underdogs triumphed 14–0. The young star conferred praise on Coach Sanford. Again the press pointed in another direction — his. For example, sports reporter Louis Lee Arms, of the *New York Sunday Tribune* wrote: "A tall tapering Negro ... dominated Ebbets Field."[15] He cited the gaping holes that Robeson opened in enemy lines lifting little Rutgers to victory. The young Knight scored one touchdown and starred on defense leading his team to a 7–1–1 record.

How did the upset occur? Robeson, as writer, explained. Football, he argued, "is method and not men ... Rutgers has the best methods taught by the greatest of football coaches, George Foster Sanford." He goes on to sing the praises of this marvelous coach, as an "advocate of clean play in life as on the field." He lauds the man: adviser, guardian and molder of characters. Above all, Robeson pinpoints teamwork and team spirit as the stuff of greatness. He analyzes every player and his contribution but himself. Foreshadowing his evolving political philosophy, young Paul Robeson put the group above the self. This uncommon man celebrated the common cause. Such selflessness is unique among athletes of today.[16]

In a silly display of pious patriotism, Walter Camp and other sports *mavens* refused to name an official All-American team. Evidently, the war to make the world safe for democracy not to mention communism and fascism precluded football honors. Walter Camp, hailed Robeson, however, as worthy of that temporarily suspended rubric: All-American. The same applied to the 1918 season, which resulted in a 5–2 record for the Scarlet Knights of the Raritan.[17] Strangely, there is far less coverage of Robeson at Rutgers during the final year of World War I. As his illustrious college career drew to a close, more attention was paid to his intellectual prowess, including the coveted Phi Beta Kappa key and prizes for oratory.[18] Nevertheless, Robeson continued to excel in the sports arena. In June 1919, a campus paper reported that Robeson hurled the javelin 137' 5" against Swarthmore College, 12 feet better than his nearest competitor.[19]

Robeson entered Columbia Law School. To pay his tuition, he assisted Fritz Pollard as coach at Lincoln University. He also joined Alpha Phi Alpha, the first black fraternity in America. While studying the law, he played professional football before the ban was imposed on blacks in 1934. His first venue was Hammond, Indiana, in 1920. He switched to the Akron pros that year and in 1921. He finished his football career with the Milwaukee Badgers in 1922. He earned anywhere from $50 to $200 per game.[20] Largely ignored, professional football did not keep records so it is difficult at best to judge Robeson's postgraduate performance. And by 1922, this "Dusky Rover" and "Football Othello" towered above his contemporaries in the sports pantheon.

Did Paul Robeson make a difference as a sports hero? Did he give us something to cheer about? In assessing his athletic career, sociologist and baseball administrator Harry Edwards observed that Paul won respect from opposing coaches with his fierce play. His coach called him "the greatest player of all time." One coach, oblivious to the explicit racism in his praise, dubbed him "a white man in black skin." On road trips, Robeson had to sleep in segregated facilities and often took meals on the team bus. In persistence and perseverance, he became a forerunner as he acknowledged: "Sports was an important part of my life in those days."[21] Prof. Lamont Yeakey forcefully argues that Paul Robeson, as athlete and scholar, smashed the myth of white supremacy.[22] True, segregation did not vanish during his glory years, but thanks to his enormous presence, black participation in once totally white intercollegiate athletics and white appreciation of black talent improved, measurably.

Not only did Robeson gain wide recognition in football; he also made his mark in baseball, basketball, and track. But football, clearly, brought him glory and Rutgers fame. In his four years, the Scarlet Knights were 22–6–3. To survive in the Darwinian world, Paul had to resort to artful elbows, quick knees, and powerful forearms to punish opponents without incurring penalties. His body became the subject of riveting attention; his intellectual accomplishments, the object of awe. The portrayal of Robeson in the nude may have contributed to a profound insight made manifest in the Harlem Renaissance in which Paul Robeson played an integral part, namely, that black is beautiful and this Black Apollo was the epitome of black beauty.[23]

There is also a disturbing afterthought. Robeson's account of his football experience in 1917 is almost too sweet in self-denial. He must have harbored deep rage that, when unleashed, caused the fire in his soul to burn incessantly. It was fed by the oxygen of other atmospheres, such as in the Soviet Union and Eastern Europe where he was lionized, admired, and loved. Because of his "service to the state," we must not extenuate or distort the injustice visited on this great man. In 1954, Rutgers University published a list of its 65 football greats.[24] No mention of Robeson can be found. In 1970, as the Cold War thawed somewhat; a committee of New Jersey sports dignitaries, prodded by Rutgers' personnel, reversed course. They nominated Robeson for the Rutgers Hall of Fame. After repeated rejection, Robeson joined the elect on August 25, 1995.[25] For Robeson, dead since 1976, it was too little, too late. For us, just in time though long overdue, it gave us something to cheer about.

Another to cheer about is Monford Merill (his given name) "Monte" Irvin, the seventh of 10 children — six boys, four girls— was born in Halesburg, Alabama, on February 2, 1919, to Cupid Alexander and Mary Eliza Irvin. That halcyon year also brought a formal end to World War I, the birth of Jackie Robinson, and a surge of race riots in a number of American cities. A victim of the sharecrop system in Alabama; Monte's father confronted his landlord over money. In dire straits, Cupid had to flee first to Georgia and later to New Jersey. Since two older children had moved to the "Garden State," Cupid followed with wife and children in tow. They eventually settled in Orange, a suburb. There, Monte attended East Orange High School, an integrated institution where he excelled in athletics. But the restaurants were segregated and movie theaters confined blacks to the balcony only.[26] Sports provided the principal passport to success in America.

Monte Irvin takes a practice swing while playing for the Newark Eagles (Negro Leagues Baseball Museum).

Earning letters in football, track, basketball, and baseball (like Paul Robeson), Irvin, at 6'1" 190 lbs., gained a reputation as his high school's greatest athlete. On graduation night, however, Monte and his date along with two other black couples could not eat at a local restaurant near school because of their color. Depressed, these youngsters left. A scout from the University of Michigan offered Monte a football scholarship. Unfortunately, he lacked the funds to reach Ann Arbor. Thus, he lost a splendid opportunity to play in the same backfield with Tommy Harmon and Forest Evershevski. He settled on Lincoln University, an all-black school in Pennsylvania where he formed a life-long friendship with future Eagles' teammate Max Manning.[27] Less than two years later, Monte left to play baseball with the Newark Eagles. Starting in high school, Monte used the pseudonym Jimmy Nelson in order to maintain his amateur status. As soon as he dropped out of college, he reverted to his real name.[28]

After he learned to pull the ball by watching Joe DiMaggio, Irvin became one of the dominant hitters in the Negro Leagues. While statistics are not always available or reliable, it is clear that Monte could match skills with the best white ballplayers. As an Eagle of Newark, Monte flew to the top of the league as a hitter with hefty averages of .403 in 1939, .377 in 1940, and .400 in 1941. Perched at third base, shortstop, and center field, Irvin became a wizard on defense as well.[29]

He honed his skills and learned some painful truths while on tour. In 1941 he and teammate Max Manning were driving through Daytona Beach, Florida, when a policeman stopped them. "Where are you goin'?" he barked. "Home," a nervous Manning replied. "Home!" Don't you know how to say, sir?" Manning froze in anger. "Yes, sir," Irvin volunteered quickly. "What's wrong with your buddy? Can't he say it?" As the officer began to unbuckle his Billy club, Irvin explained that they were learning to play baseball. They wanted no trouble. This traumatic incident, recalled nearly 60 years after it happened, revealed the survival skills of Monte Irvin. He realized that uttering the magic words, stuck in the throat of Max Manning, saved them from a beating or worse.

This is how one dealt with racism in 1941. Irvin dismissed it as "no problem ... I know the son of a bitch is ignorant ... and no skin off my teeth to say sir. It's not going to make me a lesser man."[30] In retrospect, Irvin may have rationalized his stance of accommodation. Taking the less onerous route, Irvin survived this ordeal but not without enormous psychic pain.

Unable to wrest a salary increase from tight-fisted Eagles owner, Effa Manley, Monte "jumped" to the Mexican League to join the Vera Cruz team. He led the league with a .397 average, 20 home runs, and 79 RBIs and captured the MVP award.[31]

Monte went off to war in 1943. He experienced segregation over there (Europe) as well as over here. A Company commander for example warned Monte and his black buddies to spurn social invitations and to avoid contact with white women. These absurd orders made a person feel "like you were nothing." The war left Monte with shattered nerves. Based on his pre-war baseball performance, Monte Irvin — not Jackie Robinson — should have been the designated pioneer to break the color barrier. According to one source — his daughter Pamela — Monte's wife intercepted a letter from Branch Rickey soliciting Monte's service for the Brooklyn Dodgers. Mrs. Irvin realized that Monte could not at that time shoulder the Herculean labors.[32] Rickey persisted until Effa Manley demanded monetary compensation for Monte's contract.[33]

Thus, when he returned to civilian life, he opted for more seasoning in the Negro

League and in Latin American winter ball. In 1946, he, Leon Day, Larry Doby, and Max Manning led the Newark Eagles to victory over Satchel Paige's Kansas City Monarchs in the Negro League World Series. While traveling in Mississippi in an air-conditioned bus, white farmers jeered at the "jigaboos." Irvin sensed the incongruity of the hooting crackers broiling in the southern heat while the Eagles rode in comfort. Laughter eclipsed anger.[34]

When Monte finally reached the major leagues as a New York Giant at age 30, he proved his mettle. A fine career curtailed by injury and late entry propelled Irvin into the Hall of Fame belatedly in 1973. Over eight years, he hit .293 during the regular season and .394 in two World Series: 1951 and 1954. His finest hour came in the "miracle year" of 1951 when he hit .312 with 24 home runs and a league-leading 121 RBIs. With Hank Thompson in left and Willie Mays in center, Monte formed the first all-black outfield. In the World Series, he stole home in Game 1 and proceeded to pulverize Yankees pitching at an amazing .458 clip with a then-record-setting 11 hits in 24 at-bats. The Giants lost to the Yankees in six games.[35]

After retirement, Irvin worked for Rheingold Beer in promotions and public relations. From 1968–1984 he worked as a special assistant to Baseball Commissioner Bowie Kuhn during a turbulent era sparked by free agency and other volatile issues. As the only black administrator in the commissioner's office, Irvin worked quietly behind the scenes to secure justice for his fellow Negro Leaguers. After his election to the Hall of Fame on August 6, 1973, he steered Ray Dandridge, Martin Dihigo, Rube Foster, Judy Johnson, and John Henry Lloyd through the portals of baseball immortals.[36]

A survivor, despite ill health of late, Irvin is now past 94. Unlike Robeson and Robinson, two aggressive black heroes, Monte followed a course of least or—more accurately—lesser resistance. One should remember there are many roads to glory. Mr. Irvin took the one more traveled by and that has made all the difference.[37]

Our final focal point fixes on Larry Doby. Born and raised in Camden, South Carolina, between 1923 to 1938, young Lawrence was left fatherless at age eight. Looking back in anger, he recalled his early years when whites would come to the black neighborhood and throw coins at small black children. They would also rub the children's heads in search of good luck. Larry's mother warned him against taking gifts from strangers. He listened.[38]

At 15, he arrived in Patterson, New Jersey, where he set the high school athletic world on fire with sterling performances in baseball, football, basketball, and track. He too adapted an alias—Larry Walker—to preserve his amateur status while playing professional baseball, like Irvin, for the Newark Eagles. Admitted to Long Island University on a basketball scholarship, he stayed briefly before transferring to Virginia Union. His college career was cut short by service in the U.S. Navy starting in 1943.[39]

When he returned, the svelte slugger reunited with Monte Irvin on the championship Newark Eagles for whom he played second base opposite Irvin at shortstop. This dynamic duo arguably constituted the best hitting keystone combination in baseball history. Both, however, were eventually shifted to the outfield: Irvin, first in the Negro League; Doby, later in the American League. Before entering Major League Baseball, Doby led the Negro National League with a whopping .415 batting average and 14 home runs in the first half of the 1947 season. In only 42 games, he whacked 16 doubles, knocked in 35, and scored 35.[40] Cleveland Indians owner Bill Veeck (as in wreck) was watching. This marvelous maverick had wanted to integrate baseball in 1942 with the purchase of the hapless Philadelphia Phillies but was thwarted by then Commissioner Landis.[41] In 1947 things had changed, dramatically.

Branch Rickey beat Bill Veeck to the races with the historic signing of Jackie Robinson. In 1947 as Jackie embarked on his majestic career, Veeck inked Doby to a contract and advised him how to behave. Don't argue with umpires; no "dissertations with opposing players, either of those might lead to a race riot. No associating with female Caucasians." Doby listened. Veeck watched. When he entered the Indians' locker room for the very first time, several unnamed players refused to shake his hand. Former Yankees star, Joe "Flash" Gordon broke the ice. He played catch with the Negro newcomer as did player/manager Lou Boudreau.[42]

In his debut, Doby struck out. The young slugger, at the suggestion of Coach Bill McKechnie, was converted into an outfielder.[43] One day, he misjudged a fly ball with the bases loaded. It resulted in a loss of face — the ball hit Doby in the head (actually the bill of his cap, observed Joseph Moore) — and the loss of a game.[44] Answering a challenge posed by Coach McKechnie, Doby hit a home run the very next day to win a game. Player-manager LouBoudreau helped Doby adjust along with Gordon. Later, others tried to befriend the shy slugger. Doby withdrew into silence. He experienced abuse. Opponents spit in his face. Vile epithets hounded him. He took his aggression out on the field. In 1948 his first full year in the majors, Doby hit .301 with 14 home runs and 66 RBIs.[45]

Larry played 13 stellar years with the Indians and the White Sox. Overshadowed by his peers — Mays, Mantle, Snider — Doby did not get the benefit of larger-market venues. Yet he too could — and did — hit tape-measure home runs: a 470-foot clout to dead center in Yankee Stadium and a 500-foot blast at Griffith Stadium in Washington. Statistically, his best year was 1950 when he hit .326, smashed 32 home runs, and knocked in 126 to lead the American League in the latter two categories. When he finally hung up his spikes, he had amassed 253 round-trippers to go with a .283 lifetime batting average.[46]

As a player, Doby also made history in 1957. According to biographer Joseph Moore, an incident merits consideration as a turning point in baseball history. Yankees pitcher Art Ditmar aimed a ball at Doby's head. Dusted, Doby charged the mound and sent a solid left hook to the jaw of Ditmar. Never before had a Negro player thrown the first punch at a white player in a baseball brawl. *Washington Post* writer Shirley Povich hailed the incident as a milestone. It signaled the full acceptance of blacks into baseball. The placid Doby seemed to be the least likely player to punch the face that launched a thousand stories.[47]

In 1978, Bill Veeck tabbed him again to serve as trailblazer. He appointed him manager of the Chicago White Sox. Again, he played second fiddle to a Robinson—this time to Frank, the manager of his former team in Cleveland. Despite his historic role in breaking barriers, it is evident that Doby lacked the fiery temperament of either Paul Robeson or Jackie Robinson. More like the even-tempered Irvin, he avoided confrontations. He seemed content with "loner" status. Initially, Jackie Robinson also had to keep his mouth shut. This repression, so contrary to his nature, engendered a series of ailments: high blood pressure, diabetes, arthritis, and blindness. Doby did not fully escape. He developed an ulcer.[48]

So often linked in the great chain of baseball and social history, Doby and Robinson invite different reactions. The talented if erratic poet Amiri Baraka preferred Doby as an authentic Negro.[49] Buck O'Neil, wise old man, loved all: Larry Doby, Jackie Robinson, and Satchel Paige. "I loved Jackie as a person; I love Satchel as a friend, and I love Larry as a son."[50] Doby was more typical of black athletes. "We couldn't appear uppity and we couldn't allow our intelligence or knowledge to show."[51]

After his "release" from managerial duties, Larry Doby left baseball in 1979. Don Newcombe regards that departure as a shame and a loss. Despite the shameful rebuff, Doby switched sports. He moved into pro basketball, serving as director of community relations for the New Jersey Nets.[52] After all those dues, he deserved a better fate. Doby was different. He did not disarm an adversary as Satchel Paige did with humor; Jackie Robinson with a verbal attack; Monte Irvin with sweetness; Paul Robeson with eloquence.

What do Robeson, Irvin, and Doby share in the last analysis besides the color of their skin and their content of their character? All three grew up in adversity. Robeson lost his mother at six; Doby, his father at eight. Irvin had two strong parents, but like the other two he had to battle bigotry and confront bias. Though each chose separate paths in their common quest, they kept their eyes on the same prize: social justice and fair play. Robeson battled the status quo openly. Doby avoided conflict by withdrawing into discreet silence. Irvin, a nice guy to the last, worked within the system. Despite apparent differences, they gave—and continue to give—us something to cheer about.

Notes

1. Jackie Robinson, and Alfred Duckett, *I Never Had It Made: An Autobiography* (New York: Echo Press, 1995), 255.
2. John Hoberman, *Darwin's Athletes: How Sport Has Damaged Black America and Preserved the Myth of Race* (Boston: Houghton-Mifflin Mariner Books, 1997), 3–51.
3. David K. Wiggins, "The Notion of Double-Consciousness and the Involvement of Black Athletes in American Sport," in *Ethnicity and Sports in North American History and Culture*, eds. G. Eisen and D. Wiggins (Westport, CT: Greenwood Press, 1994), 133–134.
4. Ibid., 137–138.
5. Joseph Dorinson, "Black Heroes in Sport: From Jack Johnson to Muhammad Ali," *Journal of Popular Culture* 31, no. 3 (Winter 1997): 116–117. http://dx.doi.org/10.1111/j.0022-3840.1997.3103_115.x

6. Stephen Fox, *Big Leagues: Professional Baseball, Football, and Basketball in National Memory* (New York: William Morrow, 1994), 317–321.

7. Paul Robeson, *Here I Stand* (New York: Othello Associates, 1958), 220.

8. Lloyd L. Brown, 1997, *The Young Paul Robeson: "On My Journey Now"* (Boulder, CO: Westview Press, 46–47).

9. Robert Van Gelder, *New York Times*, June 16, 1944, Sec. 2, 7.

10. Martin B. Duberman, 1988, *Paul Robeson* (New York: Alfred Knopf, 21); L. Brown, 62.

11. Philip S. Foner (ed.), 1978, *Paul Robeson Speaks...* (New York: Brunner/Mazel Publishers, 49–53).

12. As cited in Lenwood G. Davis, 1982, *A Paul Robeson Research Guide: A Selective Annotated Bibliography* (Westport, CT: Greenwood Press, 308).

13. Ibid., 310; *New York Tribune*, October 28, 1917.

14. Ibid., 311.

15. Ibid., 66–67; Foner, 1978, 51–53.

16. Brown, 1997, 81–82.

17. Francis C. Harris, 1998, "Paul Robeson" in *Paul Robeson: Artist and Citizen*, ed. J. Stewart (New Brunswick, NJ: Rutgers University press, 41–44).

18. Davis, 1982, 313.

19. Harris, 1998, 44–45.

20. Paul Robeson, 1951, "Here's My Story, Sports Was an Important Part of My Life," *Freedom* (November 1951): 1–7 as cited in L. Davis, 67.

21. Lamont H. Yeakey, 1973, *Journal of Negro Education* 42, 4 (Fall 1973), 489–503. http://dx.doi.org/10.2307/2966562

22. Lamont H. Yeakey, 1971, "The Early Years of Paul Robeson: Prelude to the Making of a Revolutionary," Master's Thesis, Columbia University.

23. Jeffrey C. Stewart, 1998, "The Black Body: Paul Robeson as a Work of Art and Politics," in *Paul Robeson: Artist and Citizen*, 135–155.

24. Duberman, 1998, 760, n. 8, 763, n. 21.

25. Harris, 1998, 45–47.

26. Monte Irvin and James A. Riley, 1996, *Nice Guys Finish First: The Autobiography of Monte Irvin* (New York: Carroll & Graf, 1966); Jack B. Moore, 1998, "Up from Sharecropping," in *Jackie Robinson: Race, Sports, and the American Dream*, eds. J. Dorinson and J. Warmund (Armonk, NY: M. E. Sharpe, 32–33).

27. Irvin and Riley, 1996, 33–34.

28. Moore, 1998, 33–34.

29. Ibid., 34; James A. Riley, 1994, *The Biographical Encyclopedia of the Negro Baseball Leagues* (New York: Carroll & Graf Publishers, 408).

30. Moore, 1998, 35.

31. Riley, 1994, 408.

32. Moore, 1998, 36–37; at the Pop Lloyd Conference in Atlantic City, Monte Irvin's daughter Pamela related the intercepted letter incident in a discussion with me.

33. Larry Moffi and Jonathan Kronstadt, 1994, *Crossing the Line: Black major Leaguers 1947–1959* (Jefferson, NC: McFarland, 40; James Overmyer, 1998, *Queen of the Negro Leagues: Effa Manley and the Newark Eagles* (Landon, MD: Scarecrow Press, 242–430.

34. Ibid., 34–35.

35. Riley, 1994, 409; Irvin claimed that Yankee luck contributed to their World Series victory over the Giants. Nowhere does he mention Giant guile as revealed in an expose by Josh Pager.

36. Irvin and Riley, 1996, 218–227.

37. I concur with Moore, 1998, 38–39 on this point.

38. Joseph Thomas Moore, 2011, *Larry Doby: The Struggle of the American League's First Black Player* (New York: Dover, 7–8).

39. Ibid., 19–25.

40. Ibid., 38; here Moore 2011cites the July 9, 1947 edition of *The Sporting News.*

41. Overmyer, 1998, 236–237.

42. Moore, 2011, 49. In an interview with Fran Healey on the Baseball Hall of Fame telecast, Doby recalled his first encounter with the Cleveland Indians.

43. Ibid., 61, 67.

44. Ibid., 78.
45. Moffi and Kronstadt, 1994, 15–17.
46. Ibid.
47. Moore, 2011, 114–15.
48. Ibid., 170.
49. Ibid., 171.
50. Ibid., 172.
51. Ibid., 172.
52. Ibid., 173–175. Again, I am indebted to Joseph Moore whose definitive biography of Larry Doby furnished most of my information as well as insights.

Blackball in Chester, Pennsylvania, 1867–1887

Historical Documents

JAMES E. BRUNSON III

IN 1867, THE ACTIVE BASE BALL CLUB, OF CHESTER, PENNSYLVANIA, "measured bats" with Philadelphia's Pythian Base Ball Club. The "Active" met a crushing defeat. The following year, Abram Brown, team secretary, corresponded with the Pythians. Brown's letter expressed a desire to join their club. It also identified teammate William Spriggs as "a heavy batter and hornet in the field." Bonds between colored baseballists of Philadelphia and Chester remained strong.

By 1877, the Keystone Social Club — Chester's "aristocrats of color" — had organized a team. The Keystone Base Ball Club, led by John Hackett and Isaac Rothwell, enjoyed a well-earned reputation. The "Keystone," "Lightfoot," "Wabash," "J. Gallon," and "J. Robinson" battled for local colored baseball supremacy. The Keystones continued the Chester–Philadelphia rivalry and competed with Wilmington, Delaware's colored nines. They also crossed bats with "white friends." Between 1867 and 1887, colored baseballists from Chester made quite an impression and continued to put strong teams in the field.

Spriggs, Hackett and Rothwell belong to a rich tradition of blackball in Chester, a small city located between Philadelphia and Wilmington, Delaware. The Rothwell boys (Albert, Charles, Isaac and George), for example, played for colored clubs of Chester, Philadelphia, and Frankford in Pennsylvania as well as for Atlantic City, Camden, and Newark in New Jersey. The Rothwell's descended from one of the earliest black families of Delaware County. Their father had served an English nobleman named Rothwell, who was associated with Lord Delaware in the early English colonization of the area. The father served three years in the Civil War and participated in several battles. He belonged to the Third United States Regiment, the first colored regiment to be recruited in Philadelphia. As late as 1951, newspapers reminisced about the Rothwell family's place in the history of Chester.

A visit to my daughters living in Norristown, Pennsylvania, and Baltimore, Maryland, inspired the compilation of these primary documents. I took the rare opportunity to imagine 19th-century baseball-team travel by trekking through several

Black Ball / DOI: 10.3172/BLB.6.129 / Volume 6 / 2013 / pp. 129–138 /
ISSN 1939-8484 (Print) / ISSN 1939-8379 (Online) /

Gilded Age cities, all astonishingly within a three hour radius— Harrisburg, Steelton, Norristown, Chester, Philadelphia, Camden, Trenton, New Brunswick, Newark, Wilmington, Baltimore, and Washington, D.C. While my travels took place over two weeks, it remains illuminating how proximity and geography affected early blackball. The primary documents provided below offer insight into the brotherhood of colored baseballists, along with their "white friends" willing to share space on the green diamond.

"Letter" (1868)

"[William Spriggs, of the Active Base Ball Club, of West Chester, Pennsylvania] is a heavy batter and hornet in the field."[1]

"Base Ball" (1877)

A game between the Keystone of South Chester and the Maple Leaf of Chester, on Saturday afternoon in South Chester resulted in a score of 27 to 22 in favor of the Keystone.[2]

"Base Ball" (1878)

A game of base-ball was played on Saturday afternoon between the Lightfoot of North Chester and Keystone of South Chester, on the grounds of the latter. Both clubs are colored, and some very good playing was done on both sides. The Keystone's thought the balls of their pitcher could not be struck by the Lightfoot, but the latter club took them by surprise when they knocked the balls all over the field. The game resulted in favor of the Lightfoot by a score of 16 to 10. The winning club was to get a ball, but the Keystone failed to produce it, which has adding nothing to their credit.[3]

"Base Ball" (1879)

The Ross nine defeated the Keystone club Saturday afternoon by a score of 17 to 1 in five innings, the shades of night preventing them from playing longer. It is difficult to tell where the score would have stood had they played the game throughout. The Ross nine will retire from the field for the winter on very good laurels, not having been defeated but once during the season. They cannot get any other clubs to play them, and they will go into winter quarters.[4]

"Dangerous Man" (1880)

At a ball given in Edgmont Hall last evening, by some colored men from Media, two women got to fighting in the dressing room, about two o'clock this morning, and a man, John Hackett [Keystone catcher], did not want anyone to interfere, and shot at Isaac Rothwell [Keystone shortstop], of this city, for attempting to separate the belligerent females. Fortunately he did not hit Rothwell. Two or three colored men pursued Hackett, and he ran down to Market Street where he jumped through the glass door in Mr. Furlong's confectionery store to get clear of his pursuers. Officer Frank Wilson came to tie scene and arrested Hackett. At a hearing before the Mayor this morning he was held in $200 for his appearance at Court.[5]

"Match Game" (1882)

There will be a match game of pool at Blackson's pool room this evening. The participants, John Jobes and [Isaac] Rothwell, are both good players, and said to be evenly matched. The prize to be contested for is a gold pin.[6]

"Festival" (1882)

The South Chester Keystone Club (colored) gave a festival in Kepner's hall last evening. There were about two hundred present. The grand cake walk took place about 12 o'clock; it was led by Mr. John Nelson and won by Mr. John Rosha, of Linwood. There were 32 couples on the walk.[7]

"South Chester Items" (1882)

The Keystone Base Ball Club will play the Ocean club of Philadelphia on the 4th of July. A good game is expected.[8]

"South Chester Items" (1882)

The game of base-ball came off between the Keystone, of South Chester, and the Orion, of Philadelphia. When the rain came on the game stood 17 to 14 in favor of the Orient. It was the closest game of the season and was watched by a large number of spectators. A great number of the friends of the Orion club came with them from Philadelphia, and it was decided by all parties that if the rain had not came on, our boys would have beaten the Philadelphia club. They held them close all the way through, and there was great cheering "on both sides. They intend, in the near future, to try it over again. The Keystone club are confident that they can beat them, and will not be satisfied until it is tried again.[9]

"South Chester Items" (1882)

The Keystone club played the Union club, on Saturday last, and the score stood at 26 to 8 in favor of the Keystone. There was a large crowd of spectators present.[10]

"South Chester Items" (1882)

The Keystone base ball club, of South Chester, will play the Our Boys club at Houston Park on Thursday. The game will be culled at 4 P.M. The Our Boys club is from Wilmington, and are said to be good players. A good game is expected. Admission 10 cents.[11]

"South Chester Items" (1882)

The base ball game between the Keystone club of South Chester, and the Our Boys Club from Wilmington, Delaware, came off on the grounds of the Houston at 4 P.M. yesterday afternoon. There was a large number of spectators present. The game stood 22 to 9 in favor of the Our Boys club. Henry Sterling and John Hackett, of the Keystone club did some very fine playing. Dix, of the Houston, was umpire. The third baseman was no good, they would have done as well with a wooden man in that position. The Keystone club felt the defeat very badly, as they were confident of beating the Wilmington club.[12]

"Base Ball Notes" (1882)

The Houston base ball club, of South Chester, and a colored club from Philadelphia [Orions], played a game of base-ball at Houston Park on Saturday afternoon. Victory was secured without effort by the Houstons, they scoring 26 runs to their opponents 6.[13]

"A Combination Cake Walk" (1882)

The Keystone Combination Club, of South Chester held a soiree and cake walk in Kepner's Hall, Third and Korlin Street last evening.[14]

"Base Ball" (1882)

The Keystone base ball club has reorganized with new and better players, and on Monday will play the Orion, the champion colored club of Philadelphia, at Houston Park. The Keystone club is composed of the following players: John Hackett, c.; Henry Sterling, p.; B. Hart, 1 b.; K. Smith, 2 d.; W. Harris, 3 d.; Isaac Rothwell, s. s.; W. Reiley, r. f.; A. Sheppard, c. f ; E. Watson, 1. f.[15]

"South Chester Items" (1882)

A game of base ball was played yesterday between the Keystone and the Orion clubs. The Keystone laid off four of their usual players and substituted others and they did not succeed in scoring. The game resulted, 27 to 0 in favor of the Orions.[16]

"In and About South Chester" (1883)

Base-ball is away up in the borough. The probabilities are that we not only will have a crack white team but also a stunning colored team. The following are the players of the J. Gallon base ball club: Catcher: John Hackett; pitcher. James Perrigan; First base: John Hart; second base: Henry Sterling; third base, David Perrigan; center field: Abraham Fields; right field: Warner Pryor; left field: William Cotman; short stop: Alexander Sheppard. The club is open to receive challenges. They would cross bats with any club in Chester or the vicinity. Address J. Gallen, captain. They will play the Blue Stockings of Upland, April 19.[17]

"Base Ball Notes" (1883)

Messrs. Hargreaves and Lutton of the Ross club are making arrangements to have the Chinese club of Philadelphia visit this city and play a game at Chester Park. As the manager of the Celestials also manages the Manhattan club, a colored team, games can only be secured with the almond-eyed ball tossers by first playing the colored club.[18]

"In and About Chester" (1883)

Another colored base-ball club is in the field and will be known as the Wabash, with William Ruley as manager. They expect to cross bats with the Keystone at an early date with prospects for an interesting match.[19]

"In and About Chester" (1883)

The Wabash base ball club are anxious for a match with the J. Gallon club, over whom they expect to win a signal victory. The Wabash has secured the services of George Williams and Daniel McDonald of Philadelphia, as pitcher and catcher. This they consider an excellent battery, and calculated to prevent their opponents from scoring a run.[20]

"A Base Ball Dispute" (1883)

EDITOR TIMES: — Judging by the heavy talk one would think that the Wabash base ball club did not know that the majority of the Gallon nine are over twenty years of age. The Wabash club first proposed to confine their game with clubs whose members are under twenty years of age, and it would no doubt be a good plan for them to stick to that proposition, for if they play the Gallon club it will be a cold day for them, and they certainly will get wiped out and left behind.[21]

"South Chester Items" (1883)

The Gallon nine are not satisfied with the result on Thursday and are of the opinion that they can yet beat the Wabash They will soon be given an opportunity to do so as another game is being planned between the two clubs, to take place at any early date.[22]

"In and About South Chester" (1883)

The Wabash and Gallon clubs will play a game of ball on Monday at Houston Park.[23]

"In and About South Chester" (1883)

There will be a game of base-ball played between the Wabash and the J. Gallon club, this afternoon.[24]

"Base Ball Notes" (1883)

Two colored clubs, the Eclipse, of Philadelphia, and the Wabash, of this city will play at Houston Park this afternoon.[25]

"Base Ball Notes" (1883)

"To-morrow afternoon the Chester and Wabash, (colored) will play at Chester Park."[26]

"South Chester Items" (1883)

The Gallon club, of South Chester, will play the Homily club, of Wilmington, to-morrow at Houston Park. A good crowd is expected. The Homily is the champion colored club, as they have not lost a game this season. A small admission will be charged to defray expenses.[27]

"Base Ball Notes" (1883)

The Ashcraft club will play the Wabash club, the champion colored team of this county, on Friday afternoon at Chester Park.[28]

"Base Ball Notes" (1883)

Chester Park was invaded yesterday afternoon by the Ashcraft club and the Wabash colored club. Both teams were uniformed and determined to vanquish each other. The game was called at 4 o'clock in the presence of an audience made up principally of colored people. But, seven innings were played, owing to the manner in which the runs and errors wore being scored by each club. The colored team carried off the honors by a score of 29 to 25.[29]

"The Wabash Defeat" (1883)

Chester Park was the scene yesterday afternoon of a game of ball between the Delaware and Wabash (colored) clubs, the Delawares had a good picked nine, which almost paralyzed their opponents in the first inning. "Everyman that went to the bat corked the ball for a base hit, and eight runs were scored in the first inning. The colored men had engaged Williams, of the Orion club of Philadelphia to pitch for them, but no one would catch for him until the second inning, when Rothwell got behind the bat. The Delawares had a heavy battery in the persons of Kitts and Howard. Speaking Kitts' pitching, one of the colored players remarked: 'Dem balls ain't got no curve, but dey's powerful swift!'" One of them caught a batter in the small of the back, and he was in for stopping there and then. By dint of hard work they scored ten runs, while the Delawares forged ahead to the tune of twenty-one, "the colored men appeared in attractive uniforms and played well, but they were overmatched. Manager Hargreaves umpired the game."[30]

"A Colored Curver" (1885)

William Green, of this city, has been engaged by the Orion Base Ball Club, a colored team, to occupy the pitcher's box. He plays at Wilmington to-day, at Dover on Saturday, and at Baltimore on Monday. William smiles at Eddy Morris' challenge and says he will wrestle any day, catch-as-catch-can for $10.[31]

"Base Ball Notes" (1885)

The Middle Ward Base Ball Club, colored, will play the North Chester team tomorrow for the championship of the county. Both teams are composed of good players. Green and Purnsley, of the Orion, will form the battery for the Middle Ward.[32]

"South Chester Chat" (1886)

The borough boasts of baring a first-class colored team for the coming season [J. Gallon], with the following players: John Hackett, John Butler, S. Hinkson, H. Smith, B. Smith, Isaac Rothwell, Louis Smith, Aaron Fields and William Furrel. They would like to play the first game of the season with the Thurlow Boys. William W. Ruley is the manager of the team.[33]

"Personal" (1886)

Messrs. Benjamin Driskett and Isaac Rothwell, of the colored aristocracy of Chester, are sniffing the salt sea air of Atlantic City. They are filling an engagement there with the colored base ball club.[34]

"Base Ball Notes" (1886)

"The T. Robinson Base Ball Club, of North Chester, defeated the J. Gallen Club, of South Chester, in a well-played game of base-ball at Thurlow Park. This was the third game in a series of four won by the Robinson. The contest was a hot one throughout. Hinckson pitched in fine form, striking out eight of the Gallen batters, and was given fine support by Burton. Perrigan pitched for the Gallen, but was hit hard at times. He was supported in almost perfect style by Hackett. Ben Smith led the batting, having six hits for a total of 13 bases." Score: Robinsons, 10; Gallons, 8.[35]

"Gallon and Delawares" (1886)

The Delaware base ball club his tried its hand with the Gallen nine of this city and suffered an overwhelming defeat. The visitors could not get on go Perrigan's curves and played a very careless game. The score:

Gallon	3	2	3	2	4	6	0	6	1–27
Delaware	2	0	0	0	2	0	0	1	1–6

Earned Runs—Gallon. 17; Delaware, 3; Home Runs—Perrigan, 1. Three base hits—Driskett, 1. Two base hits—Purnsley, 2; Hackett, 1. Base hits—Gallen, 29, with total, 40; Delaware, 9, total, 16, Umpire—Graul.[36]

"Base Ball at Thurlow" (1886)

The J. Gallon base ball club, of South Chester, will play against the Eureka Steel Works nine on Saturday afternoon at Thurlow Park. Perrigan and Hackett will be the Gallon battery.[37]

"The Coons Defeat the Thurlow Reserves" (1886)

Quite a large and enthusiastic audience of both colored and white people gathered at Thurlow Park yesterday afternoon to witness a game of base ball between the J. Gallon and the Thurlow Reserve. The Reserves expected an easy victory and made the remark that "we will do them coons up before the games over," but according to the score the "coons" seemed to have turned the bibles. The batting of Pryor and Jackson of the J. Gallon and Witsell and gross of the Reserves was among the features of the game while the fine playing of Drisket and Rothwell drew forth tumultuous applause. The score resulted in 20 to 15 in favor of the J. Gallon.[38]

"Wilmington Base Ball Club" (1887)

Wilmington, May 4—The Wilmington base ball club organized last week and is composed of the following players: Alexander Wortenberry, c; Alonzo Ward, p; Charles Lambert, 1b; Alfred Grinnage, 2b; William Gales, 3b; Horace Berry, ss; Peter Spicer, lf; J. Chippey, cf; William Maxfield, rf; Henry Berry, captain and treasurer; J. Chippey, secretary. The club is now ready to receive challenges. Address all communications to the manager, Edward L. States, 223 West Eighth Street.[39]

"Delaware Doings" (1887)

Wilmington, July 5—The Wilmington Base Ball Club defeated the West Chester Base Ball Club at West Chester on the fourth, 10 to 7.[40]

Notes

1. "Pythian Baseball Club; Scorecards" (Roll No. 8). *American Negro Historical Society Collection: Historical Society Microfilm Edition*. 1868.
2. "Base Ball," *Daily Times* (Chester, PA), June 26, 1877.
3. Ibid., Aug. 19, 1878.
4. Ibid., Oct. 6, 1879.
5. "A Dangerous Man," *Daily Times*, Nov. 26, 1880.
6. "Match Game," *Daily Times*, April 17, 1882.
7. "Festival," *Daily Times*, May 5, 1882.
8. "South Chester Items," *Daily Times*, July 1, 1882.
9. Ibid., July 4, 1882
10. Ibid., July 10, 1882
11. Ibid., Aug. 1, 1882.
12. Ibid., Aug. 4, 1882.
13. "Base Ball Notes," *Daily Times*, Aug. 22, 1882.
14. "A Combination Cake Walk," *Daily Times*, Oct. 27, 1882.
15. "Base Ball," *Daily Times*, Oct. 11, 1882.
16. "South Chester Items," *Daily Times*, Oct. 19, 1882.
17. "In and About South Chester," *Daily Times*, March 25, 1883.
18. "Base Ball Notes," *Daily Times*, May 9, 1883.
19. "In and About South Chester," *Daily Times*, June 8, 1883.
20. Ibid., June 12, 1883.
21. "A Base Ball Dispute," *Daily Times*, June 15, 1883.
22. "South Chester Items," *Daily Times*, July 7, 1883.
23. "In and About South Chester," *Daily Times*, July 12, 1883.
24. Ibid., July 21, 1883.
25. "Base Ball Notes," *Daily Times*, July 28, 1883.
26. Ibid., August 1, 1883.
27. "South Chester Items," *Daily Times*, Aug. 16, 1883.
28. "Base Ball Notes," *Daily Times*, Aug. 23, 1883.
29. Ibid., Aug. 25, 1883.
30. "The Wabash Defeat," *Daily Times*, September 1, 1883.
31. "A Colored Curver," *Daily Times*, Aug. 20, 1885.
32. "Base Ball Notes," *Daily Times*, Sept. 25, 1885.
33. "South Chester Chat," *Daily Times*, March 4, 1886.
34. "Personal," *Daily Times*, Aug. 2, 1886.
35. "Colored Clubs at the Bat," *Evening Times* (Chester, PA), Aug. 24, 1886; "Robinson and Gallen," *Daily Times*, Sept. 14, 1886; "Base Ball Notes," *Daily Times*, Sept. 15, 1886.
36. "Gallon and Delawares," *Daily Times*, Oct. 2, 1886.
37. "Base Ball at Thurlow," *Daily Times*, Oct. 7, 1886.
38. "The Coons Defeat the Thurlow Reserves," *Daily Times*, Oct. 19, 1886.
39. "Wilmington Base Ball Club," *The Freeman* (New York, NY), May 7, 1887.
40. "Delaware Doings," *The Freeman*, July 9, 1887.

Book Review

Dunkel, Tom *Color Blind: The Forgotten Team That Broke Baseball's Color Line.* New York: Atlantic Monthly, 2013.

In *Color Blind*, freelance journalist Tom Dunkel chronicles the rise and fall of the integrated team from Bismarck, North Dakota, that played in the first national semipro tournament, held in 1935. Nowhere else in the literature of the Negro Leagues is this story told in more than a few paragraphs.

Car dealership owner Neil Churchill assembled a team of the best players he could buy to bring winning baseball back to Bismarck. To the surprise of many, Satchel Paige was among those Churchill signed. (Historians today will be less surprised, familiar as they are with Paige's habit of following the money from team to team.) And it appears that Paige agreed to play without knowing that he and his peers from the Negro Leagues would take the field alongside white players. When they did so, the people of Bismarck and the other cities in the upper Midwest saw, more than a decade before Jackie Robinson, what integrated baseball might look like.

Color Blind is full of details about the history of Bismarck going back in to the 19th century. We learn about how important baseball had been to this small community, as well as to the region. The rivalry with neighboring Jamestown is well documented, as both teams tried to best the other in getting players from the Negro Leagues. Dunkel also writes about the effects of larger historical events, the Great Depression in particular, on the town and region. Money was scarce and entertainment options limited, so baseball was an outlet. For a time Churchill and others tried to run the team with local talent, but they could not sustain that effort. Pitcher Roosevelt Davis was the first Negro Leaguer Churchill brought to town. He was there when Trouppe's plane arrived and the catcher got his first glimpse of North Dakota, which was a far cry from the South he had grown up in.

Amidst all the history and baseball that Dunkel provides, he does get a little carried away at times with hyperbole, and the tone is sometimes less than serious. He describes one player as "resembling a side of beef," for instance, and compares Paige's travels to that of a tornado. Bismarck, infatuated with Paige, was "struck by cupid's arrow" and often left "heartbroken" when the pitcher would take off without warning. Paige is also likened to the prize inside a Cracker Jack box.

Dunkel's description of the on-field action is stronger. He provides gripping accounts of pitching duels between Roosevelt Davis and Barney Brown, and between

Black Ball / DOI: 10.3172/BLB.6.139 / Volume 6 / 2013 / pp. 139–140 /
ISSN 1939-8484 (Print) / ISSN 1939-8379 (Online) /

Paige and Brown, going down to the wire. You can almost hear the crack of the bat when Trouppe lines a triple down the line to bring in the winning run. This is where Dunkel is at his best, and the reader comes away believing that major league games could not have been better played or more exciting, at least to the fans in Bismarck.

Like the game accounts, the dialogue imparts the flavor of the people and times. But there's a problem here. While Dunkel purports to share several conversations between the players, he fails to identify the sources for them. And without that documentation, it is hard to say how he could have come to know what Davis and Trouppe talked about on the ride from the airport or how Paige responded when Churchill asked Trouppe to talk to the pitcher about hanging out with white women. Some of this may have come from oral history—Dunkel conducted more than 200 interviews—but, again, credit is not given.

But it should be added that *Color Blind* is not intended as a scholarly book. It aims at a broader audience than many Negro Leagues histories can hope to reach, one that includes readers interested in civil rights but who may know little or nothing about black baseball. And when *Color Blind* is compared with other, similarly oriented trade books, its one serious weakness, spotty documentation, seems less glaring. Accuracy, rather than transparency, is the better measure for these books, and Dunkel's Note on Sources suggests that his research was extensive.

While historians should read *Color Blind* carefully and critically, they should read it, all the same. Dunkel shines a light on a little-known, deeply interesting story, and his work points the way toward further research.—**Leslie Heaphy**

Future Research

Negro Leagues baseball history has nearly as many forgotten teams as overlooked players. One of those teams, the Seattle Steelheads, played in the short-lived West Coast Baseball Association. When the league held its inaugural meeting in 1946 in Oakland, California, Abe Saperstein was elected president and Olympic gold medalist Jesse Owens joined the ranks as vice president. Seattle became one of six entries, scheduled to play 110 games after paying a $500 franchise fee. Not every team paid the fee, however, and the league floundered financially from the start. Some of the league's struggles could

Seattle Steelheads, 1946 (David Eskenazi Collection).

Black Ball / DOI: 10.3172/BLB.6.141 / Volume 6 / 2013 / pp. 141–142 /
ISSN 1939-8484 (Print) / ISSN 1939-8379 (Online) / © 2013 McFarland & Company, Inc.

also be tied to the signing of Jackie Robinson and his play for the Montreal Royals in 1946. Newspapers flocked to cover Robinson's exploits and Negro Leagues coverage declined.

So who were the Steelheads? What kind of a team did they have? What kind of fan support did they get? They played their home games at Sick's Stadium on Rainier Avenue, home of the Pacific Coast League Rainiers. What arrangements did they have with the Rainiers? How much involvement did Saperstein have with the team, with so many of the players on the roster traceable to his Harlem Globetrotters baseball team? What was the relationship between Saperstein and former cop Claude Norris, who was listed on official documents as the team's owner? How did Norris come to have money to invest in a baseball club?

Little coverage of Steelheads games appeared in the *Seattle Times*. Other West Coast newspapers did little better on covering the team on the road. This is a story worthy of further investigation to broaden our understanding of black baseball in the 1940s, and in particular on the West Coast. A starting point for some research is an article by Ryan Whirty from the May 2013 issue of *Seattle Magazine* (accessible online at http://www.seattlemag.com/article/remembering-steelheads-seattles-negro-league-team).

Research on the Steelheads is also significant because it would help shed light on the other entrants in the West Coast Baseball Association. Jesse Owens, for example, was involved with the Portland Rosebuds as well as the Steelheads. Earl Warren, California governor and later Supreme Court justice, threw out the first pitch for a game between the Los Angeles White Sox and San Francisco Sea Lions. Sam Jones, of the Oakland Larks, went on to play in the major leagues. Larks pitcher Lionel Wilson served as mayor of Oakland beginning in 1977. These little tidbits provide some fascinating insights but suggest that there is much more to investigate in this league and the teams that played in it.

Prize Winners from the Fourth Annual Jerry Malloy Negro League Art Competition

The fourth annual Jerry Malloy Negro League Conference Art Competition attracted artwork from all over the nation. Art from the winners and runners-up was on display at the Yogi Berra Museum in Montclair, New Jersey, during the summer of 2013.

Winners and runners-up were selected in each of three categories: professional, amateurs, and youth. Below are images of the winning pieces, along with short biographies of the winning artists. A new category added in 2012 allows for the selection of a People's Choice Award winner. The 2013 competition resulted in two People's Choice winners, and those images are included after the other three categories.

The Winners

Youth Category, Josh Gibson, Doubleheader *by Amy Steverson*

Amy Steverson, age 15, lives in Maryville, Tennessee, and is a rising sophomore at Maryville High School. She loves painting and baseball. She is active in her church youth group and is a good student.

Her painting was inspired by her grandfather Bryan Steverson's love for the Pittsburgh Crawfords.

Judges' Comments: Artist has synthesized mirror images of Josh to great decorative effect.

"I like the reflective nature of this painting and the fact that the background and foreground have been given careful consideration. This, has philosophical as well as technical merit as a painting. I like how the player on the right is looking directly at the viewer and the player on the left is looking at the player on the right — great technique to keep the viewer's eyes roving within the frame of the painting. Very well done — keep up the good work!"

"A mirror image is difficult to render, but this artist has done it very well. Good technical skill. Gibson's jersey reads "Crawfords," referencing a Negro League team. Really nice and creative. Definitely a show piece!"

"Wow. The composition of this portrait really jumps out at you. The main character is well presented [and] the use of levels of secondary and tertiary subjects is well conceived."

Black Ball / DOI: 10.3172/BLB.6.143 / Volume 6 / 2013 / pp.143–151 /
ISSN 1939-8484 (Print) / ISSN 1939-8379 (Online) /

Crawford

Crawford

Amateur Category,* The Chicago American Giants *by John Everett

John Everett was born and raised in Toms River, New Jersey. He is a 1973 graduate of the United States Military Academy at West Point where he received a B.S. in engineering. He has an M.S. degree in telecommunications from the University of Southern Mississippi and an M.C. degree in systems engineering from The George Washington University.

Mr. Everett spent 24 years in the U.S. Army as a Green Beret in Army Special Forces, serving in 27 different countries and commanded Special Forces organizations through Special Forces Battalion. He currently serves as the senior executive responsible for the information technology infrastructure for the FBI in Washington, D.C.

He began painting as a hobby in the early 1970s. Career and family duties kept him from pursuing his hobby until 1999 when his wife encouraged him to once again take up his brush and palette and continue his artistic work. Mr. Everett is self-taught and has worked consistently to improve his skill in both oil and acrylic mediums over the past 14 years. Most of his work is inspired from photographs he has taken from around the world.

John lives in Haymarket, Virginia, and is married to the former Mary Ellen Fuller of Toms River, whom he has known since the fourth grade. They have five grown children and six grandchildren.

Judges' Comments: "Absolutely gorgeous blue color harmony enriched by interruption of pattern by two neutrally colored figures and warm-toned details. There is also an almost oriental delicacy of execution, especially in the textures. This is the product of an extremely sensitive sensibility. Beautiful — I'm speechless!"

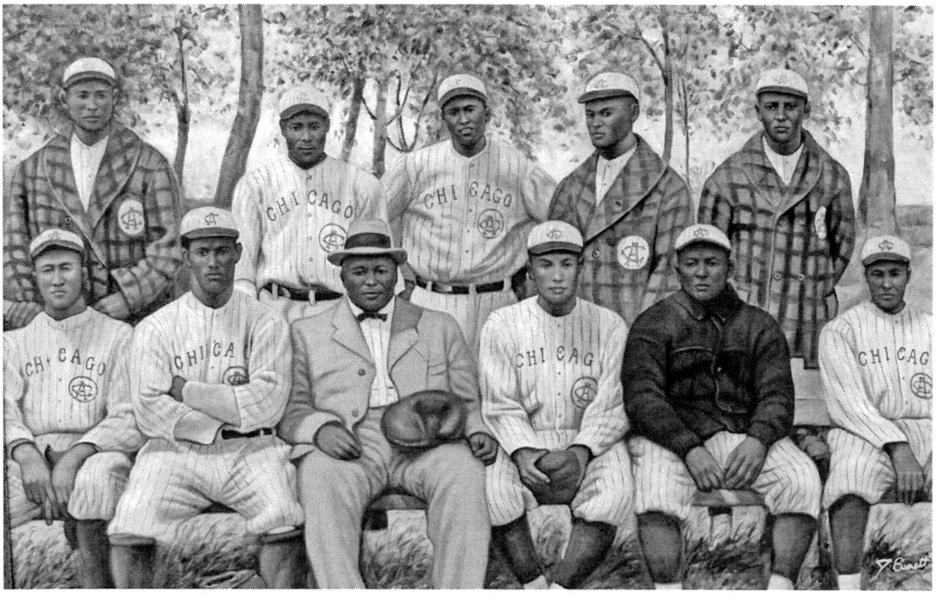

"The artist did an excellent job of using background renderings to situate this painting in a particular place. Wonderful blue uniforms pop out of the painting and draws your eye along the row of players. Very well done rendering of all players. My only suggestion would have been to include the feet of the players—however, I like the technique the artist has used as it places the viewer closer to the players, as if the viewer was a part of the team and not just observing. Fantastic job!"

"This shows a great Negro League team posing for a photograph. The artist has captured the postures and expressions very well. This wasn't a colorized photo, I assume, so the selection of color was made by the artist. This has been done very well—the beige suit of the owner contrasted with the whites and blues of the team."

"Impeccable work! The artist really makes you feel the picture is nearly viewing a real picture! Great job!

"This portrait is breathtaking. It captures the pride of the athletes. The composition, though simple, is right on point."

Professional Category, Time to Turn the Page *by Kat Flyn*

Artist's Comments: The carved wood hand is brown and the baseball is old. The stadium is second rate, framed by old Coke signs, like many stadiums played in by Negro League teams. This was the "color line" in organized baseball's history from its beginning in 1867 until the late 1940s. In 1948 Leroy "Satchel" Paige became the oldest rookie ever to play in the majors because racial segregation kept him out for most of his career. In his 1953 Topps baseball card, pictured here, he wears a St. Louis Browns jersey and is approximately 47. Even when there was talk of inducting him into the Baseball Hall of Fame in the late 1960s, the commissioner suggested a separate "Negro" wing. Because of men like Satchel Paige, the young boy (in this original 1950s photo) questioned a "separate but equal" world, symbolized by the Jim Crow character blocking his way.

Kat Flyn is an assemblage artist. Instead of "found" objects, she uses "saved" objects in her work. These artifacts, often saved by someone their entire life, are visual signs of America's social, political and cultural history—a history that many do not know or have forgotten. Often this shared history includes poverty, racism and inferior roles for women. All these artifacts that she uses in her art—an old "toy," a vintage baseball card, a worn baseball—draw the viewer in to witness our contemporary culture's subconscious prejudices.

Flyn's art has been in galleries in New York City and San Francisco. She has shown her work in museums in La Jolla and Marin, California. Her work has received Juror's Choice awards on many occasions. An Art piece on prison reform, *Hard Time*, was on exhibit at the 9th Circuit of Appeals in San Francisco. Many pieces are in private collections. Recent 2012 group exhibits have been at George Krevsky Gallery, ARC Gallery and the SF Fine Arts Fair in San Francisco.

Flyn grew up in Washington, D.C., and worked as a costume designer in Southern California for 30 years. She now works in her studio in San Francisco.

Judges' Comments: "This is visual poetry of the highest order and a poem that could only be composed about a time in America."

"The artist did a fantastic job of carving the extraordinary large left hand, referencing the ability to throw both left- and right-handed that Paige was known for.... The doll on the front is a little distracting and, to me, competes with the celebration of the piece. I like the box application as it denotes preciousness and archiving of things we value. Very well done—good job!"

"Wow! This is an outstanding piece—an unconventional memorial to Satchel Paige that contains surprises the artist was brave enough to risk. This isn't beautiful by any means, except in the sense that endurance has a certain beauty. The frame work consists of bits of old Coca-Cola crate, badly faded and battered, and a tobacco box from an era long past. The figure sitting on the frame looks to be a blackface performer from the racist vaudeville acts during the time that Paige was pitching. The opener tied to the side of the piece is a subtle, yet meaningful addition."

"Super creative! Great choice of items used to build this display! Great job!"

"This is a very powerful piece of work. The composition and use of artifacts really captures much of what was happening at the time. Very strong."

Runners-Up

Youth Category

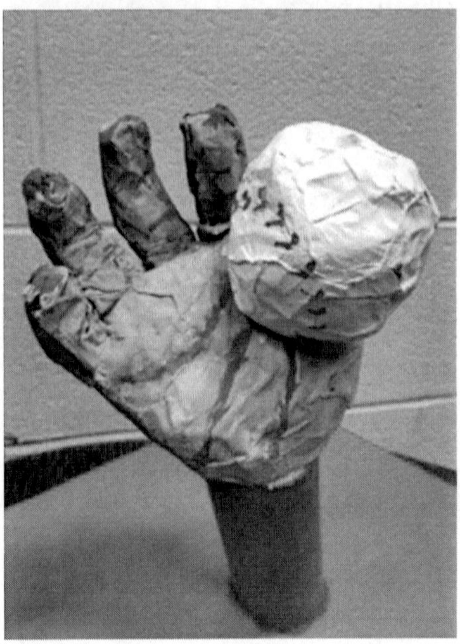

Ball and Hand **by Davion Perry.**

Jackie **by Damarion Bildon.**

Safe by Paulzair Alston.

Amateur Category

Hank Aaron and the Fans by Garth Potts.

Signed by Jackie by Milbert Brown.

Professional Category

Young Willie and the Barons by Kyle Bannister.

Josh Gibson by John Hanley.

People's Choice Award Winners

Attendees at the Jerry Malloy Negro Leagues Conference and others who viewed the winners and runners-up had a chance to vote on their favorite. This year two pieces tied for the People's Choice Award: John Hanley's *Josh Gibson* and Amy Steverson's *Josh Gibson: Doubleheader*. Congratulations to both these artists for their fine work.

Judges

A special thanks to our panel of judges for this year's art contest, including committee chair and renowned artist Benjamin Blackburn. Our judges are respected artists and experts in their fields, and we thank each of them for their time:

John Wolfe — award-winning artist

Byron Motley — musician, artist and author

David Baldwin — author, artist and former major league ball player

Jennifer Ettinger — visual artist

James Sheeley — supervisor of the Visual and Performing Arts Center for Newark Public Schools

Danielle Dronet — owner, Newark Bears

The theme for the 2014 Art Competition is "Little Known Stars of the Negro Leagues." Details for the competition can be found at www.sabr.org and www.baseballasamerica.net beginning in November.

Further Reading for This Issue

Leslie Heaphy

Bolden, Edward

"Association of Eastern Clubs Replies to Andrew Foster." *New York Amsterdam News*, 17 January 1923.
"Bolden Challenges Foster to a Debate." *Baltimore Afro-American*, 16 February 1923.
"Bolden Made Chairman of Eastern Colored Baseball League." *New York Amsterdam News*, 7 March 1923.
"Bolden Says He's for Fair, Clean Baseball." *Baltimore Afro-American*, 14 August 1926.
"Bolden to Head Eastern League." *Baltimore Afro-American*, 13 December 1924, 4.
"Bolden Tries to Defend League and Players." *New York Amsterdam News*, 29 July 1925.
"Bolden Worked at Night, Slept in Day, so He Didn't Have Time to Meet 'Rube.'" *Chicago Defender*, 24 February 1923.
Clark, William E. "Will Ed Bolden Have to Scrap the Hilldales to Save Eastern League?" *New York Age*, 6 June 1925.
"Colored Baseball Men in Sensational War of Words." *New York Amsterdam News*, 17 January 1923.
Dial, Lewis E. "Homestead Grays Withdraw from League; Bolden Elected New President at N. Y. Meeting." *New York Age*, 14 March 1936, 8.
"Ed Bolden, Manager of Hilldale, Stricken." *St. Louis Argus*, 30 September 1927, 7.
"Ed Bolden, Philadelphia Stars Owner, Dies." *Chicago Defender*, 7 October 1950, 18.
Harvey, Coley. "Bolden Was a Negro League Pioneer." http://mlb.mlb.com, 4 February 2009 and www.blackathlete.net, 3 March 2009.

Cleveland Buckeyes

"American Giants Defeat Cleveland." *Pittsburgh Courier*, 19 June 1943.
"Asheville Plays Buckeyes Aug. 17." *Chicago Defender*, 16 August 1947, 11.
"Auscos Beat Cleveland Buckeyes, 4–2, at Dayton." *The Herald-Press*, 6 July 1949, 10.
"Baseball Research Group Has Big Day in the Works." *The Chronicle-Telegram*, 15 September 1995, B5.
"Birmingham Opens Home Season with Bucks May 9." *Chicago Defender*, 4 May 1946.
"Buckeye Nine Plays Market Club Tonight." *The Herald Press*, 16 August 1943, 5.
"Buckeye Owner Protests Barring of White Player." *New Jersey Herald News*, 13 April 1946, 16.
"Buckeyes Add Stars for Game Here with Toledo Old Dutch 9." *The Lima News*, 27 August 1943, 14.
"Buckeyes Again Defeat Chicago; This Time in 10th." *Chicago Defender*, 12 June 1948.
"Buckeyes and Barons Divide." *Chicago Defender*, 14 June 1947.

Black Ball / DOI: 10.3172/BLB.6.152 / Volume 6 / 2013 / pp. 152–169 /
ISSN 1939-8484 (Print) / ISSN 1939-8379 (Online) /

"Buckeyes and Barons to Meet Next Sunday." *Syracuse Herald-American*, 27 July 1946, 43.
"Buckeyes and Chicago Split." *Chicago Defender*, 31 May 1947.
"Buckeyes Beat American Giants." *Chicago Defender*, 16 August 1947.
"Buckeyes Beat Chicago Giants in Two Games." *Chicago Tribune*, 28 April 1947, 31.
"Buckeyes Beat Chicago Twice." *Chicago Defender*, 1 July 1944.
"Buckeyes Divide with Jacksonville Red Caps." *Chicago Defender*, 6 June 1942, 20.
"Buckeyes, Eagles Split Double-Header at Newark, 4–0, 4–3, in Thrillers; W. Jefferson is the Loser." *Cleveland Call and Post*, 18 August 1945.
"Buckeyes Here on April 27." *Chicago Defender*, 19 April 1947, 19.
"Buckeyes Humble Flying Dutchmen in Lopsided Tilt." *The Holland Evening Sentinel*, 16 August 1949, 2.
"Buckeyes, Grays Clash Here in World Series." *Cleveland Call and Post*, 15 September 1945, 7B.
"Buckeyes Lose to Birmingham." *Chicago Defender*, 18 May 1946, 11.
"Buckeyes Meet Clowns at MacArthur Stadium." *Syracuse Herald-Journal*, 26 June 1947, 17.
"Buckeyes of Negro Loop Great Team." *The Helena Daily Independent*, 5 August 1940.
"Buckeyes Play in Stadium Benefit Building Fund of Future Outlook League." *Cleveland Call and Post*, 7 July 1945.
"Buckeyes Play Negro Giants in 2 Games Today." *Chicago Tribune*, 27 June 1943, A5.
"Buckeyes Rake 3 Hurlers in 19–10 Rout." *The Herald-Press*, 16 July 1949, 7.
"Buckeyes Return to Cleveland." *Mansfield News-Journal*, 13 February 1950, 8.
"Buckeyes Sign Cuban Shortstop, Outfielder." *Chicago Defender*, 23 February 1946, 9.
"Buckeyes Split Two With Cubans." *Cleveland Call and Post*, 14 April 1945, 7B.
"Buckeyes Take Title from Homestead." *The Daily Independent*, 21 September 1945, 5.
"Buckeyes to Face Black Barons at Stadium July 28." *Syracuse Post-Standard*, 14 July 1946, 12.
"Buckeyes to Open Season in Meadville." *Chicago Defender*, 30 May 1942, 19.
"Buckeyes Top Cubans in Negro Game, 10–7." *New York Times*, 22 September 1947, 30.
"Buckeyes Wallop Chicago Twice." *Cleveland Call and Post*, 30 June 1945, 7B.
"Buckeyes Win from Newark." *Chicago Defender*, 27 July 1946, 11.
"Buckeyes Win World Championship." *Chicago Defender*, 29 September 1945, 7.
"Bucks, Barons Split Two Games." *Cleveland Call and Post*, 12 May 1945.
"Bucks Beat Monarchs Twice, 1 to 0; 5 to 4." *Pittsburgh Courier*, 29 May 1943.
"Bucks, Chicago Divide Holiday Doubleheader." *Chicago Defender*, 8 June 1946, 11.
"Bucks Defeat Baron Champs." *Cleveland Call and Post*, 2 July 1945, 7B.
"Bucks Defeat Chicago Twice." *Chicago Defender*, 11 August 1945, 7.
"Bucks Glad to Aid Negro in Major Leagues." *Cleveland Call and Post*, 19 May 1945.
"Bucks Play Cubans, Rounding Out Nicely." *Cleveland Call and Post*, 21 April 1945.
"Bucks Set to Play in Cleveland, May 27." *Cleveland Call and Post*, 19 May 1945, 6B.
"Bucks Stage 3-Run Rally." *Chicago Defender*, 27 September 1947, 20.
"Bucks Top Clowns Twice, 3–0, 4–2; Smith Wins Fourth." *Pittsburgh Courier*, 5 June 1943.
"Bucks Win Series with Chicago Team." *Cleveland Call and Post*, 28 April 1945.
"Champ Buckeyes, Black Barons in Twin Bill Here." *The Syracuse Post-Standard*, 28 July 1946, 13.
"Chicago Takes on Cleveland." *Chicago Defender*, 25 May 1946, 11.
"Cleveland and Birmingham at Stadium Sunday." *Syracuse Herald-Journal*, 27 July 1946, 7.
"Cleveland at Memphis July 7." *Chicago Defender*, 6 July 1946, 11.
"Cleveland Buckeyes Ace Hurlers." *Chicago Defender*, 8 September 1945, 7.
"Cleveland Buckeyes Hammer Buds, 15–1." *The Herald Press*, 15 July 1949, 10.
"Cleveland Buckeyes Here Friday; Giants Switched." *The Herald Press*, 19 July 1945, 11.
"Cleveland Buckeyes Hit Ball all Over Lot to Beat Chicago." *Chicago Defender*, 30 June 1945, 7.
"Cleveland Buckeyes Oppose Barons Today." *Syracuse Herald-American*, 28 July 1946, 42.
"Cleveland Buckeyes Win Two Here Sunday." *Chicago Defender*, 9 August 1947.
"Cleveland Champs to Face Old Dutch Here Friday Night." *The Lima News*, 30 August 1942, 14.
"Cleveland Fans Honor Hayes; Bucks Win Two." *Chicago Defender*, 5 September 1943, 24.
"Cleveland Farm Club." *Cleveland Call and Post*, 6 April and 4 May 1946.

"Cleveland Grabs Lead in Negro World Series." *Chicago Defender*, 27 September 1947, 20.
"Cleveland Is Here Sunday." *Chicago Defender*, 23 June 1945.
"Cleveland Splits with Chicago." *Chicago Defender*, 23 June 1945.
"Cleveland to Have Negro League Ball Club in '50." *Chicago Tribune*, 1 December 1949, C4.
"Cleveland to Play Four Games with American Giants." *Chicago Defender*, 1 September 1945, 7.
"Clowns Anxiously View Buckeye Tilt." *Cleveland Call and Post*, 26 May 1945.
Cheeks, Dwayne. "The Cleveland Buckeyes Remembered: Played Second Fiddle to Tribe Until Demise." *Cleveland Plain Dealer*, 18 January 1982, 8D.
"Colored Baseball Teams to Play Here Tonight." *The Newark Advocate and American Tribune*, 21 July 1948, 14.
"Colored World Series." *Reno Evening Gazette*, 18 September 1947, 18.
"Comedians Spice Negro Baseball Here Tomorrow." *The Post-Standard*, 22 June 1947.
"Complete Plans for Night Game." *The Signal Sports*, 5 June 1943, 5.
"Cuban Stars Beat Buckeyes." *Chicago Defender*, 4 August 1945.
"Doubleheader at Stadium." *Zanesville Times Signal*, 4 June 1943.
"Dutchmen Take on the Cleveland Buckeyes Tonight." *The Holland Evening Sentinel*, 15 August 1949, 2.
"East Chicago Here Sunday, Memphis Red Sox Thursday." *The Herald-Press*, 21 July 1945, 7.
"Eastern Ohio League Leaders Are Scheduled for Action at Stadium." *The Signal Sports*, 12 June 1943, 5.
"First Lamp-Light Game of Season Scheduled for Gant Park Stadium." *The Signal Sports*, 11 June 1943, 7.
"Grays Are Beaten." *The Lima News*, 17 September 1943, 10.
"Grays in Win Over Cleveland." *Chicago Defender*, 13 April 1940, 22.
"Holland's Flying Dutchmen Meet Strong Colored Outfit Thursday." *The Holland, Michigan Evening Sentinel*, 14 July 1948, 2.
"Important Game Thursday for Cleveland Buckeyes." *The Newark Advocate and American Tribune*, 21 July 1943, 8.
Jedick, Peter. "League Park." *SABR Publication*, 1990, 20–22.
"Kansas City Beaten Twice By Cleveland." *Chicago Defender*, 29 May 1943, 11.
Kleinknecht, Merl. "Erie Has Unique Association with Old Negro Baseball Loop." *Erie Weekender*, 16 October 1982.
_____. "Wilbur Hayes and the Cleveland Buckeyes." *SABR Baseball Research Journal*, 1990.
Kuhn, Jerry. "Just Browsin' Around." *The Herald Press*, 17 May 1953, 10.
Lammers, Bill. "Champs of a Forgotten League." *Cleveland Plain Dealer Magazine*, 14 June 1992, 10–11, 14–15.
"League-Leading Colored Club Invades Colony Park." *The Herald Press*, 20 July 1945, 7.
Lenear, John H. "Indians' Celebration Honors Glory of Cleveland Buckeyes." *Cleveland Call and Post*, 22 June 1995.
"Mathers to Lead Blues Against Cleveland Team." *Syracuse Herald-American*, 13 January 1946, 23.
"Memphis at Toledo Against Buckeyes." *Chicago Defender*, 26 May 1945, 7.
"Memphis Red Sox Win 3–1, Then Lose to Cleveland, 9–4." *Syracuse Herald-Journal*, 12 July 1944.
"Memphis Sox and Buckeyes Play Tuesday." Syracuse, 1945.
"Memphis Sox at Bucks Opener." *Chicago Defender*, 26 May 1945, 7.
"Negro Baseball Teams Will Play at St. Marys." *The Lima News*, 17 June 1943, 8.
"Negro Champs Tackle Toledo Old Dutch Here in Friday Exhibition." *The Lima News*, 27 August 1943, 8.
"Negro League Team in Twin Bill Here Tonight." *Post-Standard*, 6 June 1949, 13.
"Negro World Series Opens in New York Sept. 19." *Chicago Defender*, 20 September 1947, 20.
"New Shortstop for Cleveland." *Chicago Defender*, 8 February 1947, 20.
"Niagara Falls Defeats Buckeyes at Stadium, 7–6." *Syracuse Herald-Journal*, 12 August 1944.
"19,744 See Grays Beat Bucks, 12–2." *Chicago Defender*, 20 July 1946, 10.
"No-Hit Moss May Pitch in Syracuse." *Syracuse Herald-Journal*, 5 July 1944, 22.

Porter, G. L. "Same Teams to Play Benefit Game in Cleveland, Aug. 18." *Chicago Defender*, 15 August 1942, 19.
"Rain, Cold Halt Cleveland Bucks." *Chicago Defender*, 29 April 1950.
"St. Marys Again Is Scene of Negro Baseball Contest." *The Lima News*, 19 July 1948, 19.
"Sports Flashes." *The Zanesville Signal*, 17 June 1943, 11.
"Strong Negro League Teams Play Thursday." *Syracuse Herald-Journal*, 12 August 1947, 21.
"Tribe Fans: Are You Ready for Some Baseball?" *The Chronicle-Telegram*, 7 April 1998, D1.
"Two Ball Players Killed; Four Injured." *Chicago Defender*, 12 September 1942, 1.
"Visitors Win Nightcap After Buckeyes Gain 2–1 Victory on Controversial Decision." *Cleveland Call and Post*, 23 June 1945, 6B.
"We Are Ready." *Cleveland Call and Post*, 3 March 1945.
Wilks, Mo. "Unsung Heroes of the Diamond; Cleveland Buckeyes Deserve Their Place in City's Baseball History." *Cleveland Call and Post*, 11 February 2004.
Williams, Bob. "Brilliant Opening Games Show Greatness as Buckeyes Prepare for Clowns Sunday." *Cleveland Call and Post*, 2 June 1945, 6B.
_____. "Bucks, League Leaders, Have Home-Run King in Canizares, Cuban Shortstop Game-Saver." *Cleveland Call and Post*, 16 June 1945, 6B.
_____. "First Half Champs, Buckeyes Play Birmingham Barons for First Game This Season." *Cleveland Call and Post*, 14 July 1945.
_____. "Play Clowns in Twin Bill at League Park Sun; Buckeyes Play Stadium Tuesday Night." *Cleveland Call and Post*, 21 Jul 1945.
_____. "Vastly Improved Buckeyes Strong in Every Field, May Bring Out Fans 10,000 Strong." *Cleveland Call and Post*, 26 May 1945, 7B.

Cleveland Tate Stars

"Buckeyes Win 2 Games." *Chicago Defender*, 3 September 1921.
"Buffalo Stars' Hitting Stops Before Tates." *Chicago Defender*, 1 July 1922.
"Charleston Gets 2 Homers; A. B. C.'s Down Tates Twice." *Chicago Defender*, 1922.
"Cleveland Business Man Buys Tate's Baseball Park." *Chicago Defender*, 14 July 1923.
"Cleveland Tate Stars Join National League." *Chicago Defender*, 7 July 1923.
"Cleveland Team Will Play Here Monday." *The Chronicle-Telegram*, 20 May 1920.
"Detroit Stars Stop Tates, Pennant Aspirations, 8–2." *Chicago Defender*, 27 May 1922.
Dorsey, Allen Harrison. "Another Tate Baseball Co. Meeting." *The Cleveland Gazette*, 24 June 1922.
_____. "Prime Sport News." *The Cleveland Gazette*, 11 February 1922, 18 March 1922, 22 July 1922 and 9 September 1922.
_____. "Tates Beat Cubans." *The Cleveland Gazette*, 20 May 1922.
_____. "Tates Beaten Thrice." *The Cleveland Gazette*, 13 May 1922.
_____. "Trouble Looms Big for the Tate Stars." *The Cleveland Gazette*, 26 August 1922.
Heaphy, Leslie. "Cleveland Tate Stars." *Batting Four Thousand — Baseball in the Western Reserve*, Cleveland: SABR, 2008, 34–36.
"Hilldale Downs Tate Stars in Ten Inning Game 3–2." *Chicago Defender*, 12 August 1922.
"Indianapolis Swipes 2 Games from Cleveland." *Chicago Defender*, 18 August 1923.
"Indianapolis Takes Three Out of Four from Tates." *Chicago Defender*, 2 September 1922.
"Memphis Beats Tate Stars." *Chicago Defender*, 11 August 1923.
"Memphis Red Sox Beats Tate Stars by 5 to 1 Score." *Chicago Defender*, 4 August 1923.
"The New Treasurer of the Tate Baseball Co." *The Cleveland Gazette*, 28 January 1922.
"Oberlin Club Lost Game to Clevelanders." *The Chronicle-Telegram*, 10 September 1920.
"St. Louis Takes 2 from Cleveland." *Chicago Defender*, 5 July 1924.
"Single in 11th Gives 3–2 Game to Tate Stars." *Chicago Defender*, 7 July 1923.
"Tate Baseball Company Troubles." *The Cleveland Gazette*, 1 June 1922.

"Tate Stars." *Chicago Defender*, 26 March 1927.
"Tate Stars Are Here Sunday to Battle Fosters." *Chicago Defender*, 22 July 1922.
"Tate Stars Beat Chi. Giants." *Chicago Defender*, 18 June 1921.
"Tate Stars Beat Muhics." *Chicago Defender*, 31 May 1919.
"Tate Stars Nose Out Columbus Buckeyes." *Chicago Defender*, 25 June 1921.
"Tate Stars 6; Tellings 4." *Chicago Defender*, 29 April 1922.
"Tate Stars Split Even with A. B. C.'s in Double Bill." *Chicago Defender*, 22 September 1923.
"Tate Stars Split Even with Homestead Grays." *Chicago Defender*, 19 March 1923.
"Tate Stars Start Training." *Chicago Defender*, 12 April 1919.
"Tate Stars Surprise Fans; Win 2 from Kansas City." *Chicago Defender*, 27 August 1921.
"Tate Stars Tie Up the Cleveland City Series." *Chicago Defender*, 7 October 1922.
"Tate Stars to Build New Park in Cleveland." *Chicago Defender*, 19 March 1921, 6.
"Tate Stars to Play Oberlin A. C. Wednesday." *The Chronicle-Telegram*, 7 September 1920.
"Tate Stars Win Easily." *Chicago Defender*, 21 October 1922.
"Tate Stars Win 16-Inning Game off Sutherland." *Chicago Defender*, 13 August 1921.
"Tate Stars Win Two." *Chicago Defender*, 28 July 1923.
"Tate's Defeat Rogan in Last Half of Ninth." *Chicago Defender*, 22 July 1922.
"Tates, 4; Tellings 0." *Chicago Defender*, 22 April 1922.
"The Tates Out of the League." *The Cleveland Gazette*, 30 December 1922.
"Tate's Stars Lose." *Chicago Defender*, 28 June 1919.
"Tate's Stars Take Two from Pittsburgh Keystones." *Chicago Defender*, 11 June 1921.
"Tate's Stars to Build New Park in Cleveland." *Chicago Defender*, 19 March 1921.
"Tate's Stars Win Two Games from Connors." *Chicago Defender*, 15 July 1922.
"Tate's Take Series." *The Cleveland Gazette*, 29 April 1922.
"Tates Defeat Rogan in Last Half of Ninth." *Chicago Defender*, 22 July 1922.
"Tates Take Two Games." *Chicago Defender*, 14 July 1923.
"Tates Win First Game of Season." *Chicago Defender*, 17 May 1919.
"Tates Win Second." *Chicago Defender*, 3 June 1922.
"Two Run Rally in Ninth Wins for Tate Stars." *Chicago Defender*, 2 July 1921.

Doby, Larry

Ahlqvist, Eric. "Cooperstown's Main Event." *The Cooperstown Crier*, 23 July 1998.
Alvarado, Monsy. "Ceremony, Statue Tell Doby He's First in Paterson's Heart." *The Record* (Hackensack, NJ), 2 June 2002, A-4.
Amore, Dom. "Doby Was the Second, But Challenge No Less." *The Hartford Courant*, 15 April 1997, G2.
_____. "Historic Journey." *The Hartford Courant*, 15 April 1997, G4-G5.
_____. "Windup ... and the Pitch." *The Hartford Courant*, 15 April 1997.
Anderson, Dave. "A Pioneer's Hall of Fame Wife." *New York Times*, 26 July 2001, D2.
_____. "A Serious Statesman of the Game." *New York Times*, 20 June 2003.
Araton, Harvey. "Larry Doby Knew It Was About Home." *New York Times*, 24 June 2003, D1-D2.
"Ashburn, Doby Hall Favorites." *The Frederick News*, 7 March 1995, B-2.
"Bankhead, Doby, Campy, Robinson." *Our World*, April 1948, 46.
"Baseball Legend Doby Dies at 79." *Akron Beacon Journal*, 19 June 2003.
"Baseball Legend Larry Doby, First Black in American League, Selected for Hall of Fame." *Jet*, 23 March 1998.
"Baseball Pioneer Larry Doby Remembered During Memorial Service in New Jersey." *Jet*, 14 July 2003.
Beck, Peggy. "Working in the Shadows of Rickey and Robinson: Bill Veeck, Larry Doby and the Advancement of Black Players in Baseball." In *The Cooperstown Symposium on Baseball*. Ed. by Peter Rutkoff. Jefferson, NC: McFarland, 2000, 109–135.

Berkow, Ira. "The Might Have Been in Doby's Career." *New York Times*, 8 March 1998, 30.
Bodley, Hal. "Appreciation: Hall of Famer Larry Doby." *USA Today*, 20 June 2003.
_____. "Doby Was a Man Who Made a Difference." *USA Today*, 20 June 2003, 3C.
_____. "Doby's Way to Hall of Fame Had Obstacles." *USA Today*, 4 March 1998.
_____. "4 Baseball Veterans Selected." *USA Today*, 4 March 1998.
Burton, Nsenga. "Forgotten American Hero: Larry Doby." http://charlotte.creativeloafing.com/, 20 April 2010.
Casey, Michael. "Patersonians Get Set for Doby's Hall of Fame Day." *The Record* (Hackensack, NJ), 24 July 1998, L5.
_____. "Patience Pays Off for Larry Doby." *The Record* (Hackensack, NJ), 4 March 1998, A1, A7.
Chass, Murray. "Doby Again Follows Robinson." *New York Times*, 4 March 1998, C1.
"A Civil Rights Hall of Famer Too." *Newark Star-Ledger*, 4 August 2008.
Coutros, Evonne. "Hometown Hails Hall of Fame Hero." *The Record* (Hackensack, NJ) 5 June 1998, A-4.
Cowen, Richard. "Larry Doby: 1923–2003." *The Record* (Hackensack, NJ), 24 June 2003, A1, A10.
Crayton, Grover C. "Doby's Next Stop Is Cooperstown." *Cleveland Call and Post*, 7 July 1994, 1A, 6A.
Crowe, Chris. *Just as Good: How Larry Doby Changed America's Game*. Somerville, MA: Candlewick Press, 2012.
Cunningham, Laurie. "Doby's Contributions to Baseball, America Recalled in Paterson." *Herald News*, 2 June 2002.
Davidoff, Ken. "Second to None—American League His Stage, Doby Was Thrust into Pioneer Role." *The Record* (Bergen County, NJ), 6 July 1997.
"A Day to Remember Doby." *San Jose Mercury News*, 6 July 1997.
De Vries, Jack. "Doby's Historic Career Is Second to None." *USA Today Baseball Weekly*, 1 July 1992, 35.
Doby, Larry. "Pioneer Leagues." *Sporting News*, 4 March 1997, 47.
"Doby an All-star on Another Playing Field." *Akron Beacon Journal*, 10 July 1997.
"Doby Elected to Hall." *Washington Post*, 4 March 1998.
"Doby Finally Honored." *Ledger-Enquirer*, 6 July 1997.
"Doby Headed for Hall of Fame." *Daily Record* (Morris County, NJ), 4 March 1998, C4.
"Doby Is Named to Hall." *New York Times*, 4 March 1998.
"Doby, Known for Being No. 2, Also Made Important Firsts." *Seattle Times*, 22 June 2003.
"Doby Salutes Fans During Ceremony." *The State*, 6 July 1997.
"Doby, Sutton Enter Hall of Fame Today." *Washington Post*, 26 July 1998, D7.
"Doby Takes Center Stage." *Akron Beacon Journal*, 6 July 1997.
"Doby's Rightful Recognition." *Chicago Tribune*, 4 March 1998.
"Doby's Way to Hall of Fame Had Obstacles." *USA Today*, 4 March 1998.
Dolgan, Bob. "Doby's Passing Can't Dim Images of a Tribe Hero." *Cleveland Plain Dealer*, 20 June 2003.
_____. "Tribe Great Larry Doby Dies." *Cleveland Plain Dealer*, 19 June 2003.
Editorial. "Larry Doby." *Cleveland Plain Dealer*, 20 June 2003.
Evans, Howie. "Bob Douglas Hall of Fame to Induct 3 Legends." *New York Amsterdam News*, 3 June 1995.
"Fifty Years Later, Doby Waits for Call from Hall." *USA Today Baseball Weekly* (4–10 March 1998).
"Finally Doby Gets His Due." *Tacoma News Tribune*, 4 March 1998.
Gildea, William. "Doby Elected to Hall." *The Washington Post*, 4 March 1998, C1, C5.
Ginnetti, Toni. "Veterans Send Doby to Hall." *Chicago Sun-Times*, 4 March 1998, 132.
Goodnight, Lisa. "A Fitting Tribute to the ... Silk City Slugger." *The Record*, 26 September 1997, C1, C8.
Gross, Larry. "Hall of Famer Doby Mourned." *Chicago Defender*, 21 June 2003, 48.
"Hall, Former Teammates Praise Doby." *Chicago Sun Times*, 20 June 2003, 162.
"Hall of Fame Remembers Doby." http://baseballhalloffame.org, 19 June 2003.

Hill, Justice B. "Doby, AL's First Black Player Dies." http://www.mlb.com, 19 June 2003.
_____. "Living to Tell About It." MLB.com, 10 June 2011.
_____. "Remembering a True Pioneer." http://www.mlb.com, 19 June 2003.
Holtzman, Jerome. "Doby's Rightful Recognition." *Chicago Tribune*, 4 March 1998.
Holway, John. "Rogan, Doby Receive Their Due." *Baseball America*, 30 March–12 April 1998.
"Honorable Mentions for Doby." *Newark Star-Ledger*, 7 July 1997.
"Honoring a Baseball Hero." *Chicago Sun-Times*, 20 June 2003, 43.
Hoynes, Paul. "Larry Doby Was 'Keystone' to Team's History, Says Dolan." *Cleveland Plain Dealer*, 19 June 2003.
_____. "Larry Doby's Pioneering Role with Tribe, American League Recognized." *Cleveland Plain Dealer*, 6 July 2012.
Hunt, Donald. "Baseball Great Doby Receives Postage Stamp." *Philadelphia Tribune*, 5 April 2012.
Hurd, Rick. "Why is Baseball Ignoring Doby?" *Inside Bay Area*, 8 July 2007.
"Importance of Being Second." *The Sunday Record* (NJ), 8 March 1998.
"Indians Honor Hall of Famer Larry Doby, Rename Eagle Avenue." Associated Press, 11 July 2012.
"Indians to Honor Hall of Famer, Groundbreaker Larry Doby with New Street Friday." http://ballparkbiz.wordpress.com/, 5 July 2012.
"Indians to Honor Larry Doby's Legacy." *AP*, 11 May 2007.
"Into Halls of Fame and Second Centuries." *New York Times*, 8 March 1998.
Izenberg, Jerry. "Doby's Dream Still Alive in a Paterson Field." *The Star-Ledger* (Newark, NJ), 31 May 2002, 51.
_____. "Hall Selection Caps Doby's Hard Journey." *The Star-Ledger* (Newark, NJ), 4 March 1998, 1, 12.
_____. "Isn't It Time Hall of Fame Invited Doby?" *The Star-Ledger* (Newark, NJ), 22 February 1998.
_____. "Larry Doby Should Be Honored by Newark." http:blog.nj.com/izenberg_impact/print.html, 7 July 2012.
_____. "Learning to Fly with Eagles." *The Star-Ledger* (Newark, NJ), 4 March 1998, 49, 55.
_____. "Strength and Dignity Delivered Doby to Greatness." *Newark Star-Ledger*, 19 June 2003.
"Jackie, Roy, Doby Homer." *Chicago Defender*, 30 April 1949, 14.
Jackson, John. "Forgotten Doby Will Be Remembered." *Chicago Sun-Times*, 27 June 2003, 169.
Johnson, Paul. "Helyn Doby, 76, Wife of Baseball Star." *The Record* (Hackensack, NJ), 25 July 2001.
Johnson, Paul H. "Pride Against Prejudice — Negro Leagues Find a Home at Yogi Berra Museum." *The Record* (Bergen County, NJ), 1 January 2003.
Kaegel, Dick. "'A Pioneer of a Man.'" *Kansas City Star*, 22 June 2003.
Kekis, John. "Doby, Sutton Finally Take Their Place in Hall." *Albany Times-Union*, 27 July 1998, D1, D7.
Kelly, Mike. "Importance of Being Second." *The Sunday Record* (Hackensack, NJ), 8 March 1998, 8 March 1998.
Klapisch, Bob. "Quiet Leader Voted into Hall of Fame." *The Record* (Hackensack, NJ), 4 March 1998, A1, A7.
Kleinknecht, Merl F. "Doby, Lawrence Eugene 'Larry.'" In *Biographical Dictionary of American Sports, Baseball*. Ed. by David L. Porter. Westport, CT: Greenwood Press, 2000, 393–395.
Koenig, Bill. "Fifty Years Later, Doby Waits for Call from Hall." *USA Today Baseball Weekly*, 4–10 March 1998.
_____. "MacPhail Followed Footsteps to Shrine." *USA Today Baseball Weekly*, 11–17 March 1998, 9.
"Larry Doby, American League's First Black Baseball Player, Dies at His New Jersey Home." *Jet*, 7 July 2003.
"Larry Doby Day." *Program*. 1 June 2002, Paterson, New Jersey.
"Larry Doby Exhibit at the Paterson Museum." *Bergen County Shopper*, 10 September 1997, 18 and in *Suburban News* (Bergen County, NJ), 10 December 1997.
"Larry Doby Faced Biggest Uphill Battle." *Cleveland Plain Dealer*, 19 June 2003.
"Larry Doby, Second to One." *New York Daily News*, 19 June 2003.

"Larry Doby, 79, Breaker of a Baseball Color Barrier Dies." *New York Times*, 19 June 2003.
"Law Renames State Route 120 for Baseball's Larry Doby." *The Sun Record*, 7 September 1997, A8.
"Lawmakers Act to Name Post Office for Baseball Great Doby." *The Record* (Hackensack, NJ), 25 February 1998.
"Learning to Fly with Eagles." *Newark Star-Ledger*, 4 March 1998.
Leonard, Tim. "The Glory of His Time." *The Sunday Record*, 26 July 1998, S1, S8.
Lowitt, Bruce. "Doby Excelled Despite Playing in Robinson's Shadow." TBO.com, 3 July 2007.
McClean, Tony. "14 Things You Should Know About Larry Doby." www.blackathlete.net, 8 July 2007.
McGrath, John. "Finally, Doby Gets His Due." *Tacoma News Tribune*, 4 March 1998, C1, C5.
McShane, Larry. "The Best Team You Never Saw: Newark's Eagles." AP Online, 28 May 1998.
Madden, Bill. "Following Fame-ous Footsteps." *New York Daily News*, 4 March 1998.
_____. "Yogi Remembers Happier Times with Doby." *New York Daily News*, 19 June 2003.
Maraniss, David. "Stepping Out of the Shadow." *Washington Post*, 8 July 1997, A1.
Mattura, Greg. "Best of the Best." *The Record*, 14 September 2003.
Menna, Larry K. "Doby, Larry." In *Encyclopedia of Ethnicity and Sports in The United States of America*. Eds. George Kirsch et al. Westport, CT: Greenwood Press, 2000, 133–134.
Moore, Acel. "Overshadowed by Some But Second to None, Doby Finally Gets His Due." *The Philadelphia Inquirer*, 5 March 1998, A21.
Moore, Joseph Thomas. "Heroics of '48 Left Lasting Impression." *Herald and News*, 26 July 1998.
_____. *Pride Against Prejudice: The Biography of Larry Doby*. Westport, CT: Greenwood Press, 1988.
Muder, Craig. "Waiting Ends for Doby, Sutton." *Observer-Dispatch* (Utica, NY), 27 July 1998, 1C, 3C.
"Negro Leaguer Heads to Cooperstown." *The Times Herald-Record*, 5 June 1998, 20.
"The Next One." *Sports Illustrated*, 20 June 2003, 24.
Niebart, Mike. "Doby Enters Hall with Pride." *Herald and News*, 27 July 1998, B1-B2.
_____. "Hall of Fame Will No Longer Overlook Larry Doby." *Herald and News*, 26 July 1998, A1, A11.
Noone, Mary. "Museum Honors Hometown Hero." *Herald and News*, 26 September 1997, C1, C4.
O'Toole, Andrew. "In the Shadow of No Man: Larry Doby." In *The Best Man Plays, Major League Baseball and the Black Athlete, 1901–2002*. Jefferson, NC: McFarland, 2003, 54–73.
"Overshadowed by Some But Second to None, Doby Finally Gets His Due." *Philadelphia Inquirer*, 5 March 1998.
"Paige, Doby, Minoso Here May 13, 15." *Chicago Defender*, 14 May 1949, 14.
"Paterson Museum Celebrates Larry Doby." *Herald and News*, 22 September 1997, A3.
"Patience Pays Off for Larry Doby." *The Record* (Hackensack, NJ), 4 March 1998.
Politi, Steve. "Doby Recalled as a Hall of Famer in Life." *Newark Star-Ledger*, 24 June 2003.
Quick, David. "Remembering Larry Doby." *Santa Monica Mirror* (12–18 April 2007).
"Quiet Leader Voted into Hall of Fame." *The Record* (Hackensack, NJ), 4 March 1998.
Reaves, Joseph. "Larry Doby: Proud to Bat Second." *The Arizona Republic*, 5 July 2007.
Reilly, Edward J. "Doby, Lawrence Eugene." In *Baseball: An Encyclopedia of Popular Culture*. Santa Barbara, CA: ABC-CLIO, 2000, 83.
Robinson, Bill. "Camden Makes Pitch to Honor Larry Doby." http://www.thestate.com 5 July 2002.
_____. "Doby Remains in Robinson's Shadow." *The Record*, 16 April 1997, S-5.
Rosenbaum, Dave. "Museum Honors Baseball's Larry Doby." *The Shopper News*, 12 November 1997.
Rundles, Jim. "NL's Larry Doby Finally Gets His Due." *Jackson Advocate*, 30 July–5 August 1998.
"Seven Inducted into Hall." *Washington Post*, 27 July 1998, C8.
Slear, Tom. "Larry Doby Hit for His Own Triple Crown in 1947 — Dignity." *Sports History*, 8 January 1995, 54, 56.
Smith, Claire. "Hard Work, Hard Times Lifted Sutton and Doby." *New York Times*, 27 July 1998, C1, C4.
_____. "Larry Doby, Who Broke a Color Barrier, Dies at 79." *New York Times*, 20 June 2003.

_____. "Thrown a Curve Again but He's Hanging in There." *New York Times*, 9 November 1997, 1, 5.
Smith, Red. "From Jim Crow to Cooperstown." *New York Times*, 14 February 1978, 44.
_____. "Larry Doby, Manager-in-Waiting." *New York Times*, 30 September 1974.
_____. "The Outcasts of Cooperstown." *New York Times*, 27 July 1977, 39.
Spencer, Lyle. "Doby's Numbers, Attitude Speak Volumes." MLB.com, 5 July 2007.
Spink, J.G. Taylor. "Doby's Play Makes Eagles Scream." *The Sporting News*, 20 October 1948, 2.
Stewart, Mike. "'Don't Forget Larry Doby.'" *Canton Repository*, 19 June 2003, A1, A11.
_____. "Hall of Famer Doby Dead at 79." *Chicago Sun-Times*, 19 June 2003, 139.
"Two Generations Removed, Indians Reflect on Doby's Legacy." *Cleveland Plain Dealer*, 20 June 2003.
Vanderberg, Bob. "Doby Passes On, but Memories Remain Vivid." *Chicago Tribune*, 20 June 2003, Sect. 4, 2.
Vincent, Fay. "Larry Doby Played with Dignity and without Bitterness." *New York Times*, 22 June 2003.
Walker, Ben. "Doby Helped Pave Way." *USA Today*, 19 June 2003.
_____. "Veterans Send Four to Hall." *The Record* (Hackensack, NJ), 4 March 1998.
"When Doby Made His Mark." *North Jersey Herald News*, 8 July 2007.
Whiteside, Larry. "Finally, There May Be Deserved Fame for Doby." *The Boston Globe*, 3 March 1998.

Integration

Adelson, Bruce. *Brushing Back Jim Crow, The Integration of Minor-League Baseball in the American South*. Charlottesville: University Press of Virginia, 1999.
Andrews, William. "Once Upon a Time in Atlanta." *The Chattachoochee Review* 18 (Winter 1998), 78.
"Another Branch Rickey Is Needed." *Newport Daily News*, 2 May 1974.
"Anti-Jim Crow Campaign Raches a New Stage." *Daily Worker*, 18 April 1945.
Armour, Mark. "The Effects of Integration, 1947–1986." In the *Baseball Research Journal*. Cleveland, OH: SABR, 2007.
"Ball Fan's Cure for Cellaritis; Use Negro Talent." *Chicago Defender*, 20 May 1950, 16.
Barber, Red. *1947— When All Hell Broke Loose in Baseball*. New York: Doubleday, 1982.
"Baseball Solons Deplore Attitude of Press Toward Organized League Set-up." *Norfolk Journal and Guide*, 26 March 1938, 18.
Baulch, Vivian, and Patricia Zacharias. "The Day the Tigers Finally Integrated." *The Detroit News*, 16 April 1997.
"Big League Magnate Believes Negro Baseball Has Future." *Indianapolis Recorder*, 6 August 1932, 2.
Blanchard, Jon Todd. "Negro Leagues Set Stage to Majors." *Freeman's Journal* (Kingston, NY), Summer 1990, 20–21.
Bleske, Glen, and Chris Lamb. "Covering the Integration of Baseball — A Look Back." *Editor and Publisher* 130 (No. 4), 27 January 1996.
"Bradley Wants Negroes in Organized Baseball." *Norfolk Journal and Guide*, 26 March 1938, 19.
"Breaking the Barrier One by One." *New York Times*, 15 April 1997, B15.
Briley, Ron. "The Limits of Baseball Integration." *Northern Louisiana Historical Association Journal* 28 (Fall 1997), 153–162.
Carroll, Brian. "Mediocrity Under Pressure: The Integration of the Cubs as Covered by the Chicago Defender." In *Northsiders: Essays on the History and Culture of the Cubs*. Eds. Gerald C. Wood and Andrew Hazucha. Jefferson, NC: McFarland, 2008.
"Celebrating the End of Segregated Baseball." *The Economist*, 18 January 1997, 81–82.
Center, Bill. "Integration Was Not Robinson Alone." *San Diego Union-Tribune*, 7 May 2006.

Clement, Rufus. "Racial Integration in the Field of Sports." *The Journal of Negro Education*, Vol. 23 (Sum. 1954), 222–230.
"Cleveland to Consider Negro Players." *Daily Worker*, 29 July 1942.
Clifton, Meritt. "Quebec Loop Broke Color Line in 1935." *Baseball Research Journal* #13 (1984), 67–68.
Collier, Gene. "Integrating Majors Death Knell for Black Baseball." *Pittsburgh Post Gazette*, 9 July 2006.
Cooper, Tony. "Ending Baseball's All-White Bastion in Boston." *San Francisco Chronicle*, 23 February 1993.
Corliss, Richard. "April 15, 1947: Breaking the Color Line." *Time*, 31 March 2003.
Daly, Steve. *Dem Little Bums: The Nashua Dodgers.* Concord, NH: Plaidswede Publishing, 2002.
Davis, F. M. "Honus Wagner Denies 'Color Bar' by Semi-Pro Teams in Tourney." *Pittsburgh Courier*, 31 July 1937, 16.
Deardorff, Donald L. II. "The Black Press Played a Key Role in Integrating Baseball." *St. Louis Journalism Review* 23 (No. 168), July-August 1994.
Dodson, Daniel. "The Integration of Negroes in Baseball." *Journal of Educational Sociology* 28 (October 1954): 73–82. http://dx.doi.org/10.2307/2263823
Early, Gerald. "Integration, Black Heroism and the Meaning of Jackie Robinson." *The Chronicle of Higher Education.* 23 May 1997.
Egan, Dave. "What About Trio Seeking Red Sox Tryout?" *Boston Daily Record*, 16 April 1945.
Fenster, Kenneth R. "Earl Mann, Nat Peeples, and the Failed Attempt of Integration in the Southern Association." *Nine* (Spring 2004), 73–101.
Fetter, Henry D. "From 'Stooge' to 'Czar': Judge Landis, the *Daily Worker* and the Integration of Baseball." *American Communist History* (2007), 29–63. http://dx.doi.org/10.1080/147438 90701400811
Finkelstein, Sydney, and Craig Urch. "Analysis of the Red Sox Case." Tuck School of Business, Dartmouth College, 2001.
_____. "The Boston Red Sox and the Integration of African American Players." Tuck School of Business, Dartmouth College, 2001.
"First Negro Plays in Organized Ball in Southern State." *Nevada State Journal*, 10 May 1951, 9.
Fitzpatrick, Frank. "Integration Dreams Deferred by Phillies." *Philadelphia Inquirer*, 13 July 2004, E01.
"The Flaws in the Diamonds: Celebrating the End of Segregated Baseball." *The Economist*, 18 January 1997, 81–82.
Gelman, Steve. "You Could Almost Have a Negro All Star Game." *Sport*, February 1960, 48–49.
Gorman, Bob. "David Mobley and the Rock Hill Chiefs: The Jackie Robinson of South Carolina." *The National Pastime* (2001), 51.
Grayson, Harry. "Negro Stars Would Click in Majors." *The Lowell Sun*, 25 July 1942, 7.
Gross, Milton. "Baseball's Negroes Facing Brighter Spring." *Chicago American* (December 1961), 3–23.
Heller, Dick. "Writer Sam Lacy Played Key Part Integrating Baseball." *The Washington Times*, 12 May 2003.
Hepburn, Dave. "Doin' What Comes Naturally." *Sportlife*, 1 June 1952, 15–17.
_____. "The Jackpot Boys." *Our World*, September 1948, 30–33.
Hill, Justice B. "Sportswriters Key in Integration." www.MLB.com, 11 April 2007.
Hoekstra, Dave. "Comets Forever Flying High." *Chicago Sun-Times*, 6 August 2000, 4A.
Integration File. Research Library, National Baseball Hall of Fame and Museum, Cooperstown, New York.
Ivy, Darren. *Untold Stories: Black Sport Heroes Before Integration.* Little Rock, AK: Wehco Publishing, 2002.
Jordan, David M., Larry Gerlach and John P. Rossi. "A Baseball Myth Exploded." *The National Pastime*, 17 (1998), 3–13.
Kanter, Mark. "Red Sox Break the Mold in 1967." In *The Northern Game and Beyond, Baseball in New England and Canada.* Cleveland: SABR, 2002, 11–12.

Keane, Cliff. "Robinson's Day with Sox Told." *Boston Daily Globe*, 29 April 1959.
Kennedy, Joseph S. "The Flip Side of Integration." *The Philadelphia Inquirer*, 11 July 2004, L4.
Kenyon College. *The Integration of Baseball Conference and Web Site.* April 2001.
King, Colbert I. "Race and Baseball in D.C." *Washington Post*, 2 April 2005.
Kleinknecht, Merl. "Integration of Baseball After World War II." *Baseball Research Journal* 12 (1983): 100–106.
Knee, Stuart. "Jim Crow Strikes Out: Branch Rickey and the Struggle for Integration in American Baseball." *Sport in Society* (October 2003), 71–87.
LaGuardia, Fiorella. Papers on Committee on Baseball. Municipal Archives, New York, New York.
Lamb, Chris, and Bleske, Glen. "Covering the Integration of Baseball—A Look Back." *Editor and Publisher*, 27 January 1996, 48–50.
_____. "The Road to October 23, 1945: The Press and the Integration of Baseball." *Nine* (Fall 1997), 46–68.
_____. "A Story in Black and White: Baseball and Racism in 1938." In *Cooperstown Symposium 1997*. Eds. Alvin L. Hall and Peter Rutkoff. Jefferson, NC: McFarland, 2000.
_____. "What's Wrong with Baseball.: The *Pittsburgh Courier* and the Beginning of Its Campaign to Integrate the National Pastime." *The Western Journal of Black Studies* (2002), 189–192.
Liscio, Stephanie. *Integrating Cleveland Baseball.* Jefferson, NC: McFarland, 2010.
"Marcantonio Asks Study on Negroes." *New York Times*, 25 April 1945, 28.
Massaquoi, Hans. "The Breakthrough Stars." *Ebony* Vol. 47 (August 1992), 44+.
Mayo, Jonathan. "MiLB.com Honors Black History Month." *MLB.com*, 1 February 2006.
McLaurin, Jeff. "State Assembly Honors 'Pioneers of Integration.'" *Daily Gazette* (Schenectady, NY), 5 June 1996.
Nance, Roscoe. "Integrating 'Ho-hum' Basketball Was Much Easier." *USA Today*, 16 April 1997, 11C.
"Negro Ball Stars Are Touted for Big League Jobs." *Reno Evening Gazette*, 30 July 1942, 10.
"Negro Leagues Resent Raids, McPhail Says." *Washington Post*, 28 July 1942, 19.
"Negro Leagues: The Ones We Would Have Missed." *Pittsburgh Post Gazette*, 9 July 2006.
"Negro Owners Do Not Want Clubs Raided." *Dallas Morning News*, 28 July 1942.
"Negro Trio Works Out Under Coach Hugh Duffy of Red Sox." *Boston Herald*, 17 April 1945.
"Negroes Crash 'Last Barrier'—Base Ball." *Detroit News*, 24 October 1945, 21.
"Negroes Rejected by Minor Leagues." *New York Times*, 24 February 1948, 30.
"New York Daily Mirror, in Editorial, Suggests Policy." *Indianapolis Recorder*, 11 February 1933, 2.
"98-Year-Old Ex-Red Helped Change Baseball." *Cincinnati Post*, 6 September 2000.
Ostenby, Peter M. *Other Games; Other Glory: The Memphis Red Sox and the Trauma of Integration, 1948–55.* M.A. Thesis, UNC–Chapel Hill, 1989.
Padilla, Emmanuel. "Baseball Still Lacks Blacks in Major Leagues." Bay Area Multicultural Media Academy, 23 June 2005.
Pendleton, Jason. "Jim Crow Strikes Out: Interracial Baseball in Wichita Kansas, 1920 1935." In *Baseball History From Outside the Lines, A Reader*. Ed. John E. Dreifort. Lincoln: University of Nebraska Press, 2001.
"Perhaps Opera Points Way to Nation's Game." *Indianapolis Recorder*, 5 August 1933, 2.
"Phils Willing to Sign Negroes." *Daily Worker*, 31 July 1942.
"Pirates to Host Annual African American Heritage Weekend." *Pittsburgh.pirates.mlb.com*, 8 August 2006.
Povich, Shirley. "There Are No More Shutouts of Negro Players." *Washington Post*, 23 May 1953, 13.
Pringle, Kenneth. "Landis, Robeson, and Robinson." *Sportsjones Newsletter*, 1 March 2001.
"Race." In *Slocum's Stories.* Frank E. Slocum. White Plains, NY: Bernard C. Harris, 1993, 13–21.
"Raiding Negro Loops Scored by Branham." *Dallas Morning News*, 26 October 1945.
Rea, E. B. "From the Press Box." *Norfolk Journal and Guide*, 22 January 1938, 18. Lacy's views on integration of baseball.
"Red Sox Coaches Look Over 3 Negro Players." *Boston Daily Globe*, 17 April 1945.

Reese, R. "The Socio-Political Context of the Integration of Sport in America." *Journal of African American Men* (Spring 1999).
Report of the Mayor's Committee on Baseball to Mayor F.H. LaGuardia, 31 October 1945. Negro League Files Bl.1371.70b. National Baseball Hall of Fame and Museum, Cooperstown, New York.
Rhoden, William C. "Baseball — Japan." *New York Times*, 18 August 2001, D1. Story about the Negro Leagues in the 1950s and '60s and comparing that to Japanese baseball today as their players are being drafted.
Robinson, Alan. "Blacks Broke Back of Baseball Racial Barrier." *Chicago Sun Times*, 6 October 1988, 18–19.
Rowe, Gail, and John S. Phillips. "T. H. Murnane and the Mysterious 'Darkhue White.'" In *The Northern Game and Beyond, Baseball in New England and Canada*. Cleveland: SABR, 2002, 12–15.
Rubinstein, William D. "Jackie Robinson and the Integration of Major League Baseball." *History Today*, 1 September 2003.
Ruck, Rob. "Integration Didn't Include Black Executives." *Baseball America*, 25 July 1990, 4.
Rusinack, Kelly Elaine. "Baseball on the Radical Agenda." Conference Presentation Paper. National Baseball Hall of Fame and Library, Cooperstown, New York.
Sanchez, Robert. "When Teams Integrated, Denver Pitched In." *The Denver Post*, 10 December 2004.
Scheel, Eugene. "Young Manager Took Bold Step Toward Integration." *Washington Post*, 3 August 2003.
"Segregation No Problem to Baseball Now." *New York Herald Tribune*, 4 April 1965, 7.
"Semi-Pro Baseball Drops Color Bar." *Chicago Defender*, 15 December 1945, 1.
Sherwood, John. "Recalling the Days of Baseball Apartheid." *The Journal* (Washington, DC), 16 February 1990, B1, B8.
Shropshire, Kenneth L. "Where Have You Gone, Jackie Robinson? Integration in America in the 21st Century." *Texas Law Review* (1997) 1043+.
Simon, Scott. *Jackie Robinson and the Integration of Baseball*. Hoboken, NJ: J. Wiley & Sons, 2002.
Smith, Wendell. "Red Sox Candidates Waiting to Hear from Management." *Pittsburgh Courier*, 28 April 1945.
_____. "Red Sox Consider Negroes." *Pittsburgh Courier*, 21 April 1945.
Snyder, Brad. *Beyond the Shadow of the Senators: The Untold Story of the Homestead Grays and the Integration of Baseball*. Chicago: Contemporary Books, 2003.
"Sound Basis Urged for Negro Leagues." *New York Times*, 21 January 1946, 29.
Spivey, Donald. "End of Jim Crow in Sports: The Protest at NYU, 1940–41." *Journal of Sport History* 15, Winter 1988.
Starks, Charles A. "Negro Baseball Breaking Down the Race Prejudice." *St. Louis Argus*, 1922.
Stone, Larry. "The Struggle to Integrate Baseball — 50 Years after Jackie Robinson Broke Color Barrier, Many Believe Progress in Minority Hiring Has Been Slow." *Seattle Times*, 13 April 1997.
Stout, Glenn. "Diamonds Aren't Forever." In *The Northern Game and Beyond, Baseball in New England and Canada*. Cleveland: SABR, 2002, 8–11.
Sullivan, Neil J. "Baseball and Race: The Limits of Competition." *The Journal of Negro History* (Sum. 1998) 168–77.
Swaine, Rick. *The Black Stars Who Made Baseball Whole*. Jefferson, NC: McFarland, 2006.
Taylor, Tony. "Touching All the Bases: The History of Integration in Professional Baseball in Shreveport." *North Louisiana Historical Association Journal* 15 (Winter 1984), 23–29.
Thorn, John, and Jules Tygiel. "The Signing of Jackie Robinson: The Untold Story." *Sport* (June 1988), 65–70.
"Three Negroes Given Workout by Red Sox." *Boston Evening Globe*, 16 April 1945.
Threston, Christopher. *The Integration of Baseball in Philadelphia*. Jefferson, NC: McFarland, 2002.
Tibbetts, John. "Breaking the Barrier." *World and I*, Vol. 8, Issue 2 (February 1993).
"Tri-State Has First Negro." *Statesville Daily Record*, 27 August 1952.

Treder, Steve. "A Legacy of What-Ifs: Horace Stoneham and the Integration of the Giants." *Nine* (Spring 2002), 71–107. http://dx.doi.org/10.1353/nin.2002.0023
Trudeau, Christian. "Integration in Quebec: More Than Jackie." In *Dominion Ball, Baseball Above the 49th*. Cleveland: SABR, 2005, 23–24.
"Tryouts in Pittsburgh Promised by Pirate Owner." *Daily Worker*, 28 July 1942.
Urch, Craig, and Sydney Finkelstein. "The Boston Red Sox and the Integration of African American Players." In *The Northern Game and Beyond, Baseball in New England and Canada*. Eds. Mark Kanter et al. Cleveland: SABR, 2002, 5–7.
Vollrath, Amanda. "Breaking Barriers in American Sports." *The Dog Street Journal*, 11 February 2006.
Williams, Bob. "Marcantonio Asks Commerce Department to Investigate Practices of Baseball Clubs in Employment." *Cleveland Call and Post*, 5 May 1945.
Wojnowski, Bob. "The Cost of Integration." *The Detroit News*, 14 April 1997, 1D, 6D.
"Yankees Won't Use Negro Baseball Players, Col. MacPhail Tells Mayor." *New York Age*, 22 September 1945.
Young, A. S. "Doc." "Negro Baseball Fights Bravely for Life Against Big Odds." *The Sporting News*, 7 August 1957.
Zimmerman, Jack. "Integration of Baseball Was No Easy Task." *The Lemont Metropolitan* (Illinois), 17 April 1997.

Irvin, Monte

"Baseball Legend Turns Back the Clock." *Seguin Daily News*, 10 February 2004, 5.
"Brooklyn Ready to Release Negro If Under Contract." *The Post-Standard*, 13 January 1949, 11.
Casiano, Jonathan. "Now Fielding Tributes." *The Star-Ledger*, 17 May 2006.
Chase, Chris. "'Smokey' Joe Remembered." *The Gazette Enterprise*, 10 February 2004.
Coscia, John. "Giant Honor." *Citrus County Chronicle*, 26 August 2007.
"Daguerreotypes." *The Sporting News*, 1 January 1990, 23–24.
Day, Leon, Todd Bolton, Lee Sherman, Jerry Cohen, Monte Irvin and Neal Leister. WCBM Baltimore Radio, Hieronimus & Co., February 1992. Baltimore, Maryland.
DeFilippo, Lauren. "Park Is Renamed for Irvin." *Essex Journal*, 18 May 2006, B1.
Forman, Ross. "Baseball Hall of Famer Goes to Bat for Former Negro Leaguers." *Sports Collectors Digest*, 22 March 1991, 64.
"Giants Sign Negro Pair for Jersey City Farm." *Post-Standard*, 29 January 1949.
Green, Paul. "Interview with Monte Irvin." *Sports Collectors Digest*, 16 September 1983, 42–50.
Hall, Gregory. "Baseball's Past Lives On." *The Courier-Journal*, 17 February 2005.
"Hall of Famer in Waukegon Today." *Suburban Chicago News*, 3 March 2007.
"Hall of Famer Irvin to Visit Yogi Museum." *The Montclair Times*, 6 September 2007.
Horn, Barry. "Black Star Had Talent to Be First." *The Dallas Morning News*, 10 April 1997, 1B.
Huard, Kevin. "SCD Interviews Hall of Fame Great Monte Irvin." *Sports Collectors Digest*, 22 March 1991, 80–82.
Idelson, Jeff. "Monte Irvin Shares His Thoughts." *Memories and Dreams* (May–June 2006), 12.
Irvin, Monte. Interview by Bill Marshall, 12 May 1977. Interview 77OH29 Chan 31, transcript. A.B. Chandler Oral History Project, University of Kentucky Library, Lexington, Kentucky.
Irvin, Monte. Interview by J.R. Wright, 1968. Private collection, Kalamazoo, Michigan.
Irvin, Monte. "The Time of a Lifetime." *Sports Illustrated*, 19 July 1993, 106.
Irvin, Monte, with James A. Riley. *Monte Irvin: Nice Guys Finish First*. New York: Carroll and Graf, 1996.
"Irvin, Monte." Negro League Baseball Players Association. http://www.nlbpa.com/the-athletes/irvine-monte.
Izenberg, Jerry. "Irvin Always Safe at Home." *The Star-Ledger*, 14 May 2006.

Jones, Gordie. "Irvin Doesn't Dwell on Life's What-Ifs." *The Morning Call*, 13 April 2007.
Kirkland, Kevin. "Former Negro Leagues Standout, Author Coming to Town to Speak at Event." *Pittsburgh Post-Gazette*, 13 July 2007.
"The Man: Monte Irvin." *Black Sports*, 21 July 1971, 21.
Martin, Douglas. "Irvin, Monford Merrill 'Monte.'" In *Biographical Dictionary of American Sports, Baseball*. Ed. David l. Porter. Westport, CT: Greenwood Press, 2000, 725–727.
"Memories." *Sport* (February 1994), 18.
Mizell, Hubert. "Monte Irvin Enters Hall of Fame Despite Rule That Kept Him Out of Baseball Until 30." *The Gettysburg Times*, 8 February 1973, 13.
"Monte Irvin." In *Baseball, The Biographical Encyclopedia*. Ed. David Pietrusza, Matthew Silverman, and Michael Gershman. Kingston, NY: Total Sports Publishing, 2000, 543.
Moore, Jack. "Monte Irvin: Up from Sharecropping." In *Jackie Robinson: Race, Sports, and the American Dream*. Eds. Joseph Dorinson and Joram Warmund. Armonk, NY: M.E. Sharpe, 1998: 30–40.
"Negro Leaguer Heads to Cooperstown." *The Times Herald-Record*, 5 June 1998, 20.
O'Neil John, Phil Dixon, Monte Irvin, Roy Campanella, Jimmie Crutchfield and Ann Hicks. United Talk Radio Network, Hieronimus & Co., February 1992. Baltimore, Maryland.
"Pittsburgh and the Negro Leagues: Howard Elson, Rob Ruck, Monte Irvin, Wilmer Fields and Dick Clark." KDKA Radio. 28 February 1990. Pittsburgh, Pennsylvania.
Porter, David. "Monte Irvin, Other Newark Baseball Greats Honored." *Associated Press*, 14 September 2007.
Posnanski, Joe. "A Legend Alone." *Kansas City Star*, 16 January 2004, D1, D9.
Reilly, Edward J. "Irvin, Monford." In *Baseball, An Encyclopedia of Popular Culture*. Santa Barbara, CA: ABC-CLIO, 2000, 140–42.
True, Frank C. "Baseball's Giant Killers." *Negro Digest* (July 1951), 58–62.
Watt, Richard. "Monte Irvin: Negro League All-Stars." *Sport*, February 1994, 18+.
Westcott, Rich. "Monte Irvin, Champion of Racial Equality." In *Splendor on the Diamond*. Gainesville: University Press of Florida, 2000, pp. 27–35.

Philadelphia Stars

"Auscos Take on Philadelphia Stars Here Tonight." *The Herald-Press*, 1 July 1952.
"Baltimore, Philly Stars Break Even." *Pittsburgh Courier*, 3 July 1943.
"Barney Brown Silences Grays' Big Guns as Philly Wins, 12–2." *Pittsburgh Courier*, 12 June 1943.
"Bob Katz to Hurl Against NAL Members." *St. Joseph Herald-Press*, 1 July 1952, 12.
Brown, Jim. "Philadelphia Celebrating the Philadelphia Stars and Its Negro League Baseball History." *The Fan's View* (April 2005).
"Cubs Play Noted Negro Team Tonight." *The Sedalia Democrat*, 18 May 1950, 11.
"Engage Philly Stars Tonight in Exhibition." *The Herald-Press*, 16 June 1949, 12.
"Falcons Will Play Negro '9.'" *Oshkosh Daily Northwestern*, 19 August 1952, 20.
Hochman, Stan. "Five Surviving Philly Stars, Negro Leagues to be Honored Finally." *Philadelphia Daily News*, 3 August 2004.
"K. C. Monarchs, Philly Stars to Play Here." *Dallas Morning News*, 26 June 1952.
Kram, Mark. "Stars Are Out Again." *Philadelphia Daily News*, 18 October 2004.
"Negro Nines Clash at Stadium Today." *Washington Post*, 10 June 1934, 17.
"Negro Pro Teams Meet at Burnett." *Dallas Morning News*, 6 July 1949.
"Negro Pro Teams Play this Week." *Dallas Morning News*, 3 July 1949.
"Nicetown Blanks the Stars." *Philadelphia Inquirer*, 31 July 1908.
"Phila. Stars Play Bucks." *Chicago Defender*, 30 April 1949, 14.
"Phila. Stars Threatens to Quit Negro League." *New York Age*, 31 August 1935, 8.
"Phila. Stars Lost to Tuckahoe Boys." *Philadelphia Inquirer*, 30 August 1903.

"Philadelphia and Indianapolis Negro Clubs Clash Here Tonight." *The Signal Sports,* 14 June 1949, 12.
"Philadelphia Stars Defeat Monarchs." *Dallas Morning News*, 27 June 1952.
"Philadelphia Stars Nip Houston Eagles, 6 to 5." *Dallas Morning News*, 7 July 1949.
"Philadelphia Stars: Philadelphia's Negro League Team." http://bleacherreport.com, February 2009.
"Philadelphia Stars Swamp Lincolns." *Philadelphia Inquirer*, 25 September 1922.
"Philly All-Stars Here Thursday." *Sedallia Democrat*, 17 May 1950.
"Philly Stars and Crawfords Divvy Again." *Baltimore Afro-American*, 16 September 1933, 15.
"Philly Stars in Farewell Tilt Here Sunday." *Baltimore Afro-American*, 2 September 1933, 15.
"Philly Stars Get 15 Hits to Win from Wentz Olney." *Baltimore Afro-American*, 20 April 1935, 21.
"Philly Stars Take Two from Grays." *Baltimore Afro-American*, 7 July 1934.

Rickey, Branch

Anonymous. "The Destruction of Black Baseball." *The Village Voice*, 25 October 1994, 133.
Barber, Red. "One Who Was There Recalls Branch Rickey's Fight for Civil Rights." *Christian Science Monitor,* 26 February 1986, 18.
"Branch Breaks the Ice: Brooklyn Signs Jack Roosevelt Robinson, Negro Shortstop." *Time* XLVI (5 November 1945), 77.
"Branch Rickey Discusses the Negro in Baseball Today." *Jet* 43, 9 November 1972, 46–48; *Ebony*, May 1957, 38–44.
"Branch Rickey's Box Score." *The Charlotte Observer*, 5 January 1997.
"Brooklyn's Rickey Signs Three More Negro Players." *Chicago Defender*, 8 February 1947, 20.
Brown, Jim. "Jim Brown Questions If It Was Robinson or Rickey Who Broke Baseball's Color Barrier." *Los Angeles Sentinel,* 22 February 2006.
Cohane, Tim. "A Branch Grows in Brooklyn." *Look*, 19 March 1946.
Dexter, Charles. "Branch Rickey to the Rescue." *The Star Weekly*, 3 February 1951, 4.
"Dodger President Reveals Secret Committee Report." *Christian Science Monitor*, 17 February 1948, 12.
"Faster than Jackie Robinson: Branch Rickey's Sermon's on the Mound." *New York Times*, 13 April 1997.
Feder, Sid. "Rickey's Signing of Negro Called a Revolutionary Step in Baseball." *St. Louis Post-Dispatch,* 24 October 1945, 6C.
Frommer, Harvey. *Rickey and Robinson, The Men Who Broke Baseball's Color Line.* New York: MacMillan, 1982.
Glasser, Ira. "Branch Rickey and Jackie Robinson: Precursors to the Civil Rights Movement." *The World and I* 18: 257–65, 2003.
Goudl, Paul. "Rickey No Tightwad, Sincere in Breaking Color Line." *Brooklyn Eagle*, 28 June 1953.
Holway, John. "Integration Not Rickey's Real Goal." *Washington Post*, 5 July 1986.
_____. "Myth of Branch Rickey: He Wasn't the Good Guy." *Philadelphia Inquirer*, 1 October 1994.
King, Chris. "A League of Their Own." Review of *Shades of Glory*, Lawrence D. Hogan in *Washington Post*, 4 June 2006.
Laney, Al. "Negro Players Seeking Dodger Tryouts Catch Rickey's Guard Down." *Philadelphia Evening Bulletin*, 8 February 1945.
Lowenfish, Lee. *Branch Rickey: Baseball's Ferocious Gentleman.* Lincoln: University of Nebraska Press, 2007.
Nicholson, George W. "Baseball and America Changed by Visionary Branch Rickey." *Toledo Blade,* 14 April 2007.
Nightengale, Bob. "Rickey Should Be Remembered." *The Sporting News*, 2 April 1997.
Polner, Murray. *Branch Rickey: A Biography*. New York: Atheneum, 1982.
Pratkanis, Anthony R., and Marlene E. Turner. "Nine Principles of Successful Affirmative Action:

Mr. Branch Rickey, Mr. Jackie Robinson, and the Integration of Baseball." *Nine* (Fall 1994), 36–65.

_____. "The Year Cool Papa Bell Lost the Batting Title: Mr. Branch Rickey and Mr. Jackie Robinson's Plea for Affirmative Action." *Nine* (Spring 1994), 260–276.

Rickey, Branch. Papers. Library of Congress, Washington, D.C.

Rickey, Branch B. "A Tip of the Cap from a Grandson." *New York Times*, 3 August 1997.

"Rickey Aids Negro Ball Players." *The Lowell Sun*, 12 May 1945.

Rickey and Robinson, Two Men of Conviction, Took a Big Risk With Each Other." *New York Times*, 3 August 1997, 21.

"Rickey Calls Robinson Top Ball Prospect." *Chicago Tribune*, 25 October 1945, 29.

"Rickey Cites Wire to Refute Critics." *New York Times*, 26 October 1945, 14.

"Rickey Claims That 15 Clubs Voted to Bar Negroes from the Majors." *New York Times*, 18 February 1948, 37.

"Rickey Defendant in Damage Suit for $15,427." *Berkshire County Eagle*, 1 October 1947, 24.

"Rickey Has His Eyes on a Negro Pitcher." *Joplin Globe*, 24 August 1947.

"Rickey Helps Negro League." *Detroit News*, 8 May 1945, 18.

"Rickey Reveals Formation of Negro League." *Washington Post*, 8 May 1945, 8.

"Rickey Signs Negro." *Statesville Daily Herald*, 26 August 1947.

"Rickey Takes Slap at Negro Leagues." *New York Times*, 25 October 1945, 17.

"Rickey's Friendship with 'Cha' Thomas May Have Led to Signing Jackie Robinson." *Zanesville Times-Signal*, 23 April 1948, 3.

Ryan, Cornelius. "Baseball Men Careful on Comment About Negro Player in Pro League." *Nevada State Journal*, 25 October 1945, 10.

Sperling, Godfrey. "Branch Rickey Would Be Disgusted." *Christian Science Monitor*, 4 March 1997.

"Text of MacPhail Statement." *New York Times*, 21 February 1948, 16.

"U.S. Negro League Is Launched with Brown Dodgers in Brooklyn." *New York Times*, 8 May 1945, 22.

Robeson, Paul

Brown, Lloyd L. *The Young Paul Robeson: "On My Journey Now."* Boulder, CO: Westview Press, 1997.

Clark Dick, and Larry Lester, eds. *The Negro Leagues Book*. Cleveland: SABR, 1994.

Davis, Lenwood G., ed. *A Paul Robeson Research Guide: A Selected Annotated Bibliography*. Westport, CT: Greenwood Press, 1982.

Dewey, Donald, and Nicholas Acocella. *The Biographical History of Baseball*. New York: Carroll & Graf Publishers, 1995.

Dorinson, Joseph. "Blacks in Baseball: Up from Neglect" In *The Cooperstown Symposium Baseball & American Culture, 2002*. Ed. William Simons. Jefferson, NC: McFarland, 182–193.

Dorinson, Joseph, ed. *New York Times in Education Curriculum Guide*. New York: New York Times Co., 1997.

Dorinson, Joseph, and Joram Warmund, eds. *Jackie Robinson: Race, Sports and the American Dream*. Armonk, NY: M. E. Sharpe, 1998.

Dorinson, Joseph, and William Pencak, eds. *Paul Robeson: Essays on His Life and Legacy*. Jefferson, NC: McFarland, 2002.

Duberman, Martin Bauml. *Paul Robeson*. New York: Alfred A. Knopf, 1988.

The Editors of Freedomways. *Paul Robeson: The Great Forerunner*. New York: Dodd, Mead & Co., 1985.

Eisen, George, and David K. Wiggins, eds. *Ethnicity and Sport in North American History and Culture*. Westport, CT: Greenwood Press, 1994.

Foner, Philip S., ed. *Paul Robeson Speaks: Writings, Speeches, Interviews, 1918–1974*. New York: Brunner/Mazel, 1978.

Fox, Stephen. *Big Leagues: Professional Baseball, Football and Basketball in National Memory*. New York: William Morrow & Co., 1994.
Hoberman, John. *Darwin's Athletes: How Sport Has Damaged Black America and Preserved the Myth of Race*. Boston: Houghton Mifflin Mariner, 1997.
Moffi, Larry, and Jonathan Kronstadt. *Crossing the Line: Black Major Leaguers, 1947–1959*. Jefferson, NC: McFarland, 1994.
O'Neil, Buck, with Steve Wulf and David Conrads. *I Was Right on Time*. New York: Simon & Schuster, 1996.
Powers, Joe Sr., and Mark Rogovin. *Paul Robeson Rediscovered: An Annotated Listing of His Chicago History from 1921 to 1958*. Chicago: Columbia College, 2000.
Peterson, Robert. *Only the Ball Was White*. New York: Gramercy Books, 1970.
Rogosin, Donn, *Invisibile Men: Life in Baseball's Negro Leagues*. New York: Kodansha International, 1983.
Riley, James A. *The Biographical Encyclopedia of the Negro Baseball League*. New York: Carroll & Graf, 1994.
Robeson, Paul. *Here I Stand*. Boston: Beacon Press, 1958, 1971.
Stewart, Jeffrey C., ed. *Paul Robeson: Artist and Citizen*. New Brunswick, NJ: Rutgers University Press, 1998.

Seattle Steelheads

Brewer, Jerry. "Herb Simpson, 92, Keeps Important Piece of Seattle's Baseball History Alive." *Seattle Times*, 14 August 2013.
Eskanezi, David, and Steven Rudman. "'Wayback Machine' Seattle Steelheads' Short Life." http://sportspressnw.com/2145947/2013/wayback-machine-seattle-steelheads-short-life, 5 February 2013.
Stalwick, Harry. "Baseball Lore, NW Style." *The Pacific Northwest Inlander*, 7 April 2005.
Whirty, Ryan. "Remembering the Steelheads, Seattle's Negro League Team." http://www.seattlemag.com/article/remembering-steelheads-seattles-negro-league-team (May 2013)
Williams, Darrell. "Sixty-Five Years Later, N. O.'s Simpson, 92, Surprised by Honor." *The Advocate* (N. O. Edition), 16 August 2013.

West Coast Negro League Baseball Association

"Bearded Nine Set to Play." *Oregonian*, 14 August 1946.
"Colored Circuit to Open May 14." *Oregonian*, 6 May 1946.
"Colored Stars Entertain Fans." *Bellingham Herald*, 6 July 1946.
"Horses AWOL So Jesse Runs Bases." *El Paso Herald*, 13 May 1946.
"Jesse Owens Beats Horse." *El Paso Herald*, 14 May 1946.
"La Palomas, Seattle in Long Series." *Chicago Defender*, 10 August 1946.
"Larks Take Pair." *Oregonian*, 8 July 1946.
"Negro Ball Team Overtime Victor." *Oregonian*, 15 August 1946.
"Negro Baseball Club to Play." *Oregonian*, 19 June 1946.
"Negro Diamond Circuit Opens." *Oregonian*, 11 May 1946.
"Negro League Formed on Coast." *New York Times*, 7 May 1946, 34.
"Negro Loop Opens Play." *Oregonian*, 13 May 1946.
"Negro Nine Books Action." *Oregonian*, 21 June 1946.
"Negro Players to Play Here." *Bellingham Herald*, 2 July 1946.
"Negro Teams to Play Loop Games Here." *El Paso Herald*, 10 May 1946.

"Negro Westcoasters in Exhibition Game Tonight." *Augusta Chronicle*, 11 April 1946.
"Negroes Form Coast League." *Oregonian*, 20 January 1946.
"New West Coast League Is Ready to Roll, It Says." *Los Angeles Tribune*, 16 February 1946.
"Owens Is in the Market for a Manager." *Los Angeles Tribune*, 9 February 1946.
"Owens to Back Negro Club Here." *Oregonian*, 27 January 1946.
"Pair of Pro Negro Nines Appear Here." *Spokane Spokesman Review*, 13 June 1946.
"Portland-Seattle Negro Ball Teams Play Sunday." *Oregonian*, 23 June 1946.
"Rosebuds Win, 8–3." *Seattle Daily Times*, 5 June 1946.
"Roses Divide with Seattle." *Oregonian*, 24 June 1946.
"Roses Romp on Steelheads." *Seattle Daily Times*, 15 June 1946.
"Roses Win, 4–3." *Oregonian*, 16 June 1946.
"Seattle Negro Club to Make Debut Soon." *Seattle Daily Times*, 26 May 1946.
"Steelheads 11, Roses 2." *Oregonian*, 13 June 1946.
"Steelheads Face Owens' Nine Here." *Seattle Daily Times*, 9 June 1946.
"Steelheads in Another Win." *Seattle Daily Times*, 11 June 1946.
"Steelheads Open Negro Loop Play." *Seattle Daily Times*, 2 June 1946.
"Steelheads Split." *Seattle Daily Times*, 27 May 1946.
"Steelheads to Wind Up Series Here." *Seattle Daily Times*, 6 June 1946.
"Steelies Split in Debut Here." *Seattle Daily Times*, 3 June 1946.
"Twin Bill Split." *Oregonian*, 3 June 1946.
"West Coast League Sets Fees, Rules; Opens Season May 12." *Los Angeles Tribune*, 9 March 1946.
"West Coast League to Start Season on May 12." *Chicago Defender*, 9 March 1946.

Contributors

Chris Baas is an assistant professor of landscape architecture at Ball State University and specializes in the documentation of Indiana's historic landscapes. He was recently honored by the Indiana Division of Historic Preservation and Archaeology with the Best National Register Award for his research of the Thomas Edison Concept Houses in Gary, Indiana. Before teaching, he was a landscape architect with the Indiana Department of Natural Resources, where he planned, designed, and managed projects for state properties. He is a lifetime Cincinnati Reds fan, and had the wonderful experience of working at Riverfront Stadium during the 1990 World Series.

James Edward Brunson III recently retired as the assistant vice president for the Division of Student Affairs and Enrollment Management at Northern Illinois University, where he also taught African American art history and visual culture. His articles have appeared in *Black Ball*, *Nine*, and *Base Ball: A Journal of the Early Game*. He has presented at the NASSH, Nine, Jerry Malloy Negro League, Cultural Studies Association, and Popular Culture Association /American Culture Association conferences.

Robert Cvornyek is a professor and chair of the history department at Rhode Island College where he specializes in sport history. He recently served as co-curator and principal scholar for an exhibit at the Museum of African American History in Boston titled "The Color of Baseball in Boston: A History of Black Teams, the Players, and a Sporting Community." He is currently writing a book on race and black baseball in greater Boston and is co-director of the program "It Don't Mean a Thing If It Ain't Got That Swing: Baseball, Jazz, and Black Cultural Expression." He authored "Who Killed Daddy Black?," an article on the contested death of New England's premier African American numbers king and baseball promoter in the *Boston Phoenix*.

Joseph Dorinson is a professor in the history department at Long Island University, where he has taught since 1966. He has co-edited two books, *Jackie Robinson: Race, Sports and the American Dream* (1999) and *Paul Robeson: Essays on His Life and Legacy* (2002), and has written numerous articles on a variety of subjects spanning his beloved borough of Brooklyn, black heroes, sports, politics, humor, and ethnicity. During baseball's 2000 World Series (the first "Subway Series" since 1956), Dorinson appeared on television (CNN, Fox News, New York One), was heard on the radio (NPR, WOR), and was profiled in the *New York Times* discoursing on blacks, "Reds," baseball, and the American experience.

David Krell is the baseball historian for TheSportsPost.com and a frequent speaker at the Society for American Baseball Research and the National Baseball Hall of Fame and Museum. He is also a frequent contributor to *Memories and Dreams*, the official magazine of the National Baseball Hall of Fame and Museum. He is the co-editor of the New York State Bar Association's 2013 sports law book *In the Arena*, for which he wrote the chapter about licensing and mascots. David's article series *Krell's Korner* is published in *Entertainment, Arts, and Sports Law Journal*. The articles focus on the legal and historical angles of the cases that shaped the entertainment, arts, and sports industries. He is a member of the bar in New York, New Jersey, and Pennsylvania.

Chris Lamb is a professor of journalism at Indiana University–Purdue University at Indianapolis (IUPUI). He previously taught at the College of Charleston where he also advised the student-run

Black Ball / DOI: 10.3172/BLB.6.170 / Volume 6 / 2013 / pp. 170–171 /
ISSN 1939-8484 (Print) / ISSN 1939-8379 (Online) /

newspaper. He wrote for the *Dayton Daily News*, the *Daytona Beach News Journal* and the *Knoxville News-Sentinel*. His book *Conspiracy of Silence*, which came out in 2012, focused on sportswriters and the long process of desegregating baseball.

Shawn Morris is a lifelong resident of northeast Ohio. He graduated from Kent State University with a BA in history and is currently enrolled at Cleveland State University, where he is pursuing his MA in history, concentrating on museum studies. He is a fan of all Cleveland sports.

Courtney Smith is a life-long Philadelphia sports fan and an assistant professor of history and political science at Cabrini College in Radnor, Pennsylvania, when she graduated with a degree in history and political science. Courtney received her M.A. and Ph.D. in American history from Lehigh University in Bethlehem, Pennsylvania. Her dissertation focused on Lehigh's extra-curriculur athletics from 1866 to 1998. Her master's thesis, a history of the Philadelphia Stars, forms the basis of her current scholarship projects.

Geri Strecker is an assistant professor at Ball State University, where she teaches writing for architecture and urban design. She has published articles in *NINE: A Journal of Baseball History and Culture*, *Black Ball: A Negro Leagues Journal*, and *The National Pastime*. She is finishing a book on Oscar Charleston and another on the early history of baseball in the Philippines.

Author Index

Black Ball / DOI: 10.3172/BLB.6.172 / Volume 6 / 2013 / pp. 172–174 /
ISSN 1939-8484 (Print) / ISSN 1939-8379 (Online) / © 2013 McFarland & Company, Inc.

_____. "'A Time Called Too Early': Back Baseball and the Pursuit of the American Dream." 1.1: 29–42.
Mitchem, Pamela. "Wonder Team of the Carolinas: C.L. Moore, the Asheville Blues, and Minor League Blackball in the South." 5.1: 33–51.
Morris, Peter. "Bud Fowler's Lost Years." 2.2: 10–23.
Muller, Michael. Rev. of *The Empire Strikes Out: How Baseball Sold U.S. Foreign Policy and Promoted the American Way Abroad.* 3.2: 72–74.
Nathan, Dan. "Painting Pride and Prejudice: Kadir Nelson's *We Are the Ship*." 3.1: 15–26.
Newman, Roberta. Rev. of *The Most Famous Woman in Baseball: Effa Manley and the Negro Leagues*, by Bob Luke. 5.1: 93–96.
Norris, Jason. Rev. of *South of the Color Barrier: How Jorge Pasquel and the Mexican League Pushed Baseball Toward Racial Integration*, by John Virtue. 2.2: 108–109.
Peterson, Robert. "How *Only the Ball Was White* Came to Be Written." 1.1: 7–13.
Peterson, Todd. "'An Aggregation of Conceit': The Minneapolis Keystones, 1908–1911." 2.1: 12–24.
_____. "If Given an Opportunity: The 1907 Series Between the St. Paul Gophers and the St. Paul Saints." 1.1: 43–56.
Petrovic, Paul. "'Give 'em the Razzle-Dazzle': The Negro Leagues in *The Bingo Long Traveling All-Stars and Motor Kings* and *Soul of the Game*." 3.1: 61–75.
Puerzer, Richard. "Gene Baker: Unsung Hero in the Integration of Major League Baseball." 4.1: 28–37.
Ressler, William Harris. Rev. of *Just as Good: How Larry Doby Changed America's Game*, by Chis Crow and Mike Benny. 5.2: 82–83.
_____. Rev. of *Two Pioneers: How Hank Greenberg and Jackie Robinson Transformed Baseball — and America*, by Robert Cottrell. 5.2: 80–82.
Revel, Layton, and Luis Muñoz. "On the Move with Lázaro Salazar." 2.1: 68–77.
Rushing, Lawrence. "'A Black Woman and Proud': Effa Manley and Racial Self-Identification." 4.2: 17–35.
Ryzner, Ryan. "The Black Press and Negro League Baseball in 1940s Cleveland." 2.2: 68–85.
Salazar, Anthony. Rev. of *Cuban Star: How One Negro League Owner Changed the Face of Baseball*, by Adrian Burgos. 4.2: 73–75.
Selby, Shawn. "Hot Jazz and Black Ball: Connections Between Music and Baseball in Pittsburgh and Kansas City." 3.1: 53–60.
Singletary, Wes. "A Long Way from Palatka: The Early Career of John Henry Lloyd." 2.1: 52–67.
Slade, Samantha. Rev. of *Playing America's Game: Baseball, Latinos and the Color Line*, by Adrian Burgos. 3.2: 76–78.
Sorgini, Antongiulio. Rev. of *Satchel: The Life and Times of an American Legend*, by Larry Tye. 2.2: 107–108.
Staples, Bill, Jr. "Black Giant: Biz Mackey's Texas Negro League Career." 1.1: 93–110.
Stivers, Wayne. "Biz Mackey: Catcher, Manager, Mentor Extraordinaire." 1.2: 41–56.
_____. Rev. of *Willie Wells: "El Diablo" of the Negro Leagues*, by Bob Luke. 1.2: 111–112.
Strecker, Geri. "Dave Wyatt: The First Great Black Sportswriter." 4.1: 5–14.
_____. Rev. of *Baseball's First Colored World Series: The 1924 Meeting of the Hilldale Giants and Kansas City Monarchs*, by Larry Lester. 1.1: 111.
_____. Rev. of *The Barnstorming Hawaiian Travelers: A Multiethnic Baseball Team Tours the Mainland, 1912–1916*, by Joel S. Franks. 5.2: 83–85.
_____. "The Rise and Fall of Greenlee Field: Biography of a Ballpark." 2.2: 37–67.
_____. "What Ancestry.com Can Tell Us About Black Baseball." 1.2: 95–98.
Strecker, Trey. Rev. of *Race Ball: How the Major Leagues Colonized the Black and Latin Game*, by Rob Rock. 4.2: 78–80.
_____. Rev. of *The Right Time: John Henry "Pop" Lloyd and Black Baseball*, by Wes Singletary. 5.1: 91–93.
Swaine, Rick. "The Forgotten Generation of Black Baseball Stars." 2.1: 25–36.
Trembanis, Sarah. "Signifying Baseball: Tricksters and Folklore in Black Baseball." 3.2: 21–36.

Subject Index

Asheville (NC) Blues

Baker, Gene

Ballparks

Baltimore Elite Giants

Black Press

Bolden, Ed

Bostic, Joe, Sr.

Boston Red Sox

Black Ball / DOI: 10.3172/BLB.6.X175/ Volume 6 / 2013 / pp. 175–183 /
ISSN 1939-8484 (Print) / ISSN 1939-8379 (Online) /

Henry, Prince Joe

Drescher, Rose. Rev. of *Princoirs: Official Memoirs of Prince Joe Henry, Ex-Negro Leaguer*, by Sean R. Muhammad. 3.1:88–89.

Hilldale Giants

Strecker, Geri. Rev. of *Baseball's First Colored World Series: The 1924 Meeting of the Hilldale Giants and Kansas City Monarchs*, by Larry Lester. 1.1: 111.

House of David

Harkness-Roberto, Michael. "Barnstorming: The Monarchs, the House of David and Colored House of David." 3.2: 60–69.

Houston, Texas

Brunson, James E., III. "Texas Black Ball: Galveston-Houston Rivalry (1875–1888)." 5.2: 73–79.

Howard, Elston

Briley, Ron. "'No One in the Yankee Organization Ever Made Me Conscious of My Color': Elston Howard and the Establishment Negro." 5.2: 35–50.

Indianapolis Crawfords

Garrett, Thomas R. "When Oscar Charleston, the Ethiopian Clowns and Jesse Owens Came to Portsmouth, Virginia." 3.2: 54–59.

Integration

Bowers, Courtney. Rev. of *The Integration of Major League Baseball: A Team by Team History*, by Rick Swaine. 3.2: 74–76.

Crepeau, Richard C. Rev. of *Baseball's Great Experiment: Jackie Robinson and His Legacy*, 25th Anniversary Edition, by Jules Tygiel. 1.2: 110–111.

Essington, Amy. Rev. of *Crossing the Line: Black Major Leaguers, 1947–1959*, by Larry Moffi and Jonathan Kronstadt. 1.1: 113–115.

Furcola, Marilyn. Rev. of *Pumpsie & Progress: The Red Sox, Race, and Redemption*, by Bill Nowlin. 4.2: 77–78.

Halpern, Steven. Rev. of *Blackout: The Untold Story of Jackie Robinson's First Spring Training*, by Chris Lamb. 1.1: 112.

Haupert, Michael J. "Pay, Performance, and Race During the Integration Era." 2.1: 37–51.

Haupert, Michael J., and Kenneth Winter. "Integrating Major League Baseball: A Counterfactual Analysis." 4.1: 59–80.

Keefer, Bradley S. Rev. of *Crossing the Line: Black Major Leaguers, 1947–1959*, by Larry Moffi and Jonathan Kronstadt. 4.1: 81–82.

Puerzer, Richard. "Gene Baker: Unsung Hero in the Integration of Major League Baseball." 4.1: 28–37.

Swaine, Rick. "The Forgotten Generation of Black Baseball Stars." 2.1: 25–36.

Jazz and Black Baseball

Selby, Shawn. "Hot Jazz and Black Ball: Connections Between Music and Baseball in Pittsburgh and Kansas City." 3.1: 53–60.

Jethroe, Sam

Jews and Black Baseball

Jones, William Albert "Abe"

Kansas City, Missouri

Kansas City Monarchs

Lacy, Sam

Landis, Kenesaw Mountain

Latin American Leagues

Latinos

Little Rock (AR) Black Travelers

Lloyd, John Henry "Pop"

Lynn (MA) Frasers

Bevis, Charlie. "Barnstorming Black Ballclubs vs. White Semi-Pro Lynn Frasers in 1944." 4.1: 15–27.

Mackey, Raleigh "Biz"

Luke, Bob. "Biz Mackey: Catcher, Manager, Mentor Extraordinaire." 1.2: 41–56.
Staples, Bill, Jr. "Black Giant: Biz Mackey's Texas Negro League Career." 1.1: 93–110.

Manley, Effa

Alexander, Lisa Doris. "Effa Manley and the Politics of Passing." 1.2: 83–94.
Newman, Roberta. Rev. of *The Most Famous Woman in Baseball: Effa Manley and the Negro Leagues*, by Bob Luke. 5.1: 93–96.
Rushing, Lawrence. "'A Black Woman and Proud': Effa Manley and Racial Self-Identification." 4.2: 17–35.

Mexican League

Norris, Jason. Rev. of *South of the Color Barrier: How Jorge Pasquel and the Mexican League Pushed Baseball Toward Racial Integration*, by John Virtue. 2.2: 108–109.

Miami Ethiopian Clowns

Garrett, Thomas R. "When Oscar Charleston, the Ethiopian Clowns and Jesse Owens Came to Portsmouth, Virginia." 3.2: 54–59.

Miami Marlins

Gorman, Robert. "Pitching in the Atomic Age: Satchel Paige and the Miami Marlins, 1956–1958." 3.2: 5–20.

Minneapolis Keystones

Brunson, James E., III. Rev. of *Early Black Baseball in Minnesota: The St. Paul Gophers, Minneapolis Keystones and Other Barnstorming Teams of the Deadball Era*, by Todd Peterson. 4.2: 75–77.
Peterson, Todd. "'An Aggregation of Conceit': The Minneapolis Keystones, 1908–1911." 2.1: 12–24.

Moore, Clarence L.

Mitchem, Pamela. "Wonder Team of the Carolinas: C.L. Moore, the Asheville Blues, and Minor League Blackball in the South." 5.1: 33–51.

Negro Southern League

Aiello, Thomas. "A Case for the Negro Southern League." 3.2: 37–45.

Nineteenth Century Black Baseball

Baldini, Nicole. Rev. of *Out of the Shadows: African American Baseball from the Cuban Giants to Jackie Robinson*, edited by Bill Kirwin. 4.1: 83–85.
Brown, Sharon. Rev. of *The Early Image of Black Baseball: Race and Representation in the Popular Press, 1871–1890*, by James E. Brunson III. 3.2: 70–72.
Browne, Paul. "You Can't Tell the Players: The Cuban Giants, the Gorhams and League Play." 4.2: 55–66.

Omaha, Nebraska

Owen, Jesse

Page Fence Giants

Paige, Satchel

Pasquel, Jorge

Philadelphia Pythians

Philadelphia Stars

Pittsburgh, Pennsylvania

Pompez, Alex

Portsmouth, Virginia

Garrett, Thomas R. "When Oscar Charleston, the Ethiopian Clowns and Jesse Owens Came to Portsmouth, Virginia." 3.2: 54–59.

Rickey, Branch

Heaphy, Leslie. Rev. of *Rickey and Robinson: The Preacher, the Player and America's Game*, by John C. Chalberg. 4.1: 82–83.

Robinson, Jackie

Baldini, Nicole. Rev. of *Out of the Shadows: African American Baseball from the Cuban Giants to Jackie Robinson*, edited by Bill Kirwin. 4.1: 83–85.

Crepeau, Richard C. Rev. of *Baseball's Great Experiment: Jackie Robinson and His Legacy*, 25th Anniversary Edition, by Jules Tygiel. 1.2: 110–111.

Dorinson, Joseph. "Jackie Robinson Revisited." 5.2: 51–60.

Halpern, Steven. Rev. of *Blackout: The Untold Story of Jackie Robinson's First Spring Training*, by Chris Lamb. 1.1: 112.

Heaphy, Leslie. Rev. of *Rickey and Robinson: The Preacher, the Player and America's Game*, by John C. Chalberg. 4.1: 82–83.

Hoffman, Dennis. "Impact Players: How Jackie Robinson, Mildred Brown, and Leroy Gibson Transformed the African American Experience in Omaha, Nebraska, 1946–1950." 4.1: 44–58.

Ressler, William Harris. Rev. of *Two Pioneers: How Hank Greenberg and Jackie Robinson Transformed Baseball— and America*, by Robert Cottrell. 5.2: 80–82.

Revel, Layton, and Luis Muñoz. "On the Move with Lázaro Salazar." 2.1: 68–77.

St. Paul Gophers

Brunson, James E., III. Rev. of *Early Black Baseball in Minnesota: The St. Paul Gophers, Minneapolis Keystones and Other Barnstorming Teams of the Deadball Era*, by Todd Peterson. 4.2: 75–77.

Peterson, Todd. "If Given an Opportunity: The 1907 Series Between the St. Paul Gophers and the St. Paul Saints." 1.1: 43–56.

St. Paul Saints

Peterson, Todd. "If Given an Opportunity: The 1907 Series Between the St. Paul Gophers and the St. Paul Saints." 1.1: 43–56.

Salazar, Lázaro

Revel, Layton, and Luis Muñoz. "On the Move with Lázaro Salazar." 2.1: 68–77.

Smith, Wendell

Carroll, Brian. "A Tribute to Wendell Smith." 2.1: 4–11.

Taylor, C.I.

Carroll, Brian. "C.I. Taylor and the Great Newspaper War of 1915." 4.2: 36–54.

Texas Negro Leagues

Staples, Bill, Jr. "Black Giant: Biz Mackey's Texas Negro League Career." 1.1: 93–110.